ALBERT EINSTEIN: PHILOSOPHER-SCIENTIST

VOLUME ONE

THE LIBRARY OF LIVING PHILOSOPHERS

This epoch-making series of volumes devoted to a critical analysis and discussion of the thought of the world's greatest living philosophers introduces to the reader the unique and exciting intellectual experience of sitting in a seminar with a great philosopher and his critics. The philosopher, *during his lifetime*—before it becomes necessary to guess the meaning of his words—submits to the most searching scrutiny of thought and meaning by from 17 to 30 eminent authorities, outstanding thinkers and writers from all over the world, and, in turn, *replies* to them. Adding to the value of each book in the series is an autobiography or authorized biography and a complete up-to-date bibliography of the philosopher's published writings.

THE PHILOSOPHY OF JOHN DEWEY*
THE PHILOSOPHY OF GEORGE SANTAYANA
THE PHILOSOPHY OF ALFRED NORTH WHITEHEAD*
THE PHILOSOPHY OF G. E. MOORE
THE PHILOSOPHY OF BERTRAND RUSSELL*
THE PHILOSOPHY OF ERNST CASSIRER
ALBERT EINSTEIN: PHILOSOPHER-SCIENTIST
THE PHILOSOPHY OF SARVEPALLI RADHAKRISHNAN
THE PHILOSOPHY OF C. D. BROAD
THE PHILOSOPHY OF RUDOLF CARNAP
THE PHILOSOPHY OF MARTIN BUBER
THE PHILOSOPHY OF C. I. LEWIS
THE PHILOSOPHY OF KARL POPPER
THE PHILOSOPHY OF BRAND BLANSHARD
THE PHILOSOPHY OF KARL JASPERS (Augmented Edition)
THE PHILOSOPHY OF JEAN-PAUL SARTRE

***Available only from University Microfilms International, 300 N. Zeeb Road, Ann Arbor, MI 48106 and 30/32 Mortimer Street, London W1N 7RA, England.**

Critical Comments

"This truly magnificent idea deserves a Pulitzer Prize." —*Ernest Sutherland Bates*

"The series as a whole is the greatest philosophical 'journal' that has ever been published." —*Edgar Sheffield Brightman*

"Philosophers . . . have never been in a position before to deal in a final manner, at a time when their systems were practically completed, with an organized, contemporary survey of every aspect of their doctrine . . . and to give a last clarification of their own views." —*B. A. G. Fuller*

"A unique phenomenon in the history of philosophy." —*George Albert Coe*

"The most important series of philosophical publications in this country." —*Advance*

Volumes in Preparation

THE PHILOSOPHY OF GEORG HENRIK von WRIGHT
THE PHILOSOPHY OF GABRIEL MARCEL
THE PHILOSOPHY OF W. V. QUINE

ISBN 0-87548-286-4

Karsh, Ottawa

A. Einstein.

THE LIBRARY OF LIVING PHILOSOPHERS

VOLUME VII

ALBERT EINSTEIN:

PHILOSOPHER-SCIENTIST

VOLUME ONE

EDITED BY

PAUL ARTHUR SCHILPP

NORTHWESTERN UNIVERSITY &
SOUTHERN ILLINOIS UNIVERSITY

OPEN COURT • LA SALLE, ILLINOIS • ESTABLISHED 1887

CAMBRIDGE UNIVERSITY PRESS • LONDON

ALBERT EINSTEIN: PHILOSOPHER-SCIENTIST

VOLUME ONE

THIRD EDITION

Third Printing, 1982

Library of Congress Catalog Card Number: 50-5340

Printed in the United States of America

GENERAL INTRODUCTION*

TO

"THE LIBRARY OF LIVING PHILOSOPHERS"

ACCORDING to the late F. C. S. Schiller, the greatest obstacle to fruitful discussion in philosophy is "the curious etiquette which apparently taboos the asking of questions about a philosopher's meaning while he is alive." The "interminable controversies which fill the histories of philosophy," he goes on to say, "could have been ended at once by asking the living philosophers a few searching questions."

The confident optimism of this last remark undoubtedly goes too far. Living thinkers have often been asked "a few searching questions," but their answers have not stopped "interminable controversies" about their real meaning. It is none the less true that there would be far greater clarity of understanding than is now often the case, if more such searching questions had been directed to great thinkers while they were still alive.

This, at any rate, is the basic thought behind the present undertaking. The volumes of *The Library of Living Philosophers* can in no sense take the place of the major writings of great and original thinkers. Students who would know the philosophies of such men as John Dewey, George Santayana, Alfred North Whitehead, Benedetto Croce, G. E. Moore, Bertrand Russell, Ernst Cassirer, Karl Jaspers, *et al.*, will still need to read the writings of these men. There is no substitute for first-hand contact with the original thought of the philosopher himself. Least of all does this *Library* pretend to be such a substitute. The *Library* in fact will spare neither effort nor expense in offering to the student the best possible guide to the published

* This *General Introduction*, setting forth the underlying conception of this *Library*, is purposely reprinted in each volume (with only very minor changes).

writings of a given thinker. We shall attempt to meet this aim by providing at the end of each volume in our series a complete bibliography of the published work of the philosopher in question. Nor should one overlook the fact that the essays in each volume cannot but finally lead to this same goal. The interpretative and critical discussions of the various phases of a great thinker's work and, most of all, the reply of the thinker himself, are bound to lead the reader to the works of the philosopher himself.

At the same time, there is no denying the fact that different experts find different ideas in the writings of the same philosopher. This is as true of the appreciative interpreter and grateful disciple as it is of the critical opponent. Nor can it be denied that such differences of reading and of interpretation on the part of other experts often leave the neophyte aghast before the whole maze of widely varying and even opposing interpretations. Who is right and whose interpretation shall he accept? When the doctors disagree among themselves, what is the poor student to do? If, finally, in desperation, he decides that all of the interpreters are probably wrong and that the only thing for him to do is to go back to the original writings of the philosopher himself and then make his own decision—uninfluenced (as if this were possible!) by the interpretation of any one else—the result is not that he has actually come to the meaning of the original philosopher himself, but rather that he has set up one more interpretation, which may differ to a greater or lesser degree from the interpretations already existing. It is clear that in this direction lies chaos, just the kind of chaos which Schiller has so graphically and inimitably described.[1]

It is curious that until now no way of escaping this difficulty has been seriously considered. It has not occurred to students of philosophy that one effective way of meeting the problem at least partially is to put these varying interpretations and critiques before the philosopher while he is still alive and to ask him to act at one and the same time as both defendant and judge. If the world's great living philosophers can be induced to coöper-

[1] In his essay on "Must Philosophers Disagree?" in the volume by the same title (Macmillan, London, 1934), from which the above quotations were taken.

ate in an enterprise whereby their own work can, at least to some extent, be saved from becoming merely "desiccated lecture-fodder," which on the one hand "provides innocuous sustenance for ruminant professors," and, on the other hand, gives an opportunity to such ruminants and their understudies to "speculate safely, endlessly, and fruitlessly, about what a philosopher must have meant" (Schiller), they will have taken a long step toward making their intentions clearly comprehensible.

With this in mind *The Library of Living Philosophers* expects to publish at more or less regular intervals a volume on each of the greater among the world's living philosophers. In each case it will be the purpose of the editor of *The Library* to bring together in the volume the interpretations and criticisms of a wide range of that particular thinker's scholarly contemporaries, each of whom will be given a free hand to discuss the specific phase of the thinker's work which has been assigned to him. All contributed essays will finally be submitted to the philosopher with whose work and thought they are concerned, for his careful perusal and reply. And, although it would be expecting too much to imagine that the philosopher's reply will be able to stop all differences of interpretation and of critique, this should at least serve the purpose of stopping certain of the grosser and more general kinds of misinterpretations. If no further gain than this were to come from the present and projected volumes of this *Library*, it would seem to be fully justified.

In carrying out this principal purpose of the *Library*, the editor announces that (in so far as humanly possible) each volume will conform to the following pattern:

First, a series of expository and critical articles written by the leading exponents and opponents of the philosopher's thought;

Second, the reply to the critics and commentators by the philosopher himself;

Third, an intellectual autobiography of the thinker whenever this can be secured; in any case an authoritative and authorized biography; and

Fourth, a bibliography of the writings of the philosopher to pro-

vide a ready instrument to give access to his writings and thought.

The editor has deemed it desirable to secure the services of an Advisory Board of philosophers to aid him in the selection of the subjects of future volumes. The names of the six prominent American philosophers who have consented to serve appear below. To each of them the editor expresses his deep-felt thanks.

Future volumes in this series will appear in as rapid succession as is feasible in view of the scholarly nature of this *Library*. The next three volumes in this series should be those on Benedetto Croce, Sir Sarvepalli Radhakrishnan, and Karl Jaspers.

The editor is very happy, indeed, to be able to make grateful acknowledgment for the financial assistance this volume has received. The editorial work on the Einstein volume has been largely made possible by a grant received from the Humanities Division of the General Education Board of the Rockefeller Foundation through the mediation and courtesy of the American Council of Learned Societies in Washington, D.C. To both organizations the editor desires to express his sincere gratitude and deep appreciation. However, neither the Rockefeller Foundation nor the A.C.L.S. are in any sense the authors, owners, publishers, or proprietors of this *Library,* and they are therefore not to be understood as approving by virtue of their grants any of the statements made in this volume.

Volumes I to IV (incl.) have, unfortunately, been out of print for some time now, not due to lack of demand for these volumes—there is, in fact, a steady demand for each of them—, but simply because The Library of Living Philosophers, Inc. has lacked the necessary funds to permit reprintings or new editions. It is now hoped, however, that it will be possible to print a second edition of at least the volume on *The Philosophy of John Dewey* within approximately four or five months of the date of publication of the present volume. We had strongly hoped to be able to do this in time for Professor Dewey's ninetieth birthday on October 20th, 1949. Failing in this effort we shall do our best to accomplish this end as soon as possible. It is perhaps hardly necessary to add that the *Library* would

gladly welcome gifts and donations which would enable us to reprint the other three volumes. Since November 6th, 1947, moreover, any gifts or donations made to The Library of Living Philosophers, Inc. are deductible by the donors in arriving at their taxable net income in conformity with the Internal Revenue Code of the Treasury Department of the United States of America.

P. A. S.
Editor

101-102 Fayerweather Hall
Northwestern University
Evanston, Illinois

ADVISORY BOARD

TABLE OF CONTENTS

PREFACE

THE contents of this volume speak eloquently enough for the inclusion of *Albert Einstein: Philosopher-Scientist* in this series without any superfluous words from the editor.

Almost all of the matters which need to be mentioned here are of the nature of personal privilege.

There is, first of all, the matter of gratitude for help and co-operation. Foremost here stands Professor Einstein himself. Without his consent and willingness to co-operate, this book could never have appeared. But, how to express the editor's thanks and appreciation to him—in the coldness of mere words—this is something I know not how to do. Perhaps he will understand if I state simply that my obligation and gratitude to him are beyond the possibility of verbal expression.

Among the twenty-five other contributors to this volume there are no less than six Nobel-Prize winners in science; and essays have come from as many as eleven countries (viz., Australia, Belgium, Canada, Denmark, England, France, Germany, Ireland, Scotland, Switzerland, and the U.S.A.); an essay for this volume had also been promised by a leading scientist of the U.S.S.R. (although it has not yet actually reached the editor). The editor is as deeply and sincerely obligated to these important and busy scholars the world around as he is to Professor Einstein.

It proved impossible to bring out this volume at the time originally planned. It had been hoped to lay it on Professor Einstein's birthday-table on March 14th last, on the occasion of his seventieth birthday. No one regrets this delay in publication more than does the editor.

Other regrets are no less poignant. It was a tragedy of no mean importance that Max Planck was already too seriously ill, at the time of the conception of this volume, for him to

be able to contribute an essay. Nor has the editor recovered from the sadness caused by Professor Hermann Weyl's inability to carry out his original promise to write for this book.

Three other scholars (from as many countries) finally failed to redeem their pledges given to the editor. In the case of one of these it is at least conceivable that the reason for the failure of his essay to reach us may not have lain with himself. In any case, it is regrettable that the *Library of Living Philosophers* is thus deprived from giving those essays to its interested readers. We can merely assure these readers that no stone was left unturned to secure the essays.

All these regrets are compensated for, however, by our being able to present here Professor Einstein's one and only intellectual autobiography.

Everyone who knows Professor Einstein personally is all too well aware of his extreme shyness and his honest and forthright humility. I do not believe that there would have been one chance in ten thousand that the world would ever have secured an autobiography from the hand of Professor Einstein, if the unique nature of the *Library of Living Philosophers* had not finally convinced him of the worth-whileness and significance of such an "obituary," as he calls his autobiography.

Einstein's "Autobiographical Notes" in themselves assure, therefore, the unique importance of this volume.

In a kindred category stands Professor Niels Bohr's "Discussion with Einstein,"—an essay, not merely delightfully written but of the utmost and lasting importance in its content. These recollections of conversations with Einstein on the epistemological aspects of physical science would never have come into being, were it not for the peculiar nature of this series.

One could go on in this fashion. How can one adequately praise the care, precision, directness, and beauty of Professor Einstein's "Reply" (or "Remarks," as he calls them) to his commentators and critics!

There are, however, still other persons whose kindness or aid have helped to enhance the value or increase the beauty and

correctness of this book. Professor Peter G. Bergmann, of the physics department of Syracuse University, spared neither time nor effort in helping to put Professor von Laue's paper into the same adequate and beautiful form in English as the author himself had used in his original German manuscript. Professor Arnold J. F. Siegert, of the physics department of Northwestern University, carefully checked and corrected—especially the technically scientific aspects of—my own translations of both Einstein essays. Mr. Forrest W. Williams, of Northwestern University, very kindly and ably translated the de Broglie and Bachelard essays.

Mere words of gratitude are also quite inadequate to express the editor's appreciation of the wonderfully careful and exacting work accomplished by the bibliographer of Professor Einstein's published works. Long before the present volume got under way, Miss Margaret C. Shields, at that time Librarian of the Mathematics Library of Princeton University, had been at work gathering the data which have now gone into the Bibliography, which constitutes the important Part IV of the present volume. Her labors have been endless and her efforts almost excruciatingly painstaking. The result speaks for itself. Her exhaustive bibliography of the published work of Einstein will prove to be of inestimable value to scientists and scholars for centuries to come. The abiding knowledge of this fact will be a source of deeper satisfaction to Miss Shields than any words of thanks the editor could offer.

Messrs. Surindar Suri and Kenneth G. Halvorsen saved the editor the arduous and laborious task of providing this volume with its accurate and useful index. A host of other individuals contributed their assistance during various parts of the labor of reading proof and seeing the volume through the press. To all of these the editor says a most sincere and heart-felt, "Thank you."

The order in which the essays appear in Part II was determined, in general, by the order in which Professor Einstein chose to discuss the essays in his replying "Remarks." The only exceptions to this rule are those essays to which Dr. Einstein did not reply or which came in after his "Remarks" had been

completed.

In reading and editing the contents of this volume, two possible sub-titles have come to the editor's mind again and again, namely (1) "The Scientific Battle of the Twentieth Century," and (2) "The Future of Physics." Viewed from either point of view, this book has been exciting reading, even to its editor. He may be permitted to express the hope, therefore, that the experience of other readers will be similar.

PAUL ARTHUR SCHILPP

DEPARTMENT OF PHILOSOPHY
NORTHWESTERN UNIVERSITY
EVANSTON, ILLINOIS

October 1, 1949

ACKNOWLEDGMENTS

Grateful Acknowledgment is hereby made to the authors, editors, and publishers of all of Professor Einstein's works as well as of any other books, quotations from which appear in this volume. We are particularly grateful to them for the fact that they have not required us to enumerate these volumes here by author, title, and publisher.

We also wish to express our appreciation to the editors and publishers of the numerous scientific, mathematical, and philosophical journals quoted in these pages, for the privilege of utilizing such source materials therein found relevant to the discussion of Professor Einstein's scientific and philosophical views.

PREFATORY NOTE TO THE THIRD EDITION

It has been said that no man is irreplaceable. Like most generalizations, this one too is not entirely correct. The passing of Albert Einstein, in Princeton, N. J., on April 18, 1955, certainly was an irreplaceable loss to science, to scholarship, to humanitarianism, to the cause of peace, and to the conscience of mankind. For, if the conscience of humanity could ever be said to have been represented by one single living human being, that human being was the great and truly immortal Einstein. To the editor of this LIBRARY Einstein's passing was also a great personal loss. My numerous visits and personal conversations with him constitute an indescribable legacy and indestructible memory of the greatest human being it has ever been my privilege to know personally.

Since the present (third) edition of our *Einstein* volume is the first one to be released since Einstein's even yet untimely passing, the editor felt deeply obliged to say at least that much. But all of us are pleased to know that this volume is, at long last, available again.

After all, this volume contains the only thing even so much as approximating an Autobiography that the great Einstein ever wrote. And this appears both in the great scientist's original German and in English translation, side by side and page by page (for all of 95 pages). This, by itself, is an imperishable document, which is even more significant precisely because it contains much more of Einstein's scientific thought-development than it does mere matters of personal recollection. His "Reply to Criticisms" is equally important and of permanent significance.

This third edition has been (1) corrected for errors, and (2) brought more nearly up-to-date in the Bibliography. We know that it will receive the same enthusiastic reception which greeted the first two editions of this—in a real sense timeless—volume.

The editor wishes to express his appreciation to the new

publishers of THE LIBRARY—The Hegeler Foundation and the Open Court Publishing Company—for undertaking to keep all of the volumes of THE LIBRARY permanently in print; to the Advisory Board of THE LIBRARY, for their help in planning future volumes (the present membership of the Board is listed below); and to the National Endowment for the Humanities, Washington, D. C., for generous grants for the years 1967-1970.

PAUL ARTHUR SCHILPP

DEPARTMENT OF PHILOSOPHY
SOUTHERN ILLINOIS UNIVERSITY
CARBONDALE, ILLINOIS

March 3, 1969

ADVISORY BOARD

ALBERT EINSTEIN
AUTOBIOGRAPHICAL NOTES

AUTOBIOGRAPHISCHES

HIER sitze ich, um mit 67 Jahren so etwas wie den eigenen Nekrolog zu schreiben. Dies tue ich nicht nur, weil mich Dr. Schilpp dazu überredet hat; sondern ich glaube selber dass es gut ist, den Mitstrebenden zu zeigen, wie einem das eigene Streben und Suchen im Rückblick erscheint. Nach einiger Ueberlegung fühlte ich, wie unvollkommen ein solcher Versuch ausfallen muss. Denn wie kurz und beschränkt ein Arbeitsleben ist, wie vorherrschend die Irrwege, so fällt doch die Darstellung des Mitteilungswerten nicht leicht—der jetzige Mensch von 67 ist nicht derselbe wie der von 50, 30 und 20. Jede Erinnerung ist gefärbt durch das jetzige So-Sein, also durch einen trügerischen Blickpunkt. Diese Erwägung könnte wohl abschrecken. Aber man kann doch Manches aus dem Selbst-Erleben schöpfen, was einem andern Bewusstsein nicht zugänglich ist.

Als ziemlich frühreifem jungem Menschen kam mir die Nichtigkeit des Hoffens und Strebens lebhaft zum Bewusstsein, das die meisten Menschen rastlos durchs Leben jagt. Auch sah ich bald die Grausamkeit dieses Treibens, die in jenen Jahren sorgsamer als jetzt durch Hypocrisy und glänzende Worte verdeckt war. Jeder war durch die Existenz seines Magens dazu verurteilt, an diesem Treiben sich zu beteiligen. Der Magen konnte durch solche Teilnahme wohl befriedigt werden, aber nicht der Mensch als denkendes und fühlendes Wesen. Da gab es als ersten Ausweg die Religion, die ja jedem Kinde durch die traditionelle Erziehungs-Maschine eingepflanzt wird. So kam ich—obwohl ein Kind ganz irreligiöser (jüdischer) Eltern—zu einer tiefen Religiosität, die aber im Alter von 12 Jahren bereits ein jähes Ende fand. Durch Lesen populär-

AUTOBIOGRAPHICAL NOTES*

HERE I sit in order to write, at the age of 67, something like my own obituary. I am doing this not merely because Dr. Schilpp has persuaded me to do it; but because I do, in fact, believe that it is a good thing to show those who are striving alongside of us, how one's own striving and searching appears to one in retrospect. After some reflection, I felt how insufficient any such attempt is bound to be. For, however brief and limited one's working life may be, and however predominant may be the ways of error, the exposition of that which is worthy of communication does nonetheless not come easy—today's person of 67 is by no means the same as was the one of 50, of 30, or of 20. Every reminiscence is colored by today's being what it is, and therefore by a deceptive point of view. This consideration could very well deter. Nevertheless much can be lifted out of one's own experience which is not open to another consciousness.

Even when I was a fairly precocious young man the nothingness of the hopes and strivings which chases most men restlessly through life came to my consciousness with considerable vitality. Moreover, I soon discovered the cruelty of that chase, which in those years was much more carefully covered up by hypocrisy and glittering words than is the case today. By the mere existence of his stomach everyone was condemned to participate in that chase. Moreover, it was possible to satisfy the stomach by such participation, but not man in so far as he is a thinking and feeling being. As the first way out there was religion, which is implanted into every child by way of the traditional education-machine. Thus I came—despite the fact that I was the son of entirely irreligious (Jewish) parents—to a deep religiosity, which, however, found an abrupt ending at the age

* Translated from the original German manuscript by Paul Arthur Schilpp.

wissenschaftlicher Bücher kam ich bald zu der Ueberzeugung, dass vieles in den Erzählungen der Bibel nicht wahr sein konnte. Die Folge war eine geradezu fanatische Freigeisterei, verbunden mit dem Eindruck, dass die Jugend vom Staate mit Vorbedacht belogen wird; es war ein niederschmetternder Eindruck. Das Misstrauen gegen jede Art Autorität erwuchs aus diesem Erlebnis, eine skeptische Einstellung gegen die Ueberzeugungen, welche in der jeweiligen sozialen Umwelt lebendig waren—eine Einstellung, die mich nicht wieder verlassen hat, wenn sie auch später durch bessere Einsicht in die kausalen Zusammenhänge ihre ursprünglische Schärfe verloren haben.

Es ist mir klar, dass das so verlorene religiöse Paradies der Jugend ein erster Versuch war, mich aus den Fesseln des "Nur-Persönlichen" zu befreien, aus einem Dasein, das durch Wünsche, Hoffnungen und primitive Gefühle beherrscht ist. Da gab es draussen diese grosse Welt, die unabhängig von uns Menschen da ist und vor uns steht wie ein grosses, ewiges Rätsel, wenigstens teilweise zugänglich unserem Schauen und Denken. Ihre Betrachtung winkte als eine Befreiung, und ich merkte bald, dass so Mancher, den ich schätzen und bewundern gelernt hatte, in der hingebenden Beschäftigung mit ihr innere Freiheit und Sicherheit gefunden hatte. Das gedankliche Erfassen dieser ausserpersönlichen Welt im Rahmen der uns gebotenen Möglichkeiten, schwebte mir halb bewusst, halb unbewusst als höchstes Ziel vor. Ähnlich eingestellte Menschen der Gegenwart und Vergangenheit sowie die von ihnen erlangten Einsichten waren die unverlierbaren Freunde. Der Weg zu diesem Paradies war nicht so bequem und lockend wie der Weg zum religiösen Paradies; aber er hat sich als zuverlässig erwiesen, und ich habe es nie bedauert, ihn gewählt zu haben.

Was ich da gesagt habe, ist nur in gewissem Sinne wahr, wie eine aus wenigen Strichen bestehende Zeichnung einem komplizierten, mit verwirrenden Einzelheiten ausgestatteten, Objekt nur in beschränktem Sinne gerecht werden kann. Wenn ein Individuum an gutgefügten Gedanken Freude hat, so mag sich diese Seite seines Wesens auf Kosten anderer Seiten stärker ausprägen und so seine Mentalität in steigendem Masse be-

of 12. Through the reading of popular scientific books I soon reached the conviction that much in the stories of the Bible could not be true. The consequence was a positively fanatic [orgy of] freethinking coupled with the impression that youth is intentionally being deceived by the state through lies; it was a crushing impression. Suspicion against every kind of authority grew out of this experience, a skeptical attitude towards the convictions which were alive in any specific social environment —an attitude which has never again left me, even though later on, because of a better insight into the causal connections, it lost some of its original poignancy.

It is quite clear to me that the religious paradise of youth, which was thus lost, was a first attempt to free myself from the chains of the "merely-personal," from an existence which is dominated by wishes, hopes and primitive feelings. Out yonder there was this huge world, which exists independently of us human beings and which stands before us like a great, eternal riddle, at least partially accessible to our inspection and thinking. The contemplation of this world beckoned like a liberation, and I soon noticed that many a man whom I had learned to esteem and to admire had found inner freedom and security in devoted occupation with it. The mental grasp of this extra-personal world within the frame of the given possibilities swam as highest aim half consciously and half unconsciously before my mind's eye. Similarly motivated men of the present and of the past, as well as the insights which they had achieved, were the friends which could not be lost. The road to this paradise was not as comfortable and alluring as the road to the religious paradise; but it has proved itself as trustworthy, and I have never regretted having chosen it.

What I have here said is true only within a certain sense, just as a drawing consisting of a few strokes can do justice to a complicated object, full of perplexing details, only in a very limited sense. If an individual enjoys well-ordered thoughts, it is quite possible that this side of his nature may grow more pronounced at the cost of other sides and thus may determine his mentality in increasing degree. In this case it is well possi-

stimmen. Es mag dann wohl sein, dass dies Individuum im Rückblick eine einheitliche systematische Entwicklung sieht, während das tatsächliche Erleben in kaleidoskopartiger Einzel-Situation sich abspielt. Die Mannigfaltigkeit der äusseren Situationen und die Enge des momentanen Bewusstsein-Inhaltes bringen ja eine Art Atomisierung des Lebens jedes Menschen mit sich. Bei einem Menschen meiner Art liegt der Wendepunkt der Entwicklung darin, dass das Hauptinteresse sich allmählich weitgehend loslösst vom Momentanen und Nur-Persönlichen und sich dem Streben nach gedanklicher Erfassung der Dinge zuwendet. Von diesem Gesichtspunkt aus betrachtet enthalten die obigen schematischen Bemerkungen so viel Wahres, als sich in solcher Kürze sagen lässt.

Was ist eigentlich "Denken"? Wenn beim Empfangen von Sinnes-Eindrücken Erinnerungsbilder auftauchen, so ist das noch nicht "Denken." Wenn solche Bilder Serien bilden, deren jedes Glied ein anderes wachruft, so ist dies auch noch kein "Denken." Wenn aber ein gewisses Bild in vielen solchen Reihen wiederkehrt, so wird es eben durch seine Wiederkehr zu einem ordnenden Element für solche Reihen, indem es an sich zusammenhangslose Reihen verknüpft. Ein solches Element wird zum Werkzeug, zum Begriff. Ich denke mir, dass der Uebergang vom freien Assoziieren oder "Träumen" zum Denken characterisiert ist durch die mehr oder minder dominierende Rolle, die der "Begriff" dabei spielt. Es ist an sich nicht nötig, dass ein Begriff mit einem sinnlich wahrnehmbaren und reproduzierbaren Zeichen (Wort) verknüpft sei; ist er es aber so wird dadurch Denken mitteilbar.

Mit welchem Recht—so fragt nun der Leser—operiert dieser Mensch so unbekümmert und primitiv mit Ideen auf einem so problematischen Gebiet, ohne den geringsten Versuch zu machen, etwas zu beweisen? Meine Verteidigung: all unser Denken ist von dieser Art eines freien Spiels mit Begriffen; die Berechtigung dieses Spiels liegt in dem Masse der Uebersicht über die Sinnenerlebnisse, die wir mit seiner Hilfe erreichen können. Der Begriff der "Wahrheit" kann auf ein solches Gebilde noch gar nicht angewendet werden; dieser Begriff kann nach meiner Meinung erst dann in Frage kom-

ble that such an individual in retrospect sees a uniformly systematic development, whereas the actual experience takes place in kaleidoscopic particular situations. The manifoldness of the external situations and the narrowness of the momentary content of consciousness bring about a sort of atomizing of the life of every human being. In a man of my type the turning-point of the development lies in the fact that gradually the major interest disengages itself to a far-reaching degree from the momentary and the merely personal and turns towards the striving for a mental grasp of things. Looked at from this point of view the above schematic remarks contain as much truth as can be uttered in such brevity.

What, precisely, is "thinking"? When, at the reception of sense-impressions, memory-pictures emerge, this is not yet "thinking." And when such pictures form series, each member of which calls forth another, this too is not yet "thinking." When, however, a certain picture turns up in many such series, then—precisely through such return—it becomes an ordering element for such series, in that it connects series which in themselves are unconnected. Such an element becomes an instrument, a concept. I think that the transition from free association or "dreaming" to thinking is characterized by the more or less dominating rôle which the "concept" plays in it. It is by no means necessary that a concept must be connected with a sensorily cognizable and reproducible sign (word); but when this is the case thinking becomes by means of that fact communicable.

With what right—the reader will ask—does this man operate so carelessly and primitively with ideas in such a problematic realm without making even the least effort to prove anything? My defense: all our thinking is of this nature of a free play with concepts; the justification for this play lies in the measure of survey over the experience of the senses which we are able to achieve with its aid. The concept of "truth" can not yet be applied to such a structure; to my thinking this concept can come in question only when a far-reaching agreement

men, wenn bereits eine weitgehende Einigung (Convention) über die Elemente und Regeln des Spieles vorliegen.

Es ist mir nicht zweifelhaft, dass unser Denken zum grössten Teil ohne Verwendung von Zeichen (Worte) vor sich geht und dazu noch weitgehend unbewusst. Denn wie sollten wir sonst manchmal dazu kommen, uns über ein Erlebnis ganz spontan zu "wundern"? Dies "sich wundern" scheint dann aufzutreten, wenn ein Erlebnis mit einer in uns hinreichend fixierten Begriffswelt in Konflikt kommt. Wenn solcher Konflikt hart und intensiv erlebt wird dann wirkt er in entscheidender Weise zurück auf unsere Gedankenwelt. Die Entwicklung dieser Gedankenwelt ist in gewissem Sinn eine beständige Flucht aus dem "Wunder."

Ein Wunder solcher Art erlebte ich als Kind von 4 oder 5 Jahren, als mir mein Vater einen Kompass zeigte. Dass diese Nadel in so bestimmter Weise sich benahm passte so gar nicht in die Art des Geschehens hinein, die in der unbewussten Begriffswelt Platz finden konnte (an "Berührung" geknüpftes Wirken). Ich erinnere mich noch jetzt—oder glaube mich zu erinnern—dass dies Erlebnis tiefen und bleibenden Eindruck auf mich gemacht hat. Da musste etwas hinter den Dingen sein, das tief verborgen war. Was der Mensch von klein auf vor sich sieht, darauf reagiert er nicht in solcher Art, er wundert sich nicht über das Fallen der Körper, über Wind und Regen, nicht über den Mond und nicht darüber, dass dieser nicht herunterfällt, nicht über die Verschiedenheit des Belebten und des Nicht-Belebten.

Im Alter von 12 Jahren erlebte ich ein zweites Wunder ganz verschiedener Art: An einem Büchlein über Euklidische Geometrie der Ebene, das ich am Anfang eines Schuljahres in die Hand bekam. Da waren Aussagen wie z.B. das Sich-Schneiden der drei Höhen eines Dreieckes in einem Punkt, die —obwohl an sich keineswegs evident—doch mit solcher Sicherheit bewiesen werden konnten, dass ein Zweifel ausgeschlossen zu sein schien. Diese Klarheit und Sicherheit machte einen unbeschreiblichen Eindruck auf mich. Dass die Axiome unbewiesen hinzunehmen waren beunruhigte mich nicht. Ueberhaupt genügte es mir vollkommen, wenn ich Beweise auf solche Sätze

(*convention*) concerning the elements and rules of the game is already at hand.

For me it is not dubious that our thinking goes on for the most part without use of signs (words) and beyond that to a considerable degree unconsciously. For how, otherwise, should it happen that sometimes we "wonder" quite spontaneously about some experience? This "wondering" seems to occur when an experience comes into conflict with a world of concepts which is already sufficiently fixed in us. Whenever such a conflict is experienced hard and intensively it reacts back upon our thought world in a decisive way. The development of this thought world is in a certain sense a continuous flight from "wonder."

A wonder of such nature I experienced as a child of 4 or 5 years, when my father showed me a compass. That this needle behaved in such a determined way did not at all fit into the nature of events, which could find a place in the unconscious world of concepts (effect connected with direct "touch"). I can still remember—or at least believe I can remember—that this experience made a deep and lasting impression upon me. Something deeply hidden had to be behind things. What man sees before him from infancy causes no reaction of this kind; he is not surprised over the falling of bodies, concerning wind and rain, nor concerning the moon or about the fact that the moon does not fall down, nor concerning the differences between living and non-living matter.

At the age of 12 I experienced a second wonder of a totally different nature: in a little book dealing with Euclidian plane geometry, which came into my hands at the beginning of a schoolyear. Here were assertions, as for example the intersection of the three altitudes of a triangle in one point, which —though by no means evident—could nevertheless be proved with such certainty that any doubt appeared to be out of the question. This lucidity and certainty made an indescribable impression upon me. That the axiom had to be accepted unproved did not disturb me. In any case it was quite sufficient for me if I could peg proofs upon propositions the validity of which did

stützen konnte, deren Gültigkeit mir nicht zweifelhaft erschien. Ich erinnere mich beispielsweise, dass mir der pythagoräische Satz von einem Onkel mitgeteilt wurde, bevor ich das heilige Geometrie-Büchlein in die Hand bekam. Nach harter Mühe gelang es mir, diesen Satz auf Grund der Aehnlichkeit von Dreiecken zu "beweisen"; dabei erschien es mir "evident," dass die Verhältnisse der Seiten eines rechtwinkligen Dreiecks durch einen der spitzen Winkel völlig bestimmt sein müsse. Nur was nicht in ähnlicher Weise "evident" erschien, schien mir überhaupt eines Beweises zu bedürfen. Auch schienen mir die Gegenstände, von denen die Geometrie handelt, nicht von anderer Art zu sein als die Gegenstände der sinnlichen Wahrnehmung, "die man sehen und greifen konnte." Diese primitive Auffassung, welche wohl auch der bekannten Kant'schen Fragestellung betreffend die Möglichkeit "synthetischer Urteile *a priori*" zugrundeliegt, beruht natürlich darauf, dass die Beziehung jener geometrischen Begriffe zu Gegenständen der Erfahrung (fester Stab, Strecke, etc.) unbewusst gegenwärtig war.

Wenn es so schien, dass man durch blosses Denken sichere Erkenntnis über Erfahrungsgegenstände erlangen könne, so beruhte dies "Wunder" auf einem Irrtum. Aber es ist für den, der es zum ersten Mal erlebt, wunderbar genug, dass der Mensch überhaupt imstande ist, einen solchen Grad von Sicherheit und Reinheit im blossen Denken zu erlangen, wie es uns die Griechen erstmalig in der Geometrie gezeigt haben.

Nachdem ich mich nun einmal dazu habe hinreissen lassen, den notdürftig begonnenen Nekrolog zu unterbrechen, scheue ich mich nicht hier in ein paar Sätzen mein erkenntnistheoretisches Credo auszudrücken, obwohl im Vorigen einiges davon beiläufig schon gesagt ist. Dies Credo entwickelte sich erst viel später und langsam und entspricht nicht der Einstellung, die ich in jüngeren Jahren hatte.

Ich sehe auf der einen Seite die Gesamtheit der Sinnen-Erlebnisse, auf der andern Seite die Gesamtheit der Begriffe und Sätze, die in den Büchern niedergelegt sind. Die Beziehungen zwischen den Begriffen und Sätzen unter einander sind logischer Art, und das Geschäft des logischen Denkens ist

not seem to me to be dubious. For example I remember that an uncle told me the Pythagorean theorem before the holy geometry booklet had come into my hands. After much effort I succeeded in "proving" this theorem on the basis of the similarity of triangles; in doing so it seemed to me "evident" that the relations of the sides of the right-angled triangles would have to be completely determined by one of the acute angles. Only something which did not in similar fashion seem to be "evident" appeared to me to be in need of any proof at all. Also, the objects with which geometry deals seemed to be of no different type than the objects of sensory perception, "which can be seen and touched." This primitive idea, which probably also lies at the bottom of the well known Kantian problematic concerning the possibility of "synthetic judgments *a priori*," rests obviously upon the fact that the relation of geometrical concepts to objects of direct experience (rigid rod, finite interval, etc.) was unconsciously present.

If thus it appeared that it was possible to get certain knowledge of the objects of experience by means of pure thinking, this "wonder" rested upon an error. Nevertheless, for anyone who experiences it for the first time, it is marvellous enough that man is capable at all to reach such a degree of certainty and purity in pure thinking as the Greeks showed us for the first time to be possible in geometry.

Now that I have allowed myself to be carried away sufficiently to interrupt my scantily begun obituary, I shall not hesitate to state here in a few sentences my epistemological credo, although in what precedes something has already incidentally been said about this. This credo actually evolved only much later and very slowly and does not correspond with the point of view I held in younger years.

I see on the one side the totality of sense-experiences, and, on the other, the totality of the concepts and propositions which are laid down in books. The relations between the concepts and propositions among themselves and each other are of a logical nature, and the business of logical thinking is strictly limited

strikte beschränkt auf die Herstellung der Verbindung zwischen Begriffen und Sätzen untereinander nach festgesetzten Regeln, mit denen sich die Logik beschäftigt. Die Begriffe und Sätze erhalten "Sinn" bezw. "Inhalt" nur durch ihre Beziehung zu Sinnen-Erlebnissen. Die Verbindung der letzteren mit den ersteren ist rein intuitiv, nicht selbst von logischer Natur. Der Grad der Sicherheit, mit der diese Beziehung bezw. intuitive Verknüpfung vorgenommen werden kann, und nichts anderes, unterscheidet die leere Phantasterei von der wissenschaftlichen "Wahrheit." Das Begriffssystem ist eine Schöpfung des Menschen samt den syntaktischen Regeln, welche die Struktur der Begriffssysteme ausmachen. Die Begriffssysteme sind zwar an sich logisch gänzlich willkürlich, aber gebunden durch das Ziel, eine möglischst sichere (intuitive) und vollständige Zuordnung zu der Gesamtheit der Sinnen-Erlebnisse zuzulassen; zweitens erstreben sie möglichste Sparsamkeit inbezug auf ihre logisch unabhängigen Elemente (Grundbegriffe und Axiome) d.h. nicht definierte Begriffe und nicht erschlossene Sätze.

Ein Satz ist richtig, wenn er innerhalb eines logischen Systems nach den acceptierten logischen Regeln abgeleitet ist. Ein System hat Wahrheitsgehalt, entsprechend der Sicherheit und Vollständigkeit seiner Zuordnungs-Möglichkeit zu der Erlebnis-Gesamtheit. Ein richtiger Satz erborgt seine "Wahrheit" von dem Wahrheits-Gehalt des Systems, dem er angehört.

Eine Bemerkung zur geschichtlichen Entwicklung. Hume erkannte klar, dass gewisse Begriffe, z.B. der der Kausalität, durch logische Methoden nicht aus dem Erfahrungsmaterial abgeleitet werden können. Kant, von der Unentbehrlichkeit gewisser Begriffe durchdrungen, hielt sie—so wie sie gewählt sind—für nötige Prämisse jeglichen Denkens und unterschied sie von Begriffen empirischen Ursprungs. Ich bin aber davon überzeugt, dass diese Unterscheidung irrtümlich ist, bezw. dem Problem nicht in natürlicher Weise gerecht wird. Alle Begriffe, auch die erlebnis-nächsten, sind vom logischen Gesichtspunkte aus freie Setzungen, genau wie der Begriff der Kausalität, an den sich in erster Linie die Fragestellung angeschlossen hat.

to the achievement of the connection between concepts and propositions among each other according to firmly laid down rules, which are the concern of logic. The concepts and propositions get "meaning," viz., "content," only through their connection with sense-experiences. The connection of the latter with the former is purely intuitive, not itself of a logical nature. The degree of certainty with which this relation, viz., intuitive connection, can be undertaken, and nothing else, differentiates empty phantasy from scientific "truth." The system of concepts is a creation of man together with the rules of syntax, which constitute the structure of the conceptual systems. Although the conceptual systems are logically entirely arbitrary, they are bound by the aim to permit the most nearly possible certain (intuitive) and complete co-ordination with the totality of sense-experiences; secondly they aim at greatest possible sparsity of their logically independent elements (basic concepts and axioms), i.e., undefined concepts and underived [postulated] propositions.

A proposition is correct if, within a logical system, it is deduced according to the accepted logical rules. A system has truth-content according to the certainty and completeness of its co-ordination-possibility to the totality of experience. A correct proposition borrows its "truth" from the truth-content of the system to which it belongs.

A remark to the historical development. Hume saw clearly that certain concepts, as for example that of causality, cannot be deduced from the material of experience by logical methods. Kant, thoroughly convinced of the indispensability of certain concepts, took them—just as they are selected—to be the necessary premises of every kind of thinking and differentiated them from concepts of empirical origin. I am convinced, however, that this differentiation is erroneous, i.e., that it does not do justice to the problem in a natural way. All concepts, even those which are closest to experience, are from the point of view of logic freely chosen conventions, just as is the case with the concept of causality, with which this problematic concerned itself in the first instance.

Nun zurück zum Nekrolog. Im Alter von 12-16 machte ich mich mit den Elementen der Mathematik vertraut inklusive der Prinzipien der Differential- und Integral-Rechnung. Dabei hatte ich das Glück auf Bücher zu stossen, die es nicht gar zu genau nahmen mit der logischen Strenge, dafür aber die Hauptgedanken übersichtlich hervortreten liessen. Diese Beschäftigung war im Ganzen wahrhaft fascinierend; es gab darin Höhepunkte, deren Eindruck sich mit dem der elementaren Geometrie sehr wohl messen konnte—der Grundgedanke der analytischen Geometrie, die unendlichen Reihen, der Differential- und Integral-Begriff. Auch hatte ich das Glück, die wesentlichen Ergebnisse und Methoden der gesamten Naturwissenschaft in einer vortrefflichen populären, fast durchweg aufs Qualitative sich beschränkenden Darstellung kennen zu lernen (Bernsteins naturwissenschaftliche Volksbücher, ein Werk von 5 oder 6 Bänden), ein Werk, das ich mit atemloser Spannung las. Auch etwas theoretische Physik hatte ich bereits studiert, als ich mit 17 Jahren auf das Züricher Polytechnikum kam als Student der Mathematik und Physik.

Dort hatte ich vortreffliche Lehrer (z.B. Hurwitz, Minkowski), so dass ich eigentlich eine tiefe mathematische Ausbildung hätte erlangen können. Ich aber arbeitete die meiste Zeit im physikalischen Laboratorium, fasciniert durch die direkte Berührung mit der Erfahrung. Die übrige Zeit benutzte ich hauptsächlich, um die Werke von Kirchhoff, Helmholtz, Hertz, etc. zuhause zu studieren. Dass ich die Mathematik bis zu einem gewissen Grade vernachlässigte, hatte nicht nur den Grund, dass das naturwissenschaftliche Interesse stärker war als das mathematische, sondern das folgende eigentümliche Erlebnis. Ich sah, dass die Mathematik in viele Spezialgebiete gespalten war, deren jedes diese kurze uns vergönnte Lebenszeit wegnehmen konnte. So sah ich mich in der Lage von Buridans Esel, der sich nicht für ein besonderes Bündel Heu entschliessen konnte. Dies lag offenbar daran, dass meine Intuition auf mathematischem Gebiete nicht stark genug war, um das Fundamental-Wichtige, Grundlegende sicher von dem Rest der mehr oder weniger entbehrlichen Gelehrsamkeit zu unterscheiden. Ausserdem war aber auch das Interesse für die Natur-Erkennt-

And now back to the obituary. At the age of 12-16 I familiarized myself with the elements of mathematics together with the principles of differential and integral calculus. In doing so I had the good fortune of hitting on books which were not too particular in their logical rigour, but which made up for this by permitting the main thoughts to stand out clearly and synoptically. This occupation was, on the whole, truly fascinating; climaxes were reached whose impression could easily compete with that of elementary geometry—the basic idea of analytical geometry, the infinite series, the concepts of differential and integral. I also had the good fortune of getting to know the essential results and methods of the entire field of the natural sciences in an excellent popular exposition, which limited itself almost throughout to qualitative aspects (Bernstein's *People's Books on Natural Science,* a work of 5 or 6 volumes), a work which I read with breathless attention. I had also already studied some theoretical physics when, at the age of 17, I entered the Polytechnic Institute of Zürich as a student of mathematics and physics.

There I had excellent teachers (for example, Hurwitz, Minkowski), so that I really could have gotten a sound mathematical education. However, I worked most of the time in the physical laboratory, fascinated by the direct contact with experience. The balance of the time I used in the main in order to study at home the works of Kirchhoff, Helmholtz, Hertz, etc. The fact that I neglected mathematics to a certain extent had its cause not merely in my stronger interest in the natural sciences than in mathematics but also in the following strange experience. I saw that mathematics was split up into numerous specialities, each of which could easily absorb the short lifetime granted to us. Consequently I saw myself in the position of Buridan's ass which was unable to decide upon any specific bundle of hay. This was obviously due to the fact that my intuition was not strong enough in the field of mathematics in order to differentiate clearly the fundamentally important, that which is really basic, from the rest of the more or less dispensable erudition. Beyond this, however, my interest in the knowledge of nature was also unqualifiedly stronger; and it was not clear

nis unbedingt stärker; und es wurde mir als Student nicht klar, dass der Zugang zu den tieferen prinzipiellen Erkenntnissen in der Physik an die feinsten mathematischen Methoden gebunden war. Dies dämmerte mir erst allmählich nach Jahren selbständiger wissenschaftlicher Arbeit. Freilich war auch die Physik in Spezialgebiete geteilt, deren jedes ein kurzes Arbeitsleben verschlingen konnte, ohne dass der Hunger nach tieferer Erkenntnis befriedigt würde. Die Masse des erfahrungsmässig Gegebenen und ungenügend Verbundenen war auch hier überwältigend. Aber bald lernte ich es hier, dasjenige herauszuspüren, was in die Tiefe führen konnte, von allem Andern aber abzusehen, von dem Vielen, das den Geist ausfüllt und von dem Wesentlichen ablenkt. Der Haken dabei war freilich, dass man für die Examina all diesen Wust in sich hineinstopfen musste, ob man nun wollte oder nicht. Dieser Zwang wirkte so abschreckend, dass mir nach überstandenem Endexamen jedes Nachdenken über wissenschaftliche Probleme für ein ganzes Jahr verleidet war. Dabei muss ich sagen, dass wir in der Schweiz unter solchem den wahren wissenschaftlichen Trieb erstickenden Zwang weniger zu leiden hatten, als es an vielen andern Orten der Fall ist. Es gab im Ganzen nur zwei Examina; im übrigen konnte man so ziemlich tun und lassen, was man wollte. Besonders war dies so, wenn man wie ich einen Freund hatte, der die Vorlesungen regelmässig besuchte und den Inhalt gewissenhaft ausarbeitete. Dies gab Freiheit in der Wahl der Beschäftigung bis auf wenige Monate vor dem Examen, eine Freiheit die ich weitgehend genossen habe und das mit ihr verbundene schlechte Gewissen als das weitaus kleinere Uebel gerne in den Kauf nahm. Es ist eigentlich wie ein Wunder, dass der moderne Lehrbetrieb die heilige Neugier des Forschens noch nicht ganz erdrosselt hat; denn dies delikate Pflänzchen bedarf neben Anregung hauptsächlich der Freiheit; ohne diese geht es unweigerlich zugrunde. Es ist ein grosser Irrtum zu glauben dass Freude am Schauen und Suchen durch Zwang und Pflichtgefühl gefördert werden könne. Ich denke, dass man selbst einem gesunden Raubtier seine Fressgier wegnehmen könnte, wenn es gelänge, es mit Hilfe der Peitsche fortgesetzt zum Fressen zu zwingen, wenn es keinen Hunger

to me as a student that the approach to a more profound knowledge of the basic principles of physics is tied up with the most intricate mathematical methods. This dawned upon me only gradually after years of independent scientific work. True enough, physics also was divided into separate fields, each of which was capable of devouring a short lifetime of work without having satisfied the hunger for deeper knowledge. The mass of insufficiently connected experimental data was overwhelming here also. In this field, however, I soon learned to scent out that which was able to lead to fundamentals and to turn aside from everything else, from the multitude of things which clutter up the mind and divert it from the essential. The hitch in this was, of course, the fact that one had to cram all this stuff into one's mind for the examinations, whether one liked it or not. This coercion had such a deterring effect [upon me] that, after I had passed the final examination, I found the consideration of any scientific problems distasteful to me for an entire year. In justice I must add, moreover, that in Switzerland we had to suffer far less under such coercion, which smothers every truly scientific impulse, than is the case in many another locality. There were altogether only two examinations; aside from these, one could just about do as one pleased. This was especially the case if one had a friend, as did I, who attended the lectures regularly and who worked over their content conscientiously. This gave one freedom in the choice of pursuits until a few months before the examination, a freedom which I enjoyed to a great extent and have gladly taken into the bargain the bad conscience connected with it as by far the lesser evil. It is, in fact, nothing short of a miracle that the modern methods of instruction have not yet entirely strangled the holy curiosity of inquiry; for this delicate little plant, aside from stimulation, stands mainly in need of freedom; without this it goes to wreck and ruin without fail. It is a very grave mistake to think that the enjoyment of seeing and searching can be promoted by means of coercion and a sense of duty. To the contrary, I believe that it would be possible to rob even a healthy beast of prey of its voraciousness, if it were possible, with the aid of a whip, to force the beast to devour continuously,

hat, besonders wenn man die unter solchem Zwang verabreichten Speisen entsprechend auswählte. – – –

Nun zur Physik, wie sie sich damals präsentierte. Bei aller Fruchtbarkeit im Einzelnen herrschte in prinzipiellen Dingen dogmatische Starrheit: Am Anfang (wenn es einen solchen gab), schuf Gott Newtons Bewegungsgesetze samt den notwendigen Massen und Kräften. Dies ist alles; das Weitere ergibt die Ausbildung geeigneter mathematischer Methoden durch Deduktion. Was das 19. Jahrhundert fussend auf diese Basis geleistet hat, insbesondere durch die Anwendung der partiellen Differenzialgleichungen, musste die Bewunderung jedes empfänglichen Menschen erwecken. Newton war wohl der erste, der die Leistungsfähigkeit der partiellen Differentialgleichung in seiner Theorie der Schall-Fortpflanzung offenbarte. Euler hatte schon das Fundament der Hydrodynamik geschaffen. Aber der feinere Ausbau der Mechanik diskreter Massen, als Basis der gesamten Physik, war das Werk des 19. Jahrhunderts. Was aber auf den Studenten den grössten Eindruck machte, war weniger der technische Aufbau der Mechanik und die Lösung komplizierter Probleme, sondern die Leistungen der Mechanik auf Gebieten, die dem Anscheine nach nichts mit Mechanik zu tun hatten: die mechanische Lichttheorie, die das Licht als Wellenbewegung eines quasistarren elastischen Aethers auffasste, vor allem aber die kinetische Gastheorie:—Die Unabhängigkeit der spezifischen Wärme einatomiger Gase vom Atomgewicht, die Ableitung der Gasgleichung und deren Beziehung zur spezifischen Wärme, die kinetische Theorie der Dissoziation der Gase, vor allem aber der quantitative Zusammenhang von Viskosität, Wärmeleitung und Diffusion der Gase, welche auch die absolute Grösse des Atoms lieferte. Diese Ergebnisse stützten gleichzeitig die Mechanik als Grundlage der Physik und der Atomhypothese, welch letztere ja in der Chemie schon fest verankert war. In der Chemie spielten aber nur die Verhältnisse der Atommassen eine Rolle, nicht deren absolute Grössen, sodass die Atomtheorie mehr als veranschaulichendes Gleichnis denn als Erkenntnis über den faktischen Bau der Materie betrachtet werden konnte. Abgesehen davon war es auch von

even when not hungry, especially if the food, handed out under such coercion, were to be selected accordingly. – – –

Now to the field of physics as it presented itself at that time. In spite of all the fruitfulness in particulars, dogmatic rigidity prevailed in matters of principles: In the beginning (if there was such a thing) God created Newton's laws of motion together with the necessary masses and forces. This is all; everything beyond this follows from the development of appropriate mathematical methods by means of deduction. What the nineteenth century achieved on the strength of this basis, especially through the application of the partial differential equations, was bound to arouse the admiration of every receptive person. Newton was probably first to reveal, in his theory of sound-transmission, the efficacy of partial differential equations. Euler had already created the foundation of hydrodynamics. But the more precise development of the mechanics of discrete masses, as the basis of all physics, was the achievement of the 19th century. What made the greatest impression upon the student, however, was less the technical construction of mechanics or the solution of complicated problems than the achievements of mechanics in areas which apparently had nothing to do with mechanics: the mechanical theory of light, which conceived of light as the wave-motion of a quasi-rigid elastic ether, and above all the kinetic theory of gases:—the independence of the specific heat of monatomic gases of the atomic weight, the derivation of the equation of state of a gas and its relation to the specific heat, the kinetic theory of the dissociation of gases, and above all the quantitative connection of viscosity, heat-conduction and diffusion of gases, which also furnished the absolute magnitude of the atom. These results supported at the same time mechanics as the foundation of physics and of the atomic hypothesis, which latter was already firmly anchored in chemistry. However, in chemistry only the ratios of the atomic masses played any rôle, not their absolute magnitudes, so that atomic theory could be viewed more as a visualizing symbol than as knowledge concerning the factual construction of matter. Apart from this it was also of profound

tiefem Interesse, dass die statistische Theorie der klassischen Mechanik imstande war, die Grundgesetze der Thermodynamik zu deduzieren, was dem Wesen nach schon von Boltzmann geleistet wurde.

Wir dürfen uns daher nicht wundern, dass sozusagen alle Physiker des letzten Jahrhunderts in der klassischen Mechanik eine feste und endgültige Grundlage der ganzen Physik, ja der ganzen Naturwissenschaft sahen, und dass sie nicht müde wurden zu versuchen, auch die indessen langsam sich durchsetzende Maxwell'sche Theorie des Elektromagnetismus auf die Mechanik zu gründen. Auch Maxwell und H. Hertz, die im Rückblick mit Recht als diejenigen erscheinen, die das Vertrauen auf die Mechanik als die endgültige Basis alles physikalischen Denkens erschüttert haben, haben in ihrem bewussten Denken durchaus an der Mechanik als gesicherter Basis der Physik festgehalten. Ernst Mach war es, der in seiner Geschichte der Mechanik an diesem dogmatischen Glauben rüttelte; dies Buch hat gerade in dieser Beziehung einen tiefen Einfluss auf mich als Student ausgeübt. Ich sehe Machs wahre Grösse in der unbestechlichen Skepsis und Unabhängigkeit; in meinen jungen Jahren hat mich aber auch Machs erkenntnistheoretische Einstellung sehr beeindruckt, die mir heute als im Wesentlichen unhaltbar erscheint. Er hat nämlich die dem Wesen nach konstruktive und spekulative Natur alles Denkens und im Besonderen des wissenschaftlichen Denkens nicht richtig ins Licht gestellt und infolge davon die Theorie gerade an solchen Stellen verurteilt, an welchen der konstruktiv-spekulative Charakter unverhüllbar zutage tritt, z.B. in der kinetischen Atomtheorie.

Bevor ich nun eingehe auf eine Kritik der Mechanik als Grundlage der Physik, muss erst etwas Allgemeines über die Gesichtspunkte gesagt werden, nach denen physikalische Theorien überhaupt kritisiert werden können. Der erste Gesichtspunkt liegt auf der Hand: die Theorie darf Erfahrungstatsachen nicht widersprechen. So einleuchtend diese Forderung auch zunächst erscheint, so subtil gestaltet sich ihre Anwendung. Man kann nämlich häufig, vielleicht sogar immer, an einer allgemeinen theoretischen Grundlage festhalten, indem man

interest that the statistical theory of classical mechanics was able to deduce the basic laws of thermodynamics, something which was in essence already accomplished by Boltzmann.

We must not be surprised, therefore, that, so to speak, all physicists of the last century saw in classical mechanics a firm and final foundation for all physics, yes, indeed, for all natural science, and that they never grew tired in their attempts to base Maxwell's theory of electro-magnetism, which, in the meantime, was slowly beginning to win out, upon mechanics as well. Even Maxwell and H. Hertz, who in retrospect appear as those who demolished the faith in mechanics as the final basis of all physical thinking, in their conscious thinking adhered throughout to mechanics as the secured basis of physics. It was Ernst Mach who, in his *History of Mechanics*, shook this dogmatic faith; this book exercised a profound influence upon me in this regard while I was a student. I see Mach's greatness in his incorruptible skepticism and independence; in my younger years, however, Mach's epistemological position also influenced me very greatly, a position which today appears to me to be essentially untenable. For he did not place in the correct light the essentially constructive and speculative nature of thought and more especially of scientific thought; in consequence of which he condemned theory on precisely those points where its constructive-speculative character unconcealably comes to light, as for example in the kinetic atomic theory.

Before I enter upon a critique of mechanics as the foundation of physics, something of a broadly general nature will first have to be said concerning the points of view according to which it is possible to criticize physical theories at all. The first point of view is obvious: the theory must not contradict empirical facts. However evident this demand may in the first place appear, its application turns out to be quite delicate. For it is often, perhaps even always, possible to adhere to a general theoretical foundation by securing the adaptation of the theory

durch künstliche zusätzliche Annahmen ihre Anpassung an die Tatsachen möglich macht. Jedenfalls aber hat es dieser erste Gesichtspunkt mit der Bewährung der theoretischen Grundlage an einem vorliegenden Erfahrungsmaterial zu tun.

Der zweite Gesichtspunkt hat es nicht zu schaffen mit der Beziehung zu dem Beobachtungsmaterial sondern mit den Prämissen der Theorie selbst, mit dem, was man kurz aber undeutlich als "Natürlichkeit" oder "logische Einfachheit" der Prämissen (der Grundbegriffe und zugrunde gelegten Beziehungen zwischen diesen) bezeichnen kann. Dieser Gesichtspunkt, dessen exakte Formulierung auf grosse Schwierigkeiten stösst, hat von jeher bei der Wahl und Wertung der Theorien eine wichtige Rolle gespielt. Es handelt sich dabei nicht einfach um eine Art Abzählung der logisch unabhängigen Prämissen (wenn eine solche überhaupt eindeutig möglich wäre) sondern um eine Art gegenseitiger Abwägung inkommensurabler Qualitäten. Ferner ist von Theorien mit gleich "einfacher" Grundlage diejenige als die Ueberlegene zu betrachten, welche die an sich möglichen Qualitäten von Systemen am stärksten einschränkt (d.h. die bestimmtesten Aussagen enthält). Von dem "Bereich" der Theorien brauche ich hier nichts zu sagen, da wir uns auf solche Theorien beschränken, deren Gegenstand die *Gesamtheit* der physikalischen Erscheinungen ist. Der zweite Gesichtspunkt kann kurz als der die "innere Vollkommenheit" der Theorie betreffende bezeichnet werden, während der erste Gesichtspunkt sich auf die "äussere Bewährung" bezieht. Zur "inneren Vollkommenheit" einer Theorie rechne ich auch folgendes: Wir schätzen eine Theorie höher, wenn sie nicht eine vom logischen Standpunkt willkürliche Wahl unter an sich gleichwertigen und analog gebauten Theorien ist.

Die mangelhafte Schärfe der in den letzten beiden Absätzen enthaltenen Aussagen will ich nicht mit dem Mangel an genügendem zur Verfügung stehendem Druck-Raum zu entschuldigen suchen, sondern bekenne hiermit, dass ich nicht ohne Weiteres, vielleicht überhaupt nicht fähig wäre, diese Andeutungen durch scharfe Definitionen zu ersetzen. Ich glaube aber, dass eine schärfere Formulierung möglich wäre. Jedenfalls zeigt es sich, dass zwischen den "Auguren" meist Uebereinstim-

to the facts by means of artificial additional assumptions. In any case, however, this first point of view is concerned with the confirmation of the theoretical foundation by the available empirical facts.

The second point of view is not concerned with the relation to the material of observation but with the premises of the theory itself, with what may briefly but vaguely be characterized as the "naturalness" or "logical simplicity" of the premises (of the basic concepts and of the relations between these which are taken as a basis). This point of view, an exact formulation of which meets with great difficulties, has played an important rôle in the selection and evaluation of theories since time immemorial. The problem here is not simply one of a kind of enumeration of the logically independent premises (if anything like this were at all unequivocally possible), but that of a kind of reciprocal weighing of incommensurable qualities. Furthermore, among theories of equally "simple" foundation that one is to be taken as superior which most sharply delimits the qualities of systems in the abstract (i.e., contains the most definite claims). Of the "realm" of theories I need not speak here, inasmuch as we are confining ourselves to such theories whose object is the *totality* of all physical appearances. The second point of view may briefly be characterized as concerning itself with the "inner perfection" of the theory, whereas the first point of view refers to the "external confirmation." The following I reckon as also belonging to the "inner perfection" of a theory: We prize a theory more highly if, from the logical standpoint, it is not the result of an arbitrary choice among theories which, among themselves, are of equal value and analogously constructed.

The meager precision of the assertions contained in the last two paragraphs I shall not attempt to excuse by lack of sufficient printing space at my disposal, but confess herewith that I am not, without more ado [immediately], and perhaps not at all, capable to replace these hints by more precise definitions. I believe, however, that a sharper formulation would be possible. In any case it turns out that among the "augurs" there usually is agreement in judging the "inner perfection" of the

mung besteht bezüglich der Beurteilung der "inneren Vollkommenheit" der Theorien und erst recht über den Grad der "äusseren Bewährung."

Nun zur Kritik der Mechanik als Basis der Physik.

Vom ersten Gesichtspunkte (Bewährung an den Tatsachen) musste die Einverleibung der Wellenoptik ins mechanische Weltbild ernste Bedenken erwecken. War das Licht als Wellenbewegung in einem elastischen Körper aufzufassen (Aether) so musste es ein alles durchdringendes Medium sein, wegen der Transversalität der Lichtwellen in der Hauptsache ähnlich einem festen Körper, aber inkompressibel, so dass longitudinale Wellen nicht existierten. Dieser Aether musste neben der sonstigen Materie ein Gespensterdasein führen, indem er den Bewegungen der "ponderabeln" Körper keinerlei Widerstand zu leisten schien. Um die Brechungs-Indices durchsichtiger Körper sowie die Prozesse der Emission und Absorption der Strahlung zu erklären, hätte man verwickelte Wechselwirkungen zwischen beiden Arten von Materie annehmen müssen, was nicht einmal ernstlich versucht, geschweige geleistet wurde.

Ferner nötigten die elekromagnetischen Kräfte zur Einführung elektrischer Massen, die zwar keine merkliche Trägheit besassen, aber Wechselwirkungen auf einander ausübten, und zwar, im Gegensatz zur Gravitations-Kraft, solche von polarer Art.

Was die Physiker nach langem Zaudern langsam dazu brachte, den Glauben an die Möglichkeit zu verlassen, dass die gesamte Physik auf Newtons Mechanik gegründet werden könne, war die Faraday-Maxwell'sche Elektrodynamik. Diese Theorie und ihre Bestätigung durch die Hertz'schen Versuche zeigten nämlich, dass es elektromagnetische Vorgänge gibt, die ihrem Wesen nach losgelöst sind von jeglicher ponderabeln Materie—die aus elektromagnetischen "Feldern" im leeren Raume bestehenden Wellen. Wollte man die Mechanik als Grundlage der Physik aufrecht halten, so mussten die Maxwell'schen Gleichungen mechanisch interpretiert werden. Dies wurde eifrigst aber erfolglos versucht, während sich die Gleichungen in steigendem Masse als fruchtbar erwiesen. Man gewöhnte sich daran, mit diesen Feldern als selbständigen

theories and even more so concerning the "degree" of "external confirmation."

And now to the critique of mechanics as the basis of physics.

From the first point of view (confirmation by experiment) the incorporation of wave-optics into the mechanical picture of the world was bound to arouse serious misgivings. If light was to be interpreted as undulatory motion in an elastic body (ether), this had to be a medium which permeates everything; because of the transversality of the lightwaves in the main similar to a solid body, yet incompressible, so that longitudinal waves did not exist. This ether had to lead a ghostly existence alongside the rest of matter, inasmuch as it seemed to offer no resistance whatever to the motion of "ponderable" bodies. In order to explain the refraction-indices of transparent bodies as well as the processes of emission and absorption of radiation, one would have had to assume complicated reciprocal actions between the two types of matter, something which was not even seriously tried, let alone achieved.

Furthermore, the electromagnetic forces necessitated the introduction of electric masses, which, although they had no noticeable inertia, yet interacted with each other, and whose interaction was, moreover, in contrast to the force of gravitation, of a polar type.

The factor which finally succeeded, after long hesitation, to bring the physicists slowly around to give up the faith in the possibility that all of physics could be founded upon Newton's mechanics, was the electrodynamics of Faraday and Maxwell. For this theory and its confirmation by Hertz's experiments showed that there are electromagnetic phenomena which by their very nature are detached from every ponderable matter—namely the waves in empty space which consist of electromagnetic "fields." If mechanics was to be maintained as the foundation of physics, Maxwell's equations had to be interpreted mechanically. This was zealously but fruitlessly attempted, while the equations were proving themselves fruitful in mounting degree. One got used to operating with these fields as independent substances without finding it necessary

Wesenheiten zu operieren, ohne dass man sich über ihre mechanische Natur auszuweisen brauchte; so verliess man halb unvermerkt die Mechanik als Basis der Physik, weil deren Anpassung an die Tatsachen sich schliesslich als hoffnungslos darstellte. Seitdem gibt es zweierlei Begriffselemente, einerseits materielle Punkte mit Fernkräften zwischen ihnen, andererseits das kontinuierliche Feld. Es ist ein Zwischenzustand der Physik ohne einheitliche Basis für das Ganze, der—obwohl unbefriedigend—doch weit davon entfernt ist überwunden zu sein. – – –

Nun einiges zur Kritik der Mechanik als Grundlage der Physik vom zweiten, dem inneren Gesichtspunkte aus. Solche Kritik hat bei dem heutigen Stande der Wissenschaft, d.h. nach dem Verlassen des mechanischen Fundamentes, nur noch methodisches Interesse. Sie ist aber recht geeignet eine Art des Argumentierens zu zeigen, die in der Zukunft bei der Auswahl der Theorien eine umso grössere Rolle spielen muss, je weiter sich die Grundbegriffe und Axiome von dem direkt Wahrnehmbaren entfernen, sodass das Konfrontieren der Implikationen der Theorie mit den Tatsachen immer schwieriger und langwieriger wird. Da ist in erster Linie das Mach'sche Argument zu erwähnen, das übrigens von Newton schon ganz deutlich erkannt worden war (Eimer Versuch). Alle "starren" Koordinationssysteme sind vom Standpunkt der rein geometrischen Beschreibung unter einander logisch gleichwertig. Die Gleichungen der Mechanik (z.B. schon das Trägheits-Gesetz) beanspruchen Gültigkeit nur gegenüber einer besonderen Klasse solcher Systeme, nämlich gegenüber den "Inertialsystemen." Das Koordinationssystem als körperliches Objekt ist hierbei ohne Bedeutung. Man muss also für die Notwendigkeit dieser besonderen Wahl etwas suchen, was ausserhalb der Gegenstände (Massen, Abstände) liegt, von denen die Theorie handelt. Newton führte als ursächlich bestimmend deshalb ganz explicite den "absoluten Raum" ein als allgegenwärtigen aktiven Teilnehmer bei allen mechanischen Vorgängen; unter "absolut" versteht er offenbar unbeinflusst von den Massen und ihren Bewegungen. Was den Tatbestand besonders hässlich erscheinen lässt, ist die Tatsache, dass es unendlich viele,

to give one's self an account of their mechanical nature; thus mechanics as the basis of physics was being abandoned, almost unnoticeably, because its adaptability to the facts presented itself finally as hopeless. Since then there exist two types of conceptual elements, on the one hand, material points with forces at a distance between them, and, on the other hand, the continuous field. It presents an intermediate state in physics without a uniform basis for the entirety, which—although unsatisfactory—is far from having been superseded. – – –

Now for a few remarks to the critique of mechanics as the foundation of physics from the second, the "interior," point of view. In today's state of science, i.e., after the departure from the mechanical foundation, such critique has only an interest in method left. But such a critique is well suited to show the type of argumentation which, in the choice of theories in the future will have to play an all the greater rôle the more the basic concepts and axioms distance themselves from what is directly observable, so that the confrontation of the implications of theory by the facts becomes constantly more difficult and more drawn out. First in line to be mentioned is Mach's argument, which, however, had already been clearly recognized by Newton (bucket experiment). From the standpoint of purely geometrical description all "rigid" co-ordinate systems are among themselves logically equivalent. The equations of mechanics (for example this is already true of the law of inertia) claim validity only when referred to a specific class of such systems, i.e., the "inertial systems." In this the co-ordinate system as bodily object is without any significance. It is necessary, therefore, in order to justify the necessity of the specific choice, to look for something which lies outside of the objects (masses, distances) with which the theory is concerned. For this reason "absolute space" as originally determinative was quite explicitly introduced by Newton as the omnipresent active participant in all mechanical events; by "absolute" he obviously means uninfluenced by the masses and by their motion. What makes this state of affairs appear particularly offensive is the fact that there are supposed to be infinitely many inertial systems, relative to each

gegen einander gleichförmig und rotationsfrei bewegte Inertialsysteme geben soll, die gegenüber allen andern starren Systemen ausgezeichnet sein sollen.

Mach vermutet, dass in einer wirklich vernünftigen Theorie die Trägheit, genau wie bei Newton die übrigen Kräfte, auf Wechselwirkung der Massen beruhen müsse, eine Auffassung die ich lange für im Prinzip die richtige hielt. Sie setzt aber implicite voraus, dass die basische Theorie eine solche vom allgemeinen Typus der Newton'schen Mechanik sein solle: Massen und Wirkungen zwischen diesen als ursprüngliche Begriffe. In eine konsequente Feldtheorie passt ein solcher Lösungsversuch nicht hinein, wie man unmittelbar einsieht.

Wie stichhaltig die Mach'sche Kritik aber an sich ist, kann man besonders deutlich aus folgender Analogie ersehen. Wir denken uns Leute, die eine Mechanik aufstellen, nur ein kleines Stück der Erdoberfläche kennen und auch keine Sterne wahrnehmen können. Sie werden geneigt sein, der vertikalen Dimension des Raumes besondere physikalische Eigenschaften zuzuschreiben (Richtung der Fallbeschleunigung) und auf Grund einer solchen begrifflichen Basis es begründen, dass der Erdboden überwiegend horizontal ist. Sie mögen sich nicht durch das Argument beeinflussen lassen, dass bezüglich der geometrischen Eigenschaften der Raum isotrop ist, und dass es daher unbefriedigend sei, physikalische Grundgesetze aufzustellen, gemäss welchen es eine Vorzugsrichtung geben soll; sie werden wohl geneigt sein (analog zu Newton) zu erklären, die Vertikale sei absolut, das zeige eben die Erfahrung und man müsse sich damit abfinden. Die Bevorzugung der Vertikalen gegen alle anderen Raum-Richtungen ist genau analog der Bevorzugung der Inertialsysteme gegen andere starre Koordinationssysteme.

Nun zu anderen Argumenten die sich ebenfalls auf die innere Einfachheit bezw. Natürlichkeit der Mechanik beziehen. Wenn man die Begriffe Raum (inklusive Geometrie) und Zeit ohne kritischen Zweifel hinnimmt, so besteht an sich kein Grund, die Zugrundelegung von Fernkräften zu beanstanden, wenn ein solcher Begriff auch nicht zu denjenigen Ideen passt, die man sich auf Grund der rohen Erfahrung des Alltags bildet.

other in uniform translation, which are supposed to be distinguished among all other rigid systems.

Mach conjectures that in a truly rational theory inertia would have to depend upon the interaction of the masses, precisely as was true for Newton's other forces, a conception which for a long time I considered as in principle the correct one. It presupposes implicitly, however, that the basic theory should be of the general type of Newton's mechanics: masses and their interaction as the original concepts. The attempt at such a solution does not fit into a consistent field theory, as will be immediately recognized.

How sound, however, Mach's critique is in essence can be seen particularly clearly from the following analogy. Let us imagine people construct a mechanics, who know only a very small part of the earth's surface and who also can not see any stars. They will be inclined to ascribe special physical attributes to the vertical dimension of space (direction of the acceleration of falling bodies) and, on the ground of such a conceptual basis, will offer reasons that the earth is in most places horizontal. They might not permit themselves to be influenced by the argument that as concerns the geometrical properties space is isotrope and that it is therefore supposed to be unsatisfactory to postulate basic physical laws, according to which there is supposed to be a preferential direction; they will probably be inclined (analogously to Newton) to assert the absoluteness of the vertical, as proved by experience as something with which one simply would have to come to terms. The preference given to the vertical over all other spatial directions is precisely analogous to the preference given to inertial systems over other rigid co-ordination systems.

Now to [a consideration of] other arguments which also concern themselves with the inner simplicity, i.e., naturalness, of mechanics. If one puts up with the concepts of space (including geometry) and time without critical doubts, then there exists no reason to object to the idea of action-at-a-distance, even though such a concept is unsuited to the ideas which one forms on the basis of the raw experience of daily life. However, there

Dagegen gibt es eine andere Ueberlegung, welche die Mechanik als Basis der Physik aufgefasst als primitiv erscheinen lässt. Es gibt im Wesentlichen zwei Gesetze

1) das Bewegungsgesetz
2) den Ausdruck für die Kraft bezw. die potentielle Energie.

Das Bewegungsgesetz ist präzis, aber leer, solange der Ausdruck für die Kräfte nicht gegeben ist. Für die Setzung der letzteren besteht aber ein weiter Spielraum für Willkür, besonders wenn man die an sich nicht natürliche Forderung fallen lässt, dass die Kräfte von den Koordinaten allein (und z.B. nicht von deren Differentialquotienten nach der Zeit) abhängen. Im Rahmen der Theorie ist es an sich ganz willkürlich, dass die von einem Punkte ausgehenden Gravitations- (und elektrischen) Kraftwirkungen durch die Potentialfunktion $(1/r)$ beherrscht werden. Zusätzliche Bemerkung: es ist schon lange bekannt, dass diese Funktion die zentralsymmetrische Lösung der einfachsten (drehungs-invarianten) Differentialgleichung $\Delta\varphi = 0$ ist; es wäre also naheliegend gewesen, dies als ein Anzeichen dafür zu betrachten, dass man diese Funktion als durch ein Raumgesetz bestimmt anzusehen hätte, wodurch die Willkür in der Wahl des Kraftgesetzes beseitigt worden wäre. Dies ist eigentlich die erste Erkenntnis, welche eine Abkehr von der Theorie der Fernkräfte nahelegt, welche Entwicklung —durch Faraday, Maxwell und Hertz angebahnt—unter dem äusseren Druck von Erfahrungstatsachen erst später einsetzt.

Ich möchte auch als eine innere Unsymmetrie der Theorie erwähnen, dass die im Bewegungsgesetz auftretende träge Masse auch im Kraftgesetz der Gravitation, nicht aber im Ausdruck der übrigen Kraftgesetze auftritt. Endlich möchte ich darauf hinweisen, dass die Spaltung der Energie in zwei wesensverschiedene Teile, kinetische und potentielle Energie, als unnatürlich empfunden werden muss; dies hat H. Hertz als so störend empfunden, dass er in seinem letzten Werk versuchte, die Mechanik von dem Begriff der potentiellen Energie (d.h. der Kraft) zu befreien. – – –

Genug davon. Newton verzeih' mir; du fandst den einzigen Weg der zu deiner Zeit für einen Menschen von höchster

is another consideration which causes mechanics, taken as the basis of physics, to appear as primitive. Essentially there exist two laws

1) the law of motion
2) the expression for force or potential energy.

The law of motion is precise, although empty, as long as the expression for the forces is not given. In postulating the latter, however, there exists great latitude for arbitrary [choice], especially if one omits the demand, which is not very natural in any case, that the forces depend only on the co-ordinates (and, for example, not on their differential quotients with respect to time). Within the framework of theory alone it is entirely arbitrary that the forces of gravitation (and electricity), which come from one point are governed by the potential function (1/r). Additional remark: it has long been known that this function is the central-symmetrical solution of the simplest (rotation-invariant) differential equation $\Delta\varphi = 0$; it would therefore have been a suggestive idea to regard this as a sign that this function is to be regarded as determined by a law of space, a procedure by which the arbitrariness in the choice of the law of energy would have been removed. This is really the first insight which suggests a turning away from the theory of distant forces, a development which—prepared by Faraday, Maxwell and Hertz—really begins only later on under the external pressure of experimental data.

I would also like to mention, as one internal asymmetry of this theory, that the inert mass occuring in the law of motion also appears in the expression for the gravitational force, but not in the expression for the other forces. Finally I would like to point to the fact that the division of energy into two essentially different parts, kinetic and potential energy, must be felt as unnatural; H. Hertz felt this as so disturbing that, in his very last work, he attempted to free mechanics from the concept of potential energy (i.e., from the concept of force). – – –

Enough of this. Newton, forgive me; you found the only way which, in your age, was just about possible for a man of highest thought- and creative power. The concepts, which you

Denk- und Gestaltungskraft eben noch möglich war. Die Begriffe, die du schufst, sind auch jetzt noch führend in unserem physikalischen Denken, obwohl wir nun wissen, dass sie durch andere, der Sphäre der unmittelbaren Erfahrung ferner stehende ersetzt werden müssen, wenn wir ein tieferes Begreifen der Zusammenhänge anstreben.

"Soll dies ein Nekrolog sein?" mag der erstaunte Leser fragen. Im wesentlichen ja, möchte ich antworten. Denn das Wesentliche im Dasein eines Menschen von meiner Art liegt in dem *was* er denkt und *wie* er denkt, nicht in dem, was er tut oder erleidet. Also kann der Nekrolog sich in der Hauptsache auf Mitteilung von Gedanken beschränken, die in meinem Streben eine erhebliche Rolle spielten. Eine Theorie ist desto eindrucksvoller, je grösser die Einfachheit ihrer Prämissen ist, je verschiedenartigere Dinge sie verknüpft, und je weiter ihr Anwendungsbereich ist. Deshalb der tiefe Eindruck, den die klassische Thermodynamik auf mich machte. Es ist die einzige physikalische Theorie allgemeinen Inhaltes, von der ich überzeugt bin, dass sie im Rahmen der Anwendbarkeit ihrer Grundbegriffe niemals umgestossen werden wird (zur besonderen Beachtung der grundsätzlichen Skeptiker).

Der fascinierendste Gegenstand zur Zeit meines Studiums war die Maxwell'sche Theorie. Was sie als revolutionär erscheinen liess, war der Übergang von den Fernwirkungskräften zu Feldern als Fundamentalgrössen. Die Einordnung der Optik in die Theorie des Elektromagnetismus mit ihrer Beziehung der Lichtgeschwindigkeit zum elektrischen und magnetischen absoluten Masssystem sowie die Beziehung des Brechungsexponenten zur Dielektrizitätskonstante, die qualitative zwischen Reflexionsfähigkeit und metallischer Leitfähigkeit des Körpers—es war wie eine Offenbarung. Abgesehen vom Übergang zur Feldtheorie, d.h. des Ausdrucks der elementaren Gesetze durch Differentialgleichungen, hatte Maxwell nur einen einzigen hypothetischen Schritt nötig—die Einführung des elektrischen Verschiebungsstromes im Vacuum und in den Dielektrica und seiner magnetischen Wirkung, eine Neuerung, die durch die formalen Eigenschaften der Differentialgleichungen beinahe vorgeschrieben war. In diesem Zusammenhang

created, are even today still guiding our thinking in physics, although we now know that they will have to be replaced by others farther removed from the sphere of immediate experience, if we aim at a profounder understanding of relationships.

"Is this supposed to be an obituary?" the astonished reader will likely ask. I would like to reply: essentially yes. For the essential in the being of a man of my type lies precisely in *what* he thinks and *how* he thinks, not in what he does or suffers. Consequently, the obituary can limit itself in the main to the communicating of thoughts which have played a considerable rôle in my endeavors.—A theory is the more impressive the greater the simplicity of its premises is, the more different kinds of things it relates, and the more extended is its area of applicability. Therefore the deep impression which classical thermodynamics made upon me. It is the only physical theory of universal content concerning which I am convinced that, within the framework of the applicability of its basic concepts, it will never be overthrown (for the special attention of those who are skeptics on principle).

The most fascinating subject at the time that I was a student was Maxwell's theory. What made this theory appear revolutionary was the transition from forces at a distance to fields as fundamental variables. The incorporation of optics into the theory of electromagnetism, with its relation of the speed of light to the electric and magnetic absolute system of units as well as the relation of the refraction coëfficient to the dielectric constant, the qualitative relation between the reflection coëfficient and the metallic conductivity of the body—it was like a revelation. Aside from the transition to field-theory, i.e., the expression of the elementary laws through differential equations, Maxwell needed only one single hypothetical step—the introduction of the electrical displacement current in the vacuum and in the dielectrica and its magnetic effect, an innovation which was almost prescribed by the formal properties of the differential equations. In this connection I cannot sup-

kann ich die Bemerkung nicht unterdrücken, dass das Paar Faraday-Maxwell so merkwürdige innere Aehnlichkeit hat mit dem Paar Galileo-Newton—der erste jedes Paares die Zusammenhänge intuitiv erfassend, der zweite sie exakt formulierend und quantitativ anwendend.

Was die Einsicht in das Wesen der elektromagnetischen Theorie zu jener Zeit erschwerte, war folgender eigentümlicher Umstand. Elektrische bezw. magnetische "Feldstärken" und "Verschiebungen" wurden als gleich elementare Grössen behandelt, der leere Raum als Spezialfall eines dielektrischen Körpers. Die *Materie* erschien als Träger des Feldes, nicht der *Raum*. Dadurch war impliziert, dass der Träger des Feldes einen Geschwindigkeitszustand besitze, und dies sollte natürlich auch vom "Vacuum" gelten (Aether). Hertz' Elektrodynamik bewegter Körper ist ganz auf diese grundsätzliche Einstellung gegründet.

Es war das grosse Verdienst von H. A. Lorentz, dass er hier in überzeugender Weise Wandel schuf. Im Prinzip gibt es nach ihm ein Feld nur im leeren Raume. Die atomistisch gedachte Materie ist einziger Sitz der elektrischen Ladungen; zwischen den materiellen Teilchen ist leerer Raum, der Sitz des elektromagnetischen Feldes, das erzeugt ist durch die Lage und Geschwindigkeit der auf den materiellen Teilchen sitzenden punktartigen Ladungen. Dielektrizität, Leitungsfähigkeit, etc. sind ausschliesslich durch die Art der mechanischen Bindung der Teilchen bedingt, aus welchen die Körper bestehen. Die Teilchen-Ladungen erzeugen das Feld, das andererseits Kräfte auf die Ladungen der Teilchen ausübt, die Bewegungen des letzteren gemäss Newtons Bewegungsgesetz bestimmend. Vergleicht man dies mit Newtons System, so besteht die Aenderung darin: Die Fernkräfte werden ersetzt durch das Feld, welches auch die Strahlung mitbeschreibt. Die Gravitation wird meist ihrer relativen Kleinheit wegen unberücksichtigt gelassen; ihre Berücksichtigung war aber stets möglich durch Bereicherung der Feldstruktur, bezw. Erweiterung des Maxwell'schen Feldgesetzes. Der Physiker der gegenwärtigen Generation betrachtet den von Lorentz errungenen Standpunkt als den einzig möglichen; damals aber war es ein überraschender

press the remark that the pair Faraday-Maxwell has a most remarkable inner similarity with the pair Galileo-Newton—the former of each pair grasping the relations intuitively, and the second one formulating those relations exactly and applying them quantitatively.

What rendered the insight into the essence of electromagnetic theory so much more difficult at that time was the following peculiar situation. Electric or magnetic "field intensities" and "displacements" were treated as equally elementary variables, empty space as a special instance of a dielectric body. *Matter* appeared as the bearer of the field, not *space*. By this it was implied that the carrier of the field could have velocity, and this was naturally to apply to the "vacuum" (ether) also. Hertz's electrodynamics of moving bodies rests entirely upon this fundamental attitude.

It was the great merit of H. A. Lorentz that he brought about a change here in a convincing fashion. In principle a field exists, according to him, only in empty space. Matter—considered as atoms—is the only seat of electric charges; between the material particles there is empty space, the seat of the electromagnetic field, which is created by the position and velocity of the point charges which are located on the material particles. Dielectricity, conductivity, etc., are determined exclusively by the type of mechanical tie connecting the particles, of which the bodies consist. The particle-charges create the field, which, on the other hand, exerts forces upon the charges of the particles, thus determining the motion of the latter according to Newton's law of motion. If one compares this with Newton's system, the change consists in this: action at a distance is replaced by the field, which thus also describes the radiation. Gravitation is usually not taken into account because of its relative smallness; its consideration, however, was always possible by means of the enrichment of the structure of the field, i.e., expansion of Maxwell's law of the field. The physicist of the present generation regards the point of view achieved by Lorentz as the only possible one; at that time, however, it was a surprising and

und kühner Schritt, ohne den die spätere Entwicklung nicht möglich gewesen wäre.

Betrachtet man diese Phase der Entwicklung der Theorie kritisch, so fällt der Dualismus auf, der darin liegt, dass materieller Punkt im Newton'schen Sinne und das Feld als Kontinuum als elementare Begriffe neben einander verwendet werden. Kinetische Energie und Feld-Energie erscheinen als prinzipiell verschiedene Dinge. Dies erscheint umso unbefriedigender, als gemäss der Maxwell'schen Theorie das Magnetfeld einer bewegten elektrischen Ladung Trägheit repräsentierte. Warum also nicht die *ganze* Trägheit? Dann gäbe es nur noch Feldenergie, und das Teilchen wäre nur ein Gebiet besonders grosser Dichte der Feldenergie. Dann durfte man hoffen, den Begriff des Massenpunktes samt den Bewegungsgleichungen des Teilchens aus den Feldgleichungen abzuleiten —der störende Dualismus wäre beseitigt.

H. A. Lorentz wusste dies sehr wohl. Die Maxwell'schen Gleichungen aber erlaubten nicht, das Gleichgewicht der der ein Teilchen konstituierenden Elektrizität abzuleiten. Nur andere, *nicht lineare* Gleichungen des Feldes konnten solches vielleicht leisten. Es gab aber keine Methode, derartige Feldgleichungen herauszufinden, ohne in abenteuerliche Willkür auszuarten. Jedenfalls durfte man glauben, auf dem von Faraday und Maxwell so erfolgreich begonnenen Wege nach und nach eine neue, sichere Grundlage für die gesamte Physik zu finden. – – –

Die durch die Einführung des Feldes begonnene Revolution war demnach keineswegs beendet. Da ereignete es sich, dass um die Jahrhundertwende unabhängig hiervon eine zweite fundamentale Krise einsetzte, deren Ernst durch Max Plancks Untersuchungen über die Wärmestrahlung (1900) plötzlich ins Bewusstsein trat. Die Geschichte dieses Geschehens ist umso merkwürdiger, weil sie wenigstens in ihrer ersten Phase nicht von irgend welchen überraschenden Entdeckungen experimenteller Art beeinflusst wurde.

Kirchhoff hatte auf thermodynamischer Grundlage geschlossen, dass die Energiedichte und spektrale Zusammensetzung der Strahlung in einem von undurchlässigen Wänden von der

audacious step, without which the later development would not have been possible.

If one views this phase of the development of theory critically, one is struck by the dualism which lies in the fact that the material point in Newton's sense and the field as continuum are used as elementary concepts side by side. Kinetic energy and field-energy appear as essentially different things. This appears all the more unsatisfactory inasmuch as, according to Maxwell's theory, the magnetic field of a moving electric charge represents inertia. Why not then *total* inertia? Then only field-energy would be left, and the particle would be merely an area of special density of field-energy. In that case one could hope to deduce the concept of the mass-point together with the equations of the motion of the particles from the field equations—the disturbing dualism would have been removed.

H. A. Lorentz knew this very well. However, Maxwell's equations did not permit the derivations of the equilibrium of the electricity which constitutes a particle. Only other, non-linear field equations could possibly accomplish such a thing. But no method existed by which this kind of field equations could be discovered without deteriorating into adventurous arbitrariness. In any case one could believe that it would be possible by and by to find a new and secure foundation for all of physics upon the path which had been so successfully begun by Faraday and Maxwell. – – –

Accordingly, the revolution begun by the introduction of the field was by no means finished. Then it happened that, around the turn of the century, independently of what we have just been discussing, a second fundamental crisis set in, the seriousness of which was suddenly recognized due to Max Planck's investigations into heat radiation (1900). The history of this event is all the more remarkable because, at least in its first phase, it was not in any way influenced by any surprising discoveries of an experimental nature.

On thermodynamic grounds Kirchhoff had concluded that the energy density and the spectral composition of radiation in a *Hohlraum*, surrounded by impenetrable walls of the tempera-

Temperatur T umschlossenen Hohlraum unabhängig sei von der Natur der Wände. Das heisst die nonchromatische Strahlungsdichte ϱ ist eine universelle Funktion der Frequenz ν und der absoluten Temperatur T. Damit entstand das interessante Problem der Bestimmung dieser Funktion $\varrho(\nu,T)$. Was konnte auf theoretischem Wege über diese Funktion ermittelt werden? Nach Maxwells Theorie musste die Strahlung auf die Wände einen durch die totale Energiedichte bestimmten Druck ausüben. Hieraus folgerte Boltzmann auf rein thermodynamischem Wege, dass die gesamte Energiedichte der Strahlung ($\int \varrho d\nu$) proportional T^4 sei. Er fand so eine theoretische Begründung einer bereits vorher von Stefan empirisch gefundenen Gesetzmässigkeit, bezw. er verknüpfte sie mit dem Fundament der Maxwell'schen Theorie. Hierauf fand W. Wien durch eine geistvolle thermodynamische Überlegung, die ebenfalls von der Maxwell'schen Theorie Gebrauch machte, dass die universelle Funktion ρ der beiden Variabeln ν und T von der Form sein musse

$$\rho \approx \nu^3 f\left(\frac{\nu}{T}\right),$$

wobei $f(\nu/T)$ eine universelle Funktion der einzigen Variable ν/T bedeutet. Es war klar, dass die theoretische Bestimmung dieser universellen Funktion f von fundamentaler Bedeutung war—dies war eben die Aufgabe, vor welcher Planck stand. Sorgfältige Messungen hatten zu einer recht genauen empirischen Bestimmung der Funktion f geführt. Es gelang ihm zunächst, gestützt auf diese empirischen Messungen, eine Darstellung zu finden, welche die Messungen recht gut wiedergab:

$$\rho = \frac{8\pi h\nu^3}{c^3} \frac{1}{exp(h\nu/kT) - 1}$$

wobei h und k zwei universelle Konstante sind, deren erste zur Quanten-Theorie führte. Diese Formel sieht wegen des Nenners etwas sonderbar aus. War sie auf theoretischem Wege begründbar? Planck fand tatsächlich eine Begründung, deren Unvollkommenheiten zunächst verborgen blieben, welch letz-

ture T, would be independent of the nature of the walls. That is to say, the nonchromatic density of radiation ϱ is a universal function of the frequency ν and of the absolute temperature T. Thus arose the interesting problem of determining this function $\varrho(\nu,T)$. What could theoretically be ascertained about this function? According to Maxwell's theory the radiation had to exert a pressure on the walls, determined by the total energy density. From this Boltzmann concluded by means of pure thermodynamics, that the entire energy density of the radiation ($\int \varrho d\nu$) is proportional to T^4. In this way he found a theoretical justification of a law which had previously been discovered empirically by Stefan, i.e., in this way he connected this empirical law with the basis of Maxwell's theory. Thereafter, by way of an ingenious thermodynamic consideration, which also made use of Maxwell's theory, W. Wien found that the universal function ϱ of the two variables ν and T would have to be of the form

$$\rho \approx \nu^3 f\left(\frac{\nu}{T}\right),$$

whereby $f(\nu/T)$ is a universal function of one variable ν/T only. It was clear that the theoretical determination of this universal function f was of fundamental importance—this was precisely the task which confronted Planck. Careful measurements had led to a very precise empirical determination of the function f. Relying on those empirical measurements, he succeeded in the first place in finding a statement which rendered the measurements very well indeed:

$$\rho = \frac{8\pi h\nu^3}{c^3} \frac{1}{exp(h\nu/kT) - 1}$$

whereby h and k are two universal constants, the first of which led to quantum theory. Because of the denominator this formula looks a bit queer. Was it possible to derive it theoretically? Planck actually did find a derivation, the imperfections of which remained at first hidden, which latter fact was most for-

terer Umstand ein wahres Glück war für die Entwicklung der Physik. War diese Formel richtig, so erlaubte sie mit Hilfe der Maxwell'schen Theorie die Berechnung der mittleren Energie E eines in dem Strahlungsfelde befindlichen quasi-monochromatischen Oszillators:

$$E = \frac{h\nu}{exp(h\nu/kT) - 1}$$

Planck zug es vor zu versuchen, diese letztere Grösse theoretisch zu berechnen. Bei diesem Bestreben half zunächst die Thermodynamik nicht mehr, und ebensowenig die Maxwell'sche Theorie. Was nun an dieser Formel ungemein ermutigend war, war folgender Umstand. Sie lieferte für hohe Werte der Temperatur (bei festem ν) den Ausdruck

$$E = kT.$$

Es ist dies derselbe Ausdruck, den die kinetische Gastheorie für die mittlere Energie eines in einer Dimension elastisch schwingungsfähigen Massenpunktes liefert. Diese liefert nämlich

$$E = (R/N)T,$$

wobei R die Konstante der Gasgleichung und N die Anzahl der Moleküle im Grammmolekül bedeutet, welche Konstante die absolute Grösse des Atoms ausdrückt. Die Gleichsetzung beider Ausdrücke liefert

$$N = R/k.$$

Die eine Konstante der Planck'schen Formel liefert also exakt die wahre Grösse des Atoms. Der Zahlenwert stimmte befriedigend überein mit den allerdings wenig genauen Bestimmungen von N mit Hilfe der kinetischen Gastheorie.

Dies war ein grosser Erfolg, den Planck klar erkannte. Die Sache hat aber eine bedenkliche Kehrseite, die Planck zunächst glücklicher Weise übersah. Die Ueberlegung verlangt nämlich, das die Beziehung $E = kT$ auch für kleine Temperaturen gelten müsse. Dann aber wäre es aus mit der Planck'schen Formel und mit der Konstante h. Die richtige Konsequenz aus der bestehenden Theorie wäre also gewesen: Die mittlere

tunate for the development of physics. If this formula was correct, it permitted, with the aid of Maxwell's theory, the calculation of the average energy E of a quasi-monochromatic oscillator within the field of radiation:

$$E = \frac{h\nu}{exp(h\nu/kT) - 1}$$

Planck preferred to attempt calculating this latter magnitude theoretically. In this effort, thermodynamics, for the time being, proved no longer helpful, and neither did Maxwell's theory. The following circumstance was unusually encouraging in this formula. For high temperatures (with a fixed ν) it yielded the expression

$$E = kT.$$

This is the same expression as the kinetic theory of gases yields for the average energy of a mass-point which is capable of oscillating elastically in one dimension. For in kinetic gas theory one gets

$$E = (R/N)T,$$

whereby R means the constant of the equation of state of a gas and N the number of molecules per mol, from which constant one can compute the absolute size of the atom. Putting these two expressions equal to each other one gets

$$N = R/k.$$

The one constant of Planck's formula consequently furnishes exactly the correct size of the atom. The numerical value agreed satisfactorily with the determinations of N by means of kinetic gas theory, even though these latter were not very accurate.

This was a great success, which Planck clearly recognized. But the matter has a serious drawback, which Planck fortunately overlooked at first. For the same considerations demand in fact that the relation $E = kT$ would also have to be valid for low temperatures. In that case, however, it would be all over with Planck's formula and with the constant h. From the existing theory, therefore, the correct conclusion would have

kinetische Energie des Oszillators wird entweder durch die Gastheorie falsch geliefert, was eine Widerlegung der Mechanik bedeuten würde; oder die mittlere Energie des Oszillators ergibt sich unrichtig aus der Maxwell'schen Theorie, was eine Widerlegung der letzteren bedeuten würde. Am Wahrscheinlichsten ist es unter diesen Verhältnissen, dass beide Theorien nur in der Grenze richtig, im Uebrigen aber falsch sind; so verhält es sich auch in der Tat, wie wir im Folgenden sehen werden. Hätte Planck so geschlossen, so hätte er vielleicht seine grosse Entdeckung nicht gemacht, weil seiner Ueberlegung das Fundament entzogen worden wäre.

Nun zurück zu Planck's Ueberlegung. Boltzmann hatte auf Grund der kinetischen Gastheorie gefunden, dass die Entropie abgesehen von einem konstanten Faktor gleich dem Logarithmus der "Wahrscheinlichkeit" des ins Auge gefassten Zustandes sei. Er hat damit das Wesen der im Sinne der Thermodynamik "nicht umkehrbaren" Vorgänge erkannt. Vom molekular-mechanischen Gesichtspunkte aus gesehen sind dagegen alle Vorgänge umkehrbar. Nennt man einen molekulartheoretisch definierten Zustand einen mikroskopisch beschriebenen oder kurz Mikrozustand, einen im Sinne der Thermodynamik beschriebenen Zustand einen Makrozustand, so gehören zu einem makroskopischen Zustand ungeheuer viele (Z) Zustände. Z ist dann das Mass für die Wahrscheinlichkeit eines ins Auge gefassten Makrozustandes. Diese Idee erscheint auch darum von überragender Bedeutung, dass ihre Anwendbarkeit nicht auf die mikroskopische Beschreibung auf der Grundlage der Mechanik beschränkt ist. Dies erkannte Planck und wendete das Boltzmann'sche Prinzip auf ein System an, das aus sehr vielen Resonatoren von derselben Frequenz ν besteht. Der makroskopische Zustand ist gegeben durch die Gesamtenergie der Schwingung aller Resonatoren, ein Mikrozustand durch Angabe der (momentanen) Energie jedes einzelnen Resonators. Um nun die Zahl der zu einem Makrozustand gehörigen Mikrozustände durch eine endliche Zahl ausdrücken zu können, teilte er die Gesamtenergie in eine grosse aber endliche Zahl von gleichen Energie-Elementen ε und fragte: auf wieviele Arten können diese Energie-Elemente unter die Resonatoren

been: the average kinetic energy of the oscillator is either given incorrectly by the theory of gases, which would imply a refutation of [statistical] mechanics; or else the average energy of the oscillator follows incorrectly from Maxwell's theory, which would imply a refutation of the latter. Under such circumstances it is most probable that both theories are correct only at the limits, but are otherwise false; this is indeed the situation, as we shall see in what follows. If Planck had drawn this conclusion, he probably would not have made his great discovery, because the foundation would have been withdrawn from his deductive reasoning.

Now back to Planck's reasoning. On the basis of the kinetic theory of gases Boltzmann had discovered that, aside from a constant factor, entropy is equivalent to the logarithm of the "probability" of the state under consideration. Through this insight he recognized the nature of courses of events which, in the sense of thermodynamics, are "irreversible." Seen from the molecular-mechanical point of view, however, all courses of events are reversible. If one calls a molecular-theoretically defined state a microscopically described one, or, more briefly, micro-state, and a state described in terms of thermodynamics a macro-state, then an immensely large number (Z) of states belong to a macroscopic condition. Z then is a measure of the probabality of a chosen macro-state. This idea appears to be of outstanding importance also because of the fact that its usefulness is not limited to microscopic description on the basis of mechanics. Planck recognized this and applied the Boltzmann principle to a system which consists of very many resonators of the same frequency ν. The macroscopic situation is given through the total energy of the oscillation of all resonators, a micro-condition through determination of the (instantaneous) energy of each individual resonator. In order then to be able to express the number of the micro-states belonging to a macro-state by means of a finite number, he [Planck] divided the total energy into a large but finite number of identical energy-elements ε and asked: in how many ways can these energy-elements be divided among the resonators. The logarithm of

verteilt werden. Der Logarithmus dieser Zahl liefert dann die Entropie und damit (auf thermodynamischem Wege) die Temperatur des Systems. Planck erhielt nun seine Strahlungsformel, wenn er seine Energieelemente ε von der Grösse $\varepsilon = h\nu$ wählte. Das Entscheidende dabei ist, dass das Ergebnis daran gebunden ist, dass man für ε einen bestimmten endlichen Wert nimmt, also nicht zum Limes $\varepsilon = 0$ übergeht. Diese Form der Ueberlegung lässt nicht ohne Weiteres erkennen, dass dieselbe mit der mechanischen und elektrodynamischen Basis im Widerspruch steht, auf welcher die Ableitung im Uebrigen beruht. In Wirklichkeit setzt die Ableitung aber implicite voraus, dass die Energie nur in "Quanten" von der Grösse $h\nu$ von dem einzelnen Resonator absorbiert und emittiert werden kann, dass also sowohl die Energie eines schwingungsfähigen mechanischen Gebildes als auch die Energie der Strahlung nur in solchen Quanten umgesetzt werden kann—im Gegensatz mit den Gesetzen der Mechanik und Elektrodynamik. Hierbei war der Widerspruch mit der Dynamik fundamental, während der Widerspruch mit der Elektrodynamik weniger fundamental sein konnte. Der Ausdruck für die Dichte der Strahlungsenergie ist nämlich zwar *vereinbar* mit den Maxwell'schen Gleichungen, aber keine notwendige Folge dieser Gleichungen. Dass dieser Ausdruck wichtige Mittelwerte liefert, zeigt sich ja dadurch, dass die auf ihm beruhenden Gesetze von Stefan-Boltzmann und Wien mit der Erfahrung im Einklang sind.

All dies war mir schon kurze Zeit nach dem Erscheinen von Plancks grundlegender Arbeit klar, sodass ich, ohne einen Ersatz für die klassische Mechanik zu haben, doch sehen konnte, zu was für Konsequenzen dies Gesetz der Temperaturstrahlung für den licht-elektrischen Effekt und andere verwandte Phänomene der Verwandlung von Strahlungsenergie sowie für die spezifische Wärme (insbesondere) fester Körper führt. All meine Versuche, das theoretische Fundament der Physik diesen Erkenntnissen anzupassen, scheiterten aber völlig. Es war wie wenn einem der Boden unter den Füssen weggezogen worden wäre, ohne dass sich irgendwo fester Grund zeigte, auf dem man hätte bauen können. Dass diese schwankende und widerspruchsvolle Grundlage hinreichte um einen

this number, then, furnishes the entropy and thus (via thermodynamics) the temperature of the system. Planck got his radiation-formula if he chose his energy-elements ε of the magnitude $\varepsilon = h\nu$. The decisive element in doing this lies in the fact that the result depends on taking for ε a definite finite value, i.e., that one does not go to the limit $\varepsilon = 0$. This form of reasoning does not make obvious the fact that it contradicts the mechanical and electrodynamic basis, upon which the derivation otherwise depends. Actually, however, the derivation presupposes implicitly that energy can be absorbed and emitted by the individual resonator only in "quanta" of magnitude $h\nu$, i.e., that the energy of a mechanical structure capable of oscillations as well as the energy of radiation can be transferred only in such quanta—in contradiction to the laws of mechanics and electrodynamics. The contradiction with dynamics was here fundamental; whereas the contradiction with electrodynamics could be less fundamental. For the expression for the density of radiation-energy, although it is *compatible* with Maxwell's equations, is not a necessary consequence of these equations. That this expression furnishes important average-values is shown by the fact that the Stefan-Boltzmann law and Wien's law, which are based on it, are in agreement with experience.

All of this was quite clear to me shortly after the appearance of Planck's fundamental work; so that, without having a substitute for classical mechanics, I could nevertheless see to what kind of consequences this law of temperature-radiation leads for the photo-electric effect and for other related phenomena of the transformation of radiation-energy, as well as for the specific heat of (especially) solid bodies. All my attempts, however, to adapt the theoretical foundation of physics to this [new type of] knowledge failed completely. It was as if the ground had been pulled out from under one, with no firm foundation to be seen anywhere, upon which one could have built. That this insecure and contradictory foundation was sufficient to en-

Mann mit dem einzigartigen Instinkt und Feingefühl Bohrs in den Stand zu setzen, die hauptsächlichen Gesetze der Spektrallinien und der Elektronenhüllen der Atome nebst deren Bedeutung für die Chemie aufzufinden, erschien mir wie ein Wunder—und erscheint mir auch heute noch als ein Wunder. Dies ist höchste Musikalität auf dem Gebiete des Gedankens.

Mein eingenes Interesse in jenen Jahren war weniger auf die Einzel-Folgerungen aus dem Planck'schen Ergebnis gerichtet, so wichtig diese auch sein mochten. Meine Hauptfrage war: Was für allgemeine Folgerungen können aus der Strahlungsformel betreffend die Struktur der Strahlung und überhaupt betreffend das elektromagnetische Fundament der Physik gezogen werden? Bevor ich hierauf eingehe, muss ich einige Untersuchungen kurz erwähnen, die sich auf die Brown'sche Bewegung und verwandte Gegenstände (Schwankungs-Phänomene) beziehen und sich in der Hauptsache auf die klassich Molekularmechanik gründen. Nicht vertraut mit den früher erschienen und den Gegenstand tatsächlich erschöpfenden Untersuchungen von Boltzmann und Gibbs, entwickelte ich die statistische Mechanik und die auf sie gegründete molekular-kinetische Theorie der Thermodynamik. Mein Hauptziel dabei war es, Tatsachen zu finden, welche die Existenz von Atomen von bestimmter endlicher Grösse möglichst sicher stellten. Dabei entdeckte ich, dass es nach der atomistischen Theorie eine der Beobachtung zugängliche Bewegung suspendierter mikroskopischer Teilchen geben müsse, ohne zu wissen, dass Beobachtungen über die "Brown'sche Bewegung" schon lange bekannt waren. Die einfachste Ableitung beruhte auf folgender Erwägung. Wenn die molekular-kinetische Theorie im Prinzip richtig ist, muss eine Suspension von sichtbaren Teilchen ebenso einen die Gasgesetze erfüllenden osmotischen Druck besitzen wie eine Lösung von Molekülen. Dieser osmotische Druck hängt ab von der wahren Grösse der Moleküle, d.h. von der Zahl der Moleküle in einem Gramm-Aequivalent. Ist die Suspension von ungleichmässiger Dichte, so gibt die damit vorhandene räumliche Variabilität dieses osmotischen Druckes Anlass zu einer aus-

able a man of Bohr's unique instinct and tact to discover the major laws of the spectral lines and of the electron-shells of the atoms together with their significance for chemistry appeared to me like a miracle—and appears to me as a miracle even today. This is the highest form of musicality in the sphere of thought.

My own interest in those years was less concerned with the detailed consequences of Planck's results, however important these might be. My major question was: What general conclusions can be drawn from the radiation-formula concerning the structure of radiation and even more generally concerning the electro-magnetic foundation of physics? Before I take this up, I must briefly mention a number of investigations which relate to the Brownian motion and related objects (fluctuation-phenomena) and which in essence rest upon classical molecular mechanics. Not acquainted with the earlier investigations of Boltzmann and Gibbs, which had appeared earlier and actually exhausted the subject, I developed the statistical mechanics and the molecular-kinetic theory of thermodynamics which was based on the former. My major aim in this was to find facts which would guarantee as much as possible the existence of atoms of definite finite size. In the midst of this I discovered that, according to atomistic theory, there would have to be a movement of suspended microscopic particles open to observation, without knowing that observations concerning the Brownian motion were already long familiar. The simplest derivation rested upon the following consideration. If the molecular-kinetic theory is essentially correct, a suspension of visible particles must possess the same kind of osmotic pressure fulfilling the laws of gases as a solution of molecules. This osmotic pressure depends upon the actual magnitude of the molecules, i.e., upon the number of molecules in a gram-equivalent. If the density of the suspension is inhomogeneous, the osmotic pressure is inhomogeneous, too, and gives rise to a

gleichenden Diffusionsbewegung, welche aus der bekannten Beweglichkeit der Teilchen berechenbar ist. Dieser Diffusionsvorgang kann aber andererseits auch aufgefasst werden als das Ergebnis der zunächst ihrem Betrage nach unbekannten regellosen Verlagerung der suspendierten Teilchen unter der Wirkung der thermischen Agitation. Durch Gleichsetzung der durch beide Ueberlegungen erlangten Beträge für den Diffusionsfluss erhält man quantitativ das statistiche Gesetz für jene Verlagerungen, d.h. das Gesetz der Brown'schen Bewegung. Die Uebereinstimmung dieser Betrachtung mit der Erfahrung zusammen mit der Planck'schen Bestimmung der wahren Molekülgrösse aus dem Strahlungsgesetz (für hohe Temperaturen) überzeugte die damals zahlreichen Skeptiker (Ostwald, Mach) von der Realität der Atome. Die Abneigung dieser Forscher gegen die Atomtheorie ist ohne Zweifel auf ihre positivistische philosophische Einstellung zurückzuführen. Es ist dies ein interessantes Beispiel dafür, dass selbst Forscher von kühnem Geist und von feinem Instinkt durch philosophische Vorurteile für die Interpretation von Tatsachen gehemmt werden können. Das Vorurteil—welches seither keineswegs ausgestorben ist—liegt in dem Glauben, dass die Tatsachen allein ohne freie begriffliche Konstruktion wissenschaftliche Erkenntnis liefern könnten und sollten. Solche Täuschung ist nur dadurch möglich, dass man sich der freien Wahl von solchen Begriffen nicht leicht bewusst werden kann, die durch Bewährung und langen Gebrauch unmittelbar mit dem empirischen Material verknüpft zu sein scheinen.

Der Erfolg der Theorie der Brown'schen Bewegung zeigte wieder deutlich, dass die klassische Mechanik stets dann zuverlässige Resultate lieferte, wenn sie auf Bewegungen angewandt wurde, bei welchen die höheren zeitlichen Ableitungen der Geschwindigkeit vernachlässigbar klein sind. Auf diese Erkenntnis lässt sich eine verhältnismässig direkte Methode gründen, um aus der Planck'schen Formel etwas zu erfahren über die Konstitution der Strahlung. Man darf nämlich schliessen, dass in einem Strahlungsraume ein (senkrecht zu seiner Ebene) frei bewegter, quasi monochromatisch reflektierender Spiegel eine Art Brown'sche Bewegung ausführen muss, deren

compensating diffusion, which can be calculated from the well known mobility of the particles. This diffusion can, on the other hand, also be considered as the result of the random displacement—unknown in magnitude originally—of the suspended particles due to thermal agitation. By comparing the amounts obtained for the diffusion current from both types of reasoning one reaches quantitatively the statistical law for those displacements, i.e., the law of the Brownian motion. The agreement of these considerations with experience together with Planck's determination of the true molecular size from the law of radiation (for high temperatures) convinced the sceptics, who were quite numerous at that time (Ostwald, Mach) of the reality of atoms. The antipathy of these scholars towards atomic theory can indubitably be traced back to their positivistic philosophical attitude. This is an interesting example of the fact that even scholars of audacious spirit and fine instinct can be obstructed in the interpretation of facts by philosophical prejudices. The prejudice—which has by no means died out in the meantime—consists in the faith that facts by themselves can and should yield scientific knowledge without free conceptual construction. Such a misconception is possible only because one does not easily become aware of the free choice of such concepts, which, through verification and long usage, appear to be immediately connected with the empirical material.

The success of the theory of the Brownian motion showed again conclusively that classical mechanics always offered trustworthy results whenever it was applied to motions in which the higher time derivatives of velocity are negligibly small. Upon this recognition a relatively direct method can be based which permits us to learn something concerning the constitution of radiation from Planck's formula. One may conclude in fact that, in a space filled with radiation, a (vertically to its plane) freely moving, quasi monochromatically reflecting mirror would have to go through a kind of Brownian movement, the average

mittlere kinetische Energie gleich $\frac{1}{2}(R/N)T$ ist (R = Konstante der Gasgleichung für ein Gramm-Molekül, N gleich Zahl der Moleküle in einem Gramm-Molekül, T = absolute Temperatur). Wäre die Strahlung keinen lokalen Schwankungen unterworfen, so würde der Spiegel allmählich zur Ruhe kommen, weil er auf seiner Vorderseite infolge seiner Bewegung mehr Strahlung reflektiert als auf seiner Rückseite. Er muss aber gewisse aus der Maxwell'schen Theorie berechenbare unregelmässige Schwankungen des auf ihn wirkenden Druckes dadurch erfahren, dass die die Strahlung konstituierenden Wellenbündel miteinander interferieren. Diese Rechnung zeigt nun, dass diese Druckschwankungen (insbesondere bei geringen Strahlungsdichten) keineswegs hinreichen, um dem Spiegel die mittlere kinetische Energie $\frac{1}{2}(R/N)T$ zu erteilen. Um dies Resultat zu erhalten, muss man vielmehr annehmen, dass es eine zweite aus der Maxwell'schen Theorie nicht folgende Art Druckschwankungen gibt, welche der Annahme entspricht, dass die Strahlungsenergie aus unteilbaren punktartig lokalisierten Quanten von der Energie $h\nu$ (und dem Impuls $h\nu/c$, (c = Lichtgeschwindigkeit)) besteht, die ungeteilt reflektiert werden. Diese Betrachtung zeigte in einer drastischen und direkten Weise, dass den Planck'schen Quanten eine Art unmittelbare Realität zugeschrieben werden muss, dass also die Strahlung in energetischer Beziehung eine Art Molekularstruktur besitzen muss, was natürlich mit der Maxwell'schen Theorie im Widerspruch ist. Auch Ueberlegungen über die Strahlung, die unmittelbar auf Boltzmanns Entropie-Wahrscheinlichkeits-Relation gegründet sind (Wahrscheinlichkeit = statistische zeitliche Häufigkeit gesetzt) führten zu demselben Resultat. Diese Doppelnatur von Strahlung (und materiellen Korpuskeln) ist eine Haupteigenschaft der Realität, welche die Quanten-Mechanik in einer geistreichen und verblüffend erfolgreichen Weise gedeutet hat. Diese Deutung welche von fast allen zeitgenössischen Physikern als im wesentlichen endgültig angesehen wird, erscheint mir als ein nur temporärer Ausweg; einige Bemerkungen darüber folgen später. – – –

Ueberlegungen solcher Art machten es mir schon kurz nach

kinetic energy of which equals $\frac{1}{2}(R/N)T$ ($R =$ constant of the gas-equation for one gram-molecule, N equals the number of the molecules per mol, $T =$ absolute temperature). If radiation were not subject to local fluctuations, the mirror would gradually come to rest, because, due to its motion, it reflects more radiation on its front than on its reverse side. However, the mirror must experience certain random fluctuations of the pressure exerted upon it due to the fact that the wave-packets, constituting the radiation, interfere with one another. These can be computed from Maxwell's theory. This calculation, then, shows that these pressure variations (especially in the case of small radiation-densities) are by no means sufficient to impart to the mirror the average kinetic energy $\frac{1}{2}(R/N)T$. In order to get this result one has to assume rather that there exists a second type of pressure variations, which can not be derived from Maxwell's theory, which corresponds to the assumption that radiation energy consists of indivisible point-like localized quanta of the energy $h\nu$ (and of momentum ($h\nu/c$), (c = velocity of light)), which are reflected undivided. This way of looking at the problem showed in a drastic and direct way that a type of immediate reality has to be ascribed to Planck's quanta, that radiation must, therefore, possess a kind of molecular structure in energy, which of course contradicts Maxwell's theory. Considerations concerning radiation which are based directly on Boltzmann's entropy-probability-relation (probability taken equal to statistical temporal frequency) also lead to the same result. This double nature of radiation (and of material corpuscles) is a major property of reality, which has been interpreted by quantum-mechanics in an ingenious and amazingly successful fashion. This interpretation, which is looked upon as essentially final by almost all contemporary physicists, appears to me as only a temporary way out; a few remarks to this [point] will follow later. – – –

Reflections of this type made it clear to me as long ago as

1900, d.h. kurz nach Plancks bahnbrechender Arbeit klar, dass weder die Mechanik noch die Electrodynamik (ausser in Grenzfällen) exakte Gültigkeit beanspruchen können. Nach und nach verzweifelte ich an der Möglichkeit die wahren Gesetze durch auf bekannte Tatsachen sich stützende konstruktive Bemühungen herauszufinden. Je länger und verzweifelter ich mich bemühte, desto mehr kam ich zu der Ueberzeugung, dass nur die Auffindung eines allgemeinen formalen Prinzipes uns zu gesicherten Ergebnissen führen könnte. Als Vorbild sah ich die Thermodynamik vor mir. Das allgemeine Prinzip war dort in dem Satze gegeben: die Naturgesetze sind so beschaffen, dass es unmöglich ist, ein *perpetuum mobile* (erster und zweiter Art) zu konstruieren. Wie aber ein solches allgemeines Prinzip finden? Ein solches Prinzip ergab sich nach zehn Jahren Nachdenkens aus einem Paradoxon, auf das ich schon mit 16 Jahren gestossen bin: Wenn ich einem Lichtstrahl nacheile mit der Geschwindigkeit c (Lichtgeschwindigkeit im Vacuum), so sollte ich einen solchen Lichtstrahl als ruhendes, räumlich oszillatorisches elektromagnetisches Feld wahrnehmen. So etwas scheint es aber nicht zu geben, weder auf Grund der Erfahrung noch gemäss den Maxwell'schen Gleichungen. Intuitiv klar schien es mir von vornherein, dass von einem solchen Beobachter aus beurteilt alles sich nach denselben Gesetzen abspielen müsse wie für einen relativ zu Erde ruhenden Beobachter. Denn wie sollte der erste Beobachter wissen bezw. konstatieren können, dass er sich im Zustand rascher gleichförmiger Bewegung befindet?

Man sieht, dass in diesem Paradoxon der Keim zur speziellen Relativitätstheorie schon enthalten ist. Heute weiss natürlich jeder, dass alle Versuche, dies Paradoxon befriedigend aufzuklären, zum Scheitern verurteilt waren, solange das Axiom des absoluten Charakters der Zeit, bezw. der Gleichzeitigkeit, unerkannt im Unbewussten verankert war. Dies Axiom und seine Willkür klar erkennen bedeutet eigentlich schon die Lösung des Problems. Das kritische Denken, dessen es zur Auffindung dieses zentralen Punktes bedurfte, wurde bei mir entscheidend gefördert insbesondere durch die Lektüre von David Humes und Ernst Machs philosophischen Schriften.

shortly after 1900, i.e., shortly after Planck's trailblazing work, that neither mechanics nor electrodynamics could (except in limiting cases) claim exact validity. By and by I despaired of the possibility of discovering the true laws by means of constructive efforts based on known facts. The longer and the more despairingly I tried, the more I came to the conviction that only the discovery of a universal formal principle could lead us to assured results. The example I saw before me was thermodynamics. The general principle was there given in the theorem: the laws of nature are such that it is impossible to construct a *perpetuum mobile* (of the first and second kind). How, then, could such a universal principle be found? After ten years of reflection such a principle resulted from a paradox upon which I had already hit at the age of sixteen: If I pursue a beam of light with the velocity c (velocity of light in a vacuum), I should observe such a beam of light as a spatially oscillatory electromagnetic field at rest. However, there seems to be no such thing, whether on the basis of experience or according to Maxwell's equations. From the very beginning it appeared to me intuitively clear that, judged from the standpoint of such an observer, everything would have to happen according to the same laws as for an observer who, relative to the earth, was at rest. For how, otherwise, should the first observer know, i.e., be able to determine, that he is in a state of fast uniform motion?

One sees that in this paradox the germ of the special relativity theory is already contained. Today everyone knows, of course, that all attempts to clarify this paradox satisfactorily were condemned to failure as long as the axiom of the absolute character of time, viz., of simultaneity, unrecognizedly was anchored in the unconscious. Clearly to recognize this axiom and its arbitrary character really implies already the solution of the problem. The type of critical reasoning which was required for the discovery of this central point was decisively furthered, in my case, especially by the reading of David Hume's and Ernst Mach's philosophical writings.

Man hatte sich darüber klar zu werden, was die räumlichen Koordinaten und der Zeitwert eines Ereignisses in der Physik bedeuteten. Die physikalische Deutung der räumlichen Koordinaten setzten einen starren Bezugskörper voraus, der noch dazu von mehr oder minder bestimmtem Bewegungszustande (Inertialsystem) sein musste. Bei gegebenem Inertialsystem bedeuteten die Koordinaten Ergebnisse von bestimmten Messungen mit starren (ruhenden) Stäben. (Dass die Voraussetzung der prinzipiellen Existenz starrer Stäbe eine durch approximative Erfahrung nahe gelegte aber im Prinzip willkürliche Voraussetzung ist, dessen soll man sich stets bewusst sein.) Bei solcher Interpretation der räumlichen Koordinaten wird die Frage der Gültigkeit der Euklidischen Geometrie zum physikalischen Problem.

Sucht man nun die Zeit eines Ereignisses analog zu deuten, so braucht man ein Mittel zur Messung der Zeitdifferenz (in sich determinierter periodischer Prozess realisiert durch ein System von hinreichend geringer räumlicher Abmessung). Eine relativ zum Inertialsystem ruhend angeordnete Uhr definiert eine (Orts-Zeit). Die Ortszeiten aller räumlichen Punkte zusammen genommen sind die "Zeit," die zu dem gewählten Inertialsystem gehört, wenn man noch ein Mittel gegeben hat, diese Uhren gegeneinander zu "richten." Man sieht, dass es *a priori* gar nicht nötig ist, dass die in solcher Weise definierten "Zeiten" verschiedener Inertialsysteme miteinander übereinstimmen. Man würde dies längst gemerkt haben, wenn nicht für die praktische Erfahrung des Alltags (wegen des hohen Wertes von c) das Licht nicht als Mittel für die Konstatierung absoluter Gleichzeitigkeit erschiene.

Die Voraussetzung von der (prinzipiellen) Existenz (idealer bezw. vollkommener) Massstäbe und Uhren ist nicht unabhängig voneinander, denn ein Lichtsignal, welches zwischen den Enden eines starren Stabes hin und her reflektiert wird, stellt eine ideale Uhr dar, vorausgesetzt, dass die Voraussetzung von der Konstanz der Vacuum-Lichtgeschwindigkeit nicht zu Widersprüchen führt.

Das obige Paradoxon lässt sich nun so formulieren. Nach den in der klassischen Physik verwendeten Verknüpfungsregeln

One had to understand clearly what the spatial co-ordinates and the temporal duration of events meant in physics. The physical interpretation of the spatial co-ordinates presupposed a fixed body of reference, which, moreover, had to be in a more or less definite state of motion (inertial system). In a given inertial system the co-ordinates meant the results of certain measurements with rigid (stationary) rods. (One should always be conscious of the fact that the presupposition of the existence in principle of rigid rods is a presupposition suggested by approximate experience, but which is, in principle, arbitrary.) With such an interpretation of the spatial co-ordinates the question of the validity of Euclidean geometry becomes a problem of physics.

If, then, one tries to interpret the time of an event analogously, one needs a means for the measurement of the difference in time (in itself determined periodic process realized by a system of sufficiently small spatial extension). A clock at rest relative to the system of inertia defines a local time. The local times of all space points taken together are the "time," which belongs to the selected system of inertia, if a means is given to "set" these clocks relative to each other. One sees that *a priori* it is not at all necessary that the "times" thus defined in different inertial systems agree with one another. One would have noticed this long ago, if, for the practical experience of everyday life light did not appear (because of the high value of c), as the means for the statement of absolute simultaneity.

The presupposition of the existence (in principle) of (ideal, viz., perfect) measuring rods and clocks is not independent of each other; since a lightsignal, which is reflected back and forth between the ends of a rigid rod, constitutes an ideal clock, provided that the postulate of the constancy of the light-velocity in vacuum does not lead to contradictions.

The above paradox may then be formulated as follows. According to the rules of connection, used in classical physics, of the spatial co-ordinates and of the time of events in the transi-

von räumlichen Koordinaten und Zeit von Ereignissen beim Uebergang von einem Inertialsystem zu einem andern sind die beiden Annahmen

1) Konstanz der Lichtgeschwindigkeit
2) Unabhängigkeit der Gesetze (also speziell auch des Gesetzes von der Konstanz der Lichtgeschwindigkeit) von der Wahl des Inertialsystems (spezielles Relativitätsprinzip)

miteinander unvereinbar (trotzdem beide einzeln durch die Erfahrung gestützt sind).

Die der speziellen Rel. Th. zugrunde liegende Erkenntnis ist: Die Annahmen 1) und 2) sind miteinander vereinbar, wenn für die Umrechnung von Koordinaten und Zeiten der Ereignisse neuartige Beziehungen ("Lorentz-Transformation") zugrunde gelegt werden. Bei der gegebenen physikalischen Interpretation von Koordinaten und Zeit bedeutet dies nicht etwa nur einen konventionellen Schritt sondern involviert bestimmte Hypothesen über das tatsächliche Verhalten bewegter Massstäbe und Uhren, die durch Experiment bestätigt bezw. widerlegt werden können.

Das allgemeine Prinzip der speziellen Relativitätstheorie ist in dem Postulat enthalten: Die Gesetze der Physik sind invariant mit Bezug auf Lorentz-Transformationen (für den Uebergang von einem Inertialsystem zu einem beliebigen andern Inertialsystem). Dies ist ein einschränkendes Prinzip für die Naturgesetze, vergleichbar mit dem der Thermodynamik zugrunde liegenden einschränkenden Prinzip von der Nichtexistenz des *perpetuum mobile.*

Zunächst eine Bemerkung über die Beziehung der Theorie zum "vierdimensionalen Raum." Es ist ein verbreiteter Irrtum, dass die spezielle Rel. Th. gewissermassen die Vierdimensionalität des physikalischen Kontinuums entdeckt bezw. neu eingeführt hätte. Dies ist natürlich nicht der Fall. Auch der klassischen Mechanik liegt das vierdimensionale Kontinuum von Raum und Zeit zugrunde. Nur haben im vierdimensionalen Kontinuum der klassischen Physik die "Schnitte" konstanten Zeitwertes eine absolute, d.h. von der Wahl des Bezugssystems unabhängige, Realität. Das vierdimensionale Kontinuum zer-

tion from one inertial system to another the two assumptions of

(1) the constancy of the light velocity

(2) the independence of the laws (thus specially also of the law of the constancy of the light velocity) of the choice of the inertial system (principle of special relativity)

are mutually incompatible (despite the fact that both taken separately are based on experience).

The insight which is fundamental for the special theory of relativity is this: The assumptions (1) and (2) are compatible if relations of a new type ("Lorentz-transformation") are postulated for the conversion of co-ordinates and the times of events. With the given physical interpretation of co-ordinates and time, this is by no means merely a conventional step, but implies certain hypotheses concerning the actual behavior of moving measuring-rods and clocks, which can be experimentally validated or disproved.

The universal principle of the special theory of relativity is contained in the postulate: The laws of physics are invariant with respect to the Lorentz-transformations (for the transition from one inertial system to any other arbitrarily chosen system of inertia). This is a restricting principle for natural laws, comparable to the restricting principle of the non-existence of the *perpetuum mobile* which underlies thermodynamics.

First a remark concerning the relation of the theory to "four-dimensional space." It is a wide-spread error that the special theory of relativity is supposed to have, to a certain extent, first discovered, or at any rate, newly introduced, the four-dimensionality of the physical continuum. This, of course, is not the case. Classical mechanics, too, is based on the four-dimensional continuum of space and time. But in the four-dimensional continuum of classical physics the subspaces with constant time value have an absolute reality, independent of the choice of the reference system. Because of this [fact], the four-dimensional continuum falls naturally into a three-

fällt dadurch natürlich in ein dreidimensionales und ein eindimensionales (Zeit), sodass die vierdimensionale Betrachtungsweise sich nicht als *notwendig* aufdrängt. Die spezielle Relativitätstheorie dagegen schafft eine formale Abhängigkeit zwischen der Art und Weise, wie die räumlichen Koordinaten einerseits und die Zeitkoordinate andrerseits in die Naturgesetze eingehen müssen.

Minkowskis wichtiger Beitrag zu der Theorie liegt in Folgendem: Vor Minkowskis Untersuchung hatte man an einem Gesetze eine Lorentz-Transformation auszuführen, um seine Invarianz bezüglich solcher Transformationen zu prüfen; ihm dagegen gelang es, einen solchen Formalismus einzuführen, dass die mathematische Form des Gesetzes selbst dessen Invarianz bezüglich Lorentz-Transformationen verbürgt. Er leistete durch Schaffung eines vierdimensionalen Tensorkalküls für den vierdimensionalen Raum dasselbe, was die gewöhnliche Vektorkalkül für die drei räumlichen Dimensionen leistet. Er zeigte auch, dass die Lorentz-Transformation (abgesehen von einem durch den besonderen Charakter der Zeit bedingten abweichenden Vorzeichen) nichts anderes ist als eine Drehung des Koordinatensystems im vierdimensionalen Raume.

Zunächst eine kritische Bemerkung zur Theorie, wie sie oben charakterisiert ist. Es fällt auf, dass die Theorie (ausser dem vierdimensionalen Raum) zweierlei physikalische Dinge einführt, nämlich 1) Massstäbe und Uhren, 2) alle sonstigen Dinge, z.B. das elektromagnetische Feld, den materiellen Punkt, etc. Dies ist in gewissem Sinne inkonsequent; Massstäbe und Uhren müssten eigentlich als Lösungen der Grundgleichungen (Gegenstände bestehend aus bewegten atomistischen Gebilden) dargestellt werden, nicht als gewissermassen theoretisch selbstständige Wesen. Das Vorgehen rechtfertigt sich aber dadurch, dass von Anfang an klar war, dass die Postulate der Theorie nicht stark genug sind, um aus ihr genügend vollständige Gleichungen für das physikalische Geschehen genügend frei von Willkür zu deduzieren, um auf eine solche Grundlage eine Theorie der Massstäbe und Uhren zu gründen. Wollte man nicht auf eine physikalische Deutung der Koordinaten überhaupt verzichten (was an sich möglich wäre), so

dimensional and a one-dimensional (time), so that the four-dimensional point of view does not force itself upon one as *necessary*. The special theory of relativity, on the other hand, creates a formal dependence between the way in which the spatial co-ordinates, on the one hand, and the temporal co-ordinates, on the other, have to enter into the natural laws.

Minkowski's important contribution to the theory lies in the following: Before Minkowski's investigation it was necessary to carry out a Lorentz-transformation on a law in order to test its invariance under such transformations; he, on the other hand, succeeded in introducing a formalism such that the mathematical form of the law itself guarantees its invariance under Lorentz-transformations. By creating a four-dimensional tensor-calculus he achieved the same thing for the four-dimensional space which the ordinary vector-calculus achieves for the three spatial dimensions. He also showed that the Lorentz-transformation (apart from a different algebraic sign due to the special character of time) is nothing but a rotation of the co-ordinate system in the four-dimensional space.

First, a remark concerning the theory as it is characterized above. One is struck [by the fact] that the theory (except for the four-dimensional space) introduces two kinds of physical things, i.e., (1) measuring rods and clocks, (2) all other things, e.g., the electro-magnetic field, the material point, etc. This, in a certain sense, is inconsistent; strictly speaking measuring rods and clocks would have to be represented as solutions of the basic equations (objects consisting of moving atomic configurations), not, as it were, as theoretically self-sufficient entities. However, the procedure justifies itself because it was clear from the very beginning that the postulates of the theory are not strong enough to deduce from them sufficiently complete equations for physical events sufficiently free from arbitrariness, in order to base upon such a foundation a theory of measuring rods and clocks. If one did not wish to forego a physical interpretation of the co-ordinates in general (something which, in itself, would be possible), it was better to permit such inconsistency—

war es besser, solche Inkonsequenz zuzulassen—allerdings mit der Verpflichtung, sie in einem späteren Stadium der Theorie zu eliminieren. Man darf aber die erwähnte Sünde nicht so weit legitimieren, dass man sich etwa vorstellt, dass Abstände physikalische Wesen besonderer Art seien, wesensverschieden von sonstigen physikalischen Grössen ("Physik auf Geometrie zurückführen," etc.). Wir fragen nun nach den Erkenntnissen von definitivem Charakter, den die Physik der speziellen Relativitätstheorie verdankt.

1) Es gibt keine Gleichzeitigkeit distanter Ereignisse; es gibt also auch keine unvermittelte Fernwirkung im Sinne der Newton'schen Mechanik. Die Einführung von Fernwirkungen, die sich mit Lichtgeschwindigkeit ausbreiten, bleibt zwar nach dieser Theorie denkbar, erscheint aber unnatürlich; in einer derartigen Theorie könnte es nämlich keinen vernünftigen Ausdruck für das Energieprinzip geben. Es erscheint deshalb unvermeidlich, dass die physikalische Realität durch kontinuierliche Raumfunktionen zu beschreiben ist. Der materielle Punkt dürfte deshalb als Grundbegriff der Theorie nicht mehr in Betracht kommen.

2) Die Sätze der Erhaltung des Impulses und der Erhaltung der Energie werden zu einem einzigen Satz verschmolzen. Die träge Masse eines abgeschlossenen Systems ist mit seiner Energie identisch, sodass die Masse als selbstständiger Begriff eliminiert ist.

Bemerkung. Die Lichtgeschwindigkeit c ist eine der Grössen, welche in physikalischen Gleichungen als "universelle Konstante" auftritt. Wenn man aber als Zeiteinheit statt der Sekunde die Zeit einführt, in welcher das Licht 1 cm zurücklegt, so tritt c in den Gleichungen nicht mehr auf. Man kann in diesem Sinne sagen, dass die Konstante c nur eine *scheinbare* universelle Konstante ist.

Es ist offenkundig und allgemein angenommen, dass man auch noch zwei andere universelle Konstante dadurch aus der Physik eliminieren könnte, dass man an Stelle des Gramms und Centimeters passend gewählte "natürliche" Einheiten einführt (z.B. Masse und Radius des Elektrons).

Denkt man sich dies ausgeführt, so würden in den Grund-

with the obligation, however, of eliminating it at a later stage of the theory. But one must not legalize the mentioned sin so far as to imagine that intervals are physical entities of a special type, intrinsically different from other physical variables ("reducing physics to geometry," etc.).

We now shall inquire into the insights of definite nature which physics owes to the special theory of relativity.

(1) There is no such thing as simultaneity of distant events; consequently there is also no such thing as immediate action at a distance in the sense of Newtonian mechanics. Although the introduction of actions at a distance, which propogate with the speed of light, remains thinkable, according to this theory, it appears unnatural; for in such a theory there could be no such thing as a reasonable statement of the principle of conservation of energy. It therefore appears unavoidable that physical reality must be described in terms of continuous functions in space. The material point, therefore, can hardly be conceived any more as the basic concept of the theory.

(2) The principles of the conservation of momentum and of the conservation of energy are fused into one single principle. The inert mass of a closed system is identical with its energy, thus eliminating mass as an independent concept.

Remark. The speed of light c is one of the quantities which occurs as "universal constant" in physical equations. If, however, one introduces as unit of time instead of the second the time in which light travels 1 cm, c no longer occurs in the equations. In this sense one could say that the constant c is only an *apparently* universal constant.

It is obvious and generally accepted that one could eliminate two more universal constants from physics by introducing, instead of the gram and the centimeter, properly chosen "natural" units (for example, mass and radius of the electron).

If one considers this done, then only "dimension-less" con-

Gleichungen der Physik nur mehr "dimensionslose" Konstante auftreten können. Bezüglich dieser möchte ich einen Satz aussprechen, der vorläufig auf nichts anderes gegründet werden kann als auf ein Vertrauen in die Einfachheit, bezw. Verständlichkeit, der Natur: derartige *willkürliche* Konstante gibt es nicht; d.h. die Natur ist so beschaffen, dass man für sie logisch derart stark determinierte Gesetze aufstellen kann, dass in diesen Gesetzen nur rational völlig bestimmte Konstante auftreten (also nicht Konstante, deren Zahlwerte verändert werden könnten, ohne die Theorie zu zerstören). – – –

Die spezielle Relativitätstheorie verdankt ihre Entstehung den Maxwell'schen Gleichungen des elektromagnetischen Feldes. Umgekehrt werden die letzteren erst durch die spezielle Relativitätstheorie in befriedigender Weise formal begriffen. Es sind die einfachsten Lorentz-invarianten Feldgleichungen, die für einen aus einem Vektorfeld abgeleiteten schief symmetrischen Tensor aufgestellt werden können. Dies wäre an sich befriedigend, wenn wir nicht aus den Quanten-Erscheinungen wüssten, dass die Maxwell'sche Theorie den energetischen Eigenschaften der Strahlung nicht gerecht wird. Wie aber die Maxwell'sche Theorie in natürlicher Weise modifiziert werden könnte, dafür liefert auch die spezielle Relativitätstheorie keinen hinreichenden Anhaltspunkt. Auch auf die Mach'sche Frage: "wie kommt es, dass die Inertialsysteme gegenüber anderen Koordinationssystemen physikalisch ausgezeichnet sind?" liefert diese Theorie keine Antwort.

Dass die spezielle Relativitätstheorie nur der erste Schritt einer notwendigen Entwicklung sei, wurde mir erst bei der Bemühung völlig klar die Gravitation im Rahmen dieser Theorie darzustellen. In der feldartig interpretierten klassischen Mechanik erscheint das Potential der Gravitation als ein *skalares* Feld (die einfachste theoretische Möglichkeit eines Feldes mit einer einzigen Komponente). Eine solche Skalar-Theorie des Gravitationsfeldes kann zunächst leicht invariant gemacht werden inbezug auf die Gruppe der Lorentz-Transformationen. Folgendes Programm erscheint also natürlich: Das physikalische Gesamtfeld besteht aus einem Skalarfeld (Gravitation) und einem Vektorfeld (elektromagnetisches

stants could occur in the basic equations of physics. Concerning such I would like to state a theorem which at present can not be based upon anything more than upon a faith in the simplicity, i.e., intelligibility, of nature: there are no *arbitrary* constants of this kind; that is to say, nature is so constituted that it is possible logically to lay down such strongly determined laws that within these laws only rationally completely determined constants occur (not constants, therefore, whose numerical value could be changed without destroying the theory). – – –

The special theory of relativity owes its origin to Maxwell's equations of the electromagnetic field. Inversely the latter can be grasped formally in satisfactory fashion only by way of the special theory of relativity. Maxwell's equations are the simplest Lorentz-invariant field equations which can be postulated for an anti-symmetric tensor derived from a vector field. This in itself would be satisfactory, if we did not know from quantum phenomena that Maxwell's theory does not do justice to the energetic properties of radiation. But how Maxwell's theory would have to be modified in a natural fashion, for this even the special theory of relativity offers no adequate foothold. Also to Mach's question: "how does it come about that inertial systems are physically distinguished above all other co-ordinate systems?" this theory offers no answer.

That the special theory of relativity is only the first step of a necessary development became completely clear to me only in my efforts to represent gravitation in the framework of this theory. In classical mechanics, interpreted in terms of the field, the potential of gravitation appears as a *scalar* field (the simplest theoretical possibility of a field with a single component). Such a scalar theory of the gravitational field can easily be made invariant under the group of Lorentz-transformations. The following program appears natural, therefore: The total physical field consists of a scalar field (gravitation) and a vector field (electromagnetic field); later insights may eventually

Feld); spätere Erkenntnisse mögen eventuell die Einführung noch komplizierterer Feldarten nötig machen, aber darum brauchte man sich zunächst nicht zu kümmern.

Die Möglichkeit der Realisierung dieses Programms war aber von vornherein zweifelhaft, weil die Theorie folgende Dinge vereinigen musste.

1) Aus allgemeinen Ueberlegungen der speziellen Relativitätstheorie war klar, dass die *träge* Masse eines physikalischen Systems mit der Gesamtenergie (also z.B. mit der kinetischen Energie) wachse.

2) Aus sehr präzisen Versuchen (insbesondere aus den Eötvös'schen Drehwage-Versuchen) war mit sehr grosser Präzision empirisch bekannt, dass die *schwere* Masse eines Körpers seiner *trägen* Masse genau gleich sei.

Aus 1) und 2) folgte, dass die *Schwere* eines Systems in genau bekannter Weise von seiner Gesamtenergie abhänge. Wenn die Theorie dies nicht oder nicht in natürlicher Weise leistete, so war sie zu verwerfen. Die Bedingung lässt sich am natürlichsten so aussprechen: die Fall-Beschleunigung eines Systems in einem gegebenen Schwerefelde ist von der Natur des fallenden Systems (speziell also auch von seinem Energie-Inhalte) unabhängig.

Es zeigte sich nun, dass im Rahmen des skizzierten Programmes diesem elementaren Sachverhalte überhaupt nicht oder jedenfalls nicht in natürlicher Weise Genüge geleistet werden konnte. Dies gab mir die Ueberzeugung, dass im Rahmen der speziellen Relativitätstheorie kein Platz sei für eine befriedigende Theorie der Gravitation.

Nun fiel mir ein: Die Tatsache der Gleichheit der trägen und schweren Masse, bezw. die Tatsache der Unabhängigkeit der Fallbeschleunigung von der Natur der fallenden Substanz, lässt sich so ausdrücken: In einem Gravitationsfelde (geringer räumlicher Ausdehnung) verhalten sich die Dinge so wie in einem gravitationsfreien Raume, wenn man in diesem statt eines "Inertialsystems" ein gegen ein solches beschleunigtes Bezugssystem einführt.

Wenn man also das Verhalten der Körper inbezug auf das

make necessary the introduction of still more complicated types of fields; but to begin with one did not need to bother about this.

The possibility of the realization of this program was, however, dubious from the very first, because the theory had to combine the following things:

(1) From the general considerations of special relativity theory it was clear that the *inert* mass of a physical system increases with the total energy (therefore, e.g., with the kinetic energy).

(2) From very accurate experiments (specially from the torsion balance experiments of Eötvös) it was empirically known with very high accuracy that the gravitational mass of a body is exactly equal to its *inert* mass.

It followed from (1) and (2) that the *weight* of a system depends in a precisely known manner on its total energy. If the theory did not accomplish this or could not do it naturally, it was to be rejected. The condition is most naturally expressed as follows: the acceleration of a system falling freely in a given gravitational field is independent of the nature of the falling system (specially therefore also of its energy content).

It then appeared that, in the framework of the program sketched, this elementary state of affairs could not at all or at any rate not in any natural fashion, be represented in a satisfactory way. This convinced me that, within the frame of the special theory of relativity, there is no room for a satisfactory theory of gravitation.

Now it came to me: The fact of the equality of inert and heavy mass, i.e., the fact of the independence of the gravitational acceleration of the nature of the falling substance, may be expressed as follows: In a gravitational field (of small spatial extension) things behave as they do in a space free of gravitation, if one introduces in it, in place of an "inertial system," a reference system which is accelerated relative to an inertial system.

If then one conceives of the behavior of a body, in reference

letztere Bezugssystem als durch ein "wirkliches" (nicht nur scheinbares) Gravitationsfeld bedingt auffasst, so kann man dieses Bezugssystem mit dem gleichen Rechte als ein "Inertialsystem" betrachten wie das ursprüngliche Bezugssystem.

Wenn man also beliebig ausgedehnte, nicht von vornherein durch räumliche Grenzbedingungen eingeschränkte, Gravitationsfelder als möglich betrachtet, so wird der Begriff des Inertialsystems völlig leer. Der Begriff "Beschleunigung gegenüber dem Raume" verliert dann jede Bedeutung und damit auch das Trägheitsprinzip samt dem Mach'schen Paradoxon.

So führt die Tatsache der Gleichheit der trägen und schweren Masse ganz natürlich zu den Auffassungen, dass die Grund-Forderung der speziellen Relativitätstheorie (Invarianz der Gesetze bezüglich Lorentz-Transformationen) zu eng sei, d.h. dass man eine Invarianz der Gesetze auch bezüglich *nicht linearer* Transformationen der Koordinaten im vierdimensionalen Kontinuum zu postulieren habe.

Dies trug sich 1908 zu. Warum brauchte es weiterer 7 Jahre für die Aufstellung der allgemeinen Rel. Theorie? Der hauptsächliche Grund liegt darin, dass man sich nicht so leicht von der Auffassung befreit, dass den Koordinaten eine unmittelbare metrische Bedeutung zukommen müsse. Die Wandlung vollzog sich ungefähr in folgender Weise.

Wir gehen aus von einem leeren, feldfreien Raume, wie er —auf ein Inertialsystem bezogen—im Sinne der speziellen Relativitätstheorie als der einfachste aller denkbaren physikalischen Tatbestände auftritt. Denken wir uns nun ein Nicht-Inertialsystem dadurch eingeführt, dass das neue System gegen das Inertialsystem (in dreidimensionaler Beschreibungsart) in einer Richtung (geeignet definiert) gleichförmig beschleunigt ist, so besteht inbezug auf dieses System ein statisches paralleles Schwerefeld. Das Bezugssystem kann dabei als starr gewählt werden, in den dreidimensionalen metrischen Beziehungen von euklidischem Charakter. Aber jene Zeit, in welcher das Feld statisch erscheint, wird *nicht* durch *gleich beschaffene* ruhende Uhren gemessen. Aus diesem speziellen Beispiel erkennt man schon, dass die unmittelbare metrische Bedeutung der Koordinaten verloren geht, wenn man überhaupt nichtlineare

to the latter reference system, as caused by a "real" (not merely apparent) gravitational field, it is possible to regard this reference system as an "inertial system" with as much justification as the original reference system.

So, if one regards as possible, gravitational fields of arbitrary extension which are not initially restricted by spatial limitations, the concept of the "inertial system" becomes completely empty. The concept, "acceleration relative to space," then loses every meaning and with it the principle of inertia together with the entire paradox of Mach.

The fact of the equality of inert and heavy mass thus leads quite naturally to the recognition that the basic demand of the special theory of relativity (invariance of the laws under Lorentz-transformations) is too narrow, i.e., that an invariance of the laws must be postulated also relative to *non-linear* transformations of the co-ordinates in the four-dimensional continuum.

This happened in 1908. Why were another seven years required for the construction of the general theory of relativity? The main reason lies in the fact that it is not so easy to free oneself from the idea that co-ordinates must have an immediate metrical meaning. The transformation took place in approximately the following fashion.

We start with an empty, field-free space, as it occurs—related to an inertial system—in the sense of the special theory of relativity, as the simplest of all imaginable physical situations. If we now think of a non-inertial system introduced by assuming that the new system is uniformly accelerated against the inertial system (in a three-dimensional description) in one direction (conveniently defined), then there exists with reference to this system a static parallel gravitational field. The reference system may thereby be chosen as rigid, of Euclidian type, in three-dimensional metric relations. But the time, in which the field appears as static, is *not* measured by *equally constituted* stationary clocks. From this special example one can already recognize that the immediate metric significance of the co-ordinates is lost if one admits non-linear transforma-

Transformationen der Koordinaten zulässt. Letzteres *muss* man aber, wenn man der Gleichheit von schwerer und träger Masse durch das Fundament der Theorie gerecht werden will, und wenn man das Mach'sche Paradoxon bezüglich der Inertialsysteme überwinden will.

Wenn man nun aber darauf verzichten muss, den Koordinaten eine unmittelbare metrische Bedeutung zu geben (Koordinatendifferenzen = messbare Längen bezw. Zeiten), so wird man nicht umhin können, alle durch kontinuierliche Transformationen der Koordinaten erzeugbare Koordinatensysteme als gleichwertig zu behandeln.

Die allgemeine Relativitätstheorie geht demgemäss von dem Grundsatz aus: Die Naturgesetze sind durch Gleichungen auszudrücken, die kovariant sind bezüglich der Gruppe der kontinuierlichen Koordinaten-Transformationen. Diese Gruppe tritt also hier an die Stelle der Gruppe der Lorentz-Transformationen der speziellen Relativitätstheorie, welch letztere Gruppe eine Untergruppe der ersteren bildet.

Diese Forderung für sich alleine genügt natürlich nicht als Ausgangspunkt für eine Ableitung der Grundgleichungen der Physik. Zunächst kann man sogar bestreiten, dass die Forderung allein eine wirkliche Beschränkung für die physikalischen Gesetze enthalte; denn es wird stets möglich sein, ein zunächst nur für gewisse Koordinatensysteme postuliertes Gesetz so umzuformulieren, dass die neue Formulierung der Form nach allgemein kovariant wird. Ausserdem ist es von vornherein klar, dass sich unendlich viele Feldgesetze formulieren lassen, die diese Kovarianz-Eigenschaft haben. Die eminente heuristische Bedeutung des allgemeinen Relativitätsprinzips liegt aber darin, dass es uns zu der Aufsuchung jener Gleichungssysteme führt, welche *in allgemein kovarianter* Formulierung *möglichst einfach* sind; unter diesen haben wir die Feldgesetze des physikalischen Raumes zu suchen. Felder, die durch solche Transformationen ineinander übergeführt werden können, beschreiben denselben realen Sachverhalt.

Die Hauptfrage für den auf diesem Gebiete Suchenden ist diese: Von welcher mathematischen Art sind die Grössen (Funktionen der Koordinaten), welche die physikalischen

tions of co-ordinates at all. To do the latter is, however, *obligatory* if one wants to do justice to the equality of gravitational and inert mass by means of the basis of the theory, and if one wants to overcome Mach's paradox as concerns the inertial systems.

If, then, one must give up the attempt to give the co-ordinates an immediate metric meaning (differences of co-ordinates = measurable lengths, viz., times), one will not be able to avoid treating as equivalent all co-ordinate systems, which can be created by the continuous transformations of the co-ordinates.

The general theory of relativity, accordingly, proceeds from the following principle: Natural laws are to be expressed by equations which are covariant under the group of continuous co-ordinate transformations. This group replaces the group of the Lorentz-transformations of the special theory of relativity, which forms a sub-group of the former.

This demand by itself is of course not sufficient to serve as point of departure for the derivation of the basic concepts of physics. In the first instance one may even contest [the idea] that the demand by itself contains a real restriction for the physical laws; for it will always be possible thus to reformulate a law, postulated at first only for certain co-ordinate systems, such that the new formulation becomes formally universally co-variant. Beyond this it is clear from the beginning that an infinitely large number of field-laws can be formulated which have this property of covariance. The eminent heuristic significance of the general principles of relativity lies in the fact that it leads us to the search for those systems of equations which are *in their general covariant* formulation the *simplest ones possible;* among these we shall have to look for the field equations of physical space. Fields which can be transformed into each other by such transformations describe the same real situation.

The major question for anyone doing research in this field is this: Of which mathematical type are the variables (functions of the co-ordinates) which permit the expression of the physical

Eigenschaften des Raumes auszudrücken gestatten ("Struktur")? Dann erst: welchen Gleichungen genügen jene Grössen?

Wir können heute diese Fragen noch keineswegs mit Sicherheit beantworten. Der bei der ersten Formulierung der allgemeinen Rel. Theorie eingeschlagene Weg lässt sich so kennzeichnen. Wenn wir auch nicht wissen, durch was für Feldvariable (Struktur) der physikalische Raum zu charakterisieren ist, so kennen wir doch mit Sicherheit einen speziellen Fall: den des "feldfreien" Raumes in der speziellen Relativitätstheorie. Ein solcher Raum ist dadurch charakterisiert, dass für ein passend gewähltes Koordinatensystem der zu zwei benachbarten Punkten gehörige Ausdruck

$$ds^2 = dx_1^2 + dx_2^2 + dx_3^2 - dx_4^2 \tag{1}$$

eine messbare Grösse darstellt (Abstandsquadrat), also eine reale physikalische Bedeutung hat. Auf ein beliebiges System bezogen drückt sich diese Grösse so aus

$$ds^2 = g_{ik}dx_i dx_k \tag{2}$$

wobei die Indices von 1 bis 4 laufen. Die g_{ik} bilden einen symmetrischen Tensor. Wenn, nach Ausführung einer Transformation am Felde (1), die ersten Ableitungen der g_{ik} nach den Koordinaten nicht verschwinden, so besteht, mit Bezug auf dies Koordinatensystem, ein Gravitationsfeld im Sinne der obigen Ueberlegung, und zwar ein Gravitationsfeld ganz spezieller Art. Dies besondere Feld lässt sich dank der Riemann'schen Untersuchung n-dimensionaler metrischer Räume invariant charakterisieren:

1) Der aus den Koeffizienten der Metric (2) gebildete Riemann'sche Krümmungstensor R_{iklm} verschwindet.
2) Die Bahn eines Massenpunktes ist inbezug auf das Inertialsystem (inbezug auf welches (1) gilt) eine gerade Linie, also eine Extremale (Geodete). Letzteres ist aber bereits eine auf (2) sich stützende Charakterisierung des Bewegungsgesetzes.

Das *allgemeine* Gesetz des physikalischen Raumes muss nun eine Verallgemeinerung des soeben charakterisierten Gesetzes sein. Ich nahm nun an, dass es zwei Stufen der Verallgemeinerung gibt:

properties of space ("structure")? Only after that: Which equations are satisfied by those variables?

The answer to these questions is today by no means certain. The path chosen by the first formulation of the general theory of relativity can be characterized as follows. Even though we do not know by what type field-variables (structure) physical space is to be characterized, we do know with certainty a special case: that of the "field-free" space in the special theory of relativity. Such a space is characterized by the fact that for a properly chosen co-ordinate system the expression

$$ds^2 = dx_1^2 + dx_2^2 + dx_3^2 - dx_4^2 \qquad (1)$$

belonging to two neighboring points, represents a measurable quantity (square of distance), and thus has a real physical meaning. Referred to an arbitrary system this quantity is expressed as follows:

$$ds^2 = g_{ik}dx_i dx_k \qquad (2)$$

whereby the indices run from 1 to 4. The g_{ik} form a (real) symmetrical tensor. If, after carrying out a transformation on field (1), the first derivatives of the g_{ik} with respect to the co-ordinates do not vanish, there exists a gravitational field with reference to this system of co-ordinates in the sense of the above consideration, a gravitational field, moreover, of a very special type. Thanks to Riemann's investigation of n-dimensional metrical spaces this special field can be invariantly characterized:

(1) Riemann's curvature-tensor R_{iklm}, formed from the coefficients of the metric (2) vanishes.

(2) The orbit of a mass-point in reference to the inertial system (relative to which (1) is valid) is a straight line, therefore an extremal (geodetic). The latter, however, is already a characterization of the law of motion based on (2).

The *universal* law of physical space must now be a generalization of the law just characterized. I now assume that there are two steps of generalization:

a) reines Gravitationsfeld

b) allgemeines Feld (in welchem auch Grössen auftreten, die irgendwie dem elektromagnetischen Felde entsprechen).

Der Fall a) war dadurch charakterisiert, dass das Feld zwar immer noch durch eine Riemann-Metrik (2) bezw. durch einen symmetrischen Tensor darstellbar ist, wobei es aber (ausser im Infinitesimalen) keine Darstellung in der Form (1) gibt. Dies bedeutet, dass im Falle a) der Riemann-Tensor *nicht* verschwindet. Es ist aber klar, dass in diesem Falle ein Feldgesetz gelten muss, das eine Verallgemeinerung (Abschwächung) dieses Gesetzes ist. Soll auch dies Gesetz von der zweiten Differentiationsordnung und in den zweiten Ableitungen linear sein, so kam nur die durch einmalige Kontraktion zu gewinnende Gleichung

$$0 = R_{kl} = g^{im} R_{iklm}$$

als Feldgleichung im Falle a) in Betracht. Es erscheint ferner natürlich anzunehmen, dass auch im Falle a) die geodätische Linie immer noch das Bewegungsgesetz des materiellen Punktes darstelle.

Es erschien mir damals aussichtslos, den Versuch zu wagen, das Gesamtfeld b) darzustellen und für dieses Feldgesetze zu ermitteln. Ich zog es deshalb vor, einen vorläufigen formalen Rahmen für eine Darstellung der ganzen physikalischen Realität hinzustellen; dies war nötig, um wenigstens vorläufig die Brauchbarkeit des Grundgedankens der allgemeinen Relativität untersuchen zu können. Dies geschah so.

In der Newton'schen Theorie kann man als Feldgesetz der Gravitation

$$\Delta\varphi = 0$$

schreiben (φ = Gravitationspotential) an solchen Orten, wo die Dichte ϱ der Materie verschwindet. Allgemein wäre zu setzen (Poissonsche Gleichung)

$$\Delta\varphi = 4\pi k\varrho \cdot \quad (\varrho = \text{Massen-Dichte}).$$

Im Falle der relativistischen Theorie des Gravitationsfeldes tritt R_{ik} an die Stelle von $\Delta\varphi$. Auf die rechte Seite haben wir

(a) pure gravitational field

(b) general field (in which quantities corresponding somehow to the electromagnetic field occur, too).

The instance (a) was characterized by the fact that the field can still be represented by a Riemann-metric (2), i.e., by a symmetric tensor, whereby, however, there is no representation in the form (1) (except in infinitesimal regions). This means that in the case (a) the Riemann-tensor does not vanish. It is clear, however, that in this case a field-law must be valid, which is a generalization (loosening) of this law. If this law also is to be of the second order of differentiation and linear in the second derivations, then only the equation, to be obtained by a single contraction

$$0 = R_{kl} = g^{im} R_{iklm}$$

came under consideration as field-equation in the case of (a). It appears natural, moreover, to assume that also in the case of (a) the geodetic line is still to be taken as representing the law of motion of the material point.

It seemed hopeless to me at that time to venture the attempt of representing the total field (b) and to ascertain field-laws for it. I preferred, therefore, to set up a preliminary formal frame for the representation of the entire physical reality; this was necessary in order to be able to investigate, at least preliminarily, the usefulness of the basic idea of general relativity. This was done as follows.

In Newton's theory one can write the field-law of gravitation thus:

$$\Delta\varphi = 0$$

(φ = gravitation-potential) at points, where the density of matter, ϱ, vanishes. In general one may write (Poisson equation)

$$\Delta\varphi = 4\pi k\varrho \cdot \quad (\varrho = \text{mass-density}).$$

In the case of the relativistic theory of the gravitational field R_{ik} takes the place of $\Delta\varphi$. On the right side we shall then have

dann an die Stelle von ϱ ebenfalls einen Tensor zu setzen. Da wir aus der speziellen Rel. Th. wissen, dass die (träge) Masse gleich ist der Energie, so wird auf die rechte Seite der Tensor der Energie-Dichte zu setzen sein—genauer der gesamten Energiedichte, soweit sie nicht dem reinen Gravitationsfelde angehört. Man gelangt so zu den Feldgleichungen

$$R_{ik} - \frac{1}{2} g_{ik} R = -k T_{ik}.$$

Das zweite Glied der linken Seite ist aus formalen Gründen zugefügt; die linke Seite ist nämlich so geschrieben, dass ihre Divergenz im Sinne des absoluten Differentialkalküls identisch verschwindet. Die rechte Seite ist eine formale Zusammenfassung aller Dinge, deren Erfassung im Sinne einer Feldtheorie noch problematisch ist. Natürlich war ich keinen Augenblick darüber im Zweifel, dass diese Fassung nur ein Notbehelf war, um dem allgemeinen Relativitätsprinzip einen vorläufigen geschlossenen Ausdruck zu geben. Es war ja nicht wesentlich *mehr* als eine Theorie des Gravitationsfeldes, das einigermassen künstlich von einem Gesamtfelde noch unbekannter Struktur isoliert wurde.

Wenn irgend etwas—abgesehen von der Forderung der Invarianz der Gleichungen bezüglich der Gruppe der kontinuierlichen Koordinaten-Transformationen—in der skizzierten Theorie möglicherweise endgültige Bedeutung beanspruchen kann, so ist es die Theorie des Grenzfalles des reinen Gravitationsfeldes und dessen Beziehung zu der metrischen Struktur des Raumes. Deshalb soll im unmittelbar Folgenden nur von den Gleichungen des reinen Gravitationsfeldes die Rede sein.

Das Eigenartige an diesen Gleichungen ist einerseits ihr komplizierter Bau, besonders ihr nichtlinearer Charakter inbezug auf die Feldvariabeln und deren Ableitungen, andererseits, die fast zwingende Notwendigkeit, mit welcher die Transformationsgruppe dies komplizierte Feldgesetz bestimmt. Wenn man bei der speziellen Relativitätstheorie, d.h. bei der Invarianz bezüglich der Lorentz-Gruppe, stehen geblieben wäre, so würde auch im Rahmen dieser engeren Gruppe das Feldgesetz $R_{ik} = 0$ invariant sein. Aber vom Standpunkte der engeren Gruppe bestünde zunächst keinerlei Anlass dafür, dass

to place a tensor also in place of ϱ. Since we know from the special theory of relativity that the (inert) mass equals energy, we shall have to put on the right side the tensor of energy-density—more precisely the entire energy-density, insofar as it does not belong to the pure gravitational field. In this way one gets the field-equations

$$R_{ik} - \frac{1}{2} g_{ik} R = -k T_{ik}.$$

The second member on the left side is added because of formal reasons; for the left side is written in such a way that its divergence disappears identically in the sense of the absolute differential calculus. The right side is a formal condensation of all things whose comprehension in the sense of a field-theory is still problematic. Not for a moment, of course, did I doubt that this formulation was merely a makeshift in order to give the general principle of relativity a preliminary closed expression. For it was essentially not anything *more* than a theory of the gravitational field, which was somewhat artificially isolated from a total field of as yet unknown structure.

If anything in the theory as sketched—apart from the demand of the invariance of the equations under the group of the continuous co-ordinate-transformations—can possibly make the claim to final significance, then it is the theory of the limiting case of the pure gravitational field and its relation to the metric structure of space. For this reason, in what immediately follows we shall speak only of the equations of the pure gravitational field.

The peculiarity of these equations lies, on the one hand, in their complicated construction, especially their non-linear character as regards the field-variables and their derivatives, and, on the other hand, in the almost compelling necessity with which the transformation-group determines this complicated field-law. If one had stopped with the special theory of relativity, i.e., with the invariance under the Lorentz-group, then the field-law $R_{ik} = 0$ would remain invariant also within the frame of this narrower group. But, from the point of view of the nar-

die Gravitation durch eine so komplizierte Struktur dargestellt werden müsse, wie sie der symmetrische Tensor g_{ik} darstellt. Würde man aber doch hinreichende Gründe dafür finden, so gäbe es eine unübersehbare Zahl von Feldgesetzen aus Grössen g_{ik}, die alle kovariant sind bezüglich Lorentz-Transformationen (nicht aber gegenüber der allgemeinen Gruppe). Selbst aber wenn man von all den denkbaren Lorentz-invarianten Gesetzen zufällig gerade das zu der weiteren Gruppe gehörige Gesetz erraten hätte, so wäre man immer noch nicht auf der durch das allgemeine Relativitätsprinzip erlangten Stufe der Erkenntnis. Denn vom Standpunkt der Lorentz-Gruppe wären zwei Lösungen fälschlich als physikalisch voneinander verschieden zu betrachten, wenn sie durch eine nichtlineare Koordinaten-Transformation ineinander transformierbar sind, d.h. vom Standpunkt der weiteren Gruppe nur verschiedene Darstellungen desselben Feldes sind.

Noch eine allgemeine Bemerkung über Struktur und Gruppe. Es ist klar, dass man im Allgemeinen eine Theorie als umso vollkommener beurteilen wird, eine je einfachere "Struktur" sie zugrundelegt und je weiter die Gruppe ist, bezüglich welcher die Feldgleichungen invariant sind. Man sieht nun, dass diese beiden Forderungen einander im Wege sind. Gemäss der speziellen Relativitätstheorie (Lorentz-Gruppe) kann man z.B. für die denkbar einfachste Struktur (skalares Feld) ein kovariantes Gesetz aufstellen, während es in der allgemeinen Relativitätstheorie (weitere Gruppe der kontinuierlichen Koordinaten-Transformationen) erst für die kompliziertere Struktur des symmetrischen Tensors ein invariantes Feldgesetz gibt. Wir haben *physikalische* Gründe dafür angegeben, dass Invarianz gegenüber der weiteren Gruppe in der Physik gefordert werden muss;[1] vom rein mathematischen Gesichtspunkte aus sehe ich keinen Zwang, die einfachere Struktur der Weite der Gruppe zum Opfer zu bringen.

Die Gruppe der allgemeinen Relativität bringt es zum ersten

[1] Bei der engeren Gruppe zu bleiben und gleichzeitig die kompliziertere Struktur der allgemeinen Rel. Theorie zugrunde zu legen, bedeutet eine naive Inkonsequenz. Sünde bleibt Sünde, auch wenn sie von sonst respektabeln Männern begangen wird.

rower group there would at first exist no reason for representing gravitation by so complicated a structure as is represented by the symmetric tensor g_{ik}. If, nonetheless, one would find sufficient reasons for it, there would then arise an immense number of field-laws out of quantities g_{ik}, all of which are covariant under Lorentz-transformations (not, however, under the general group). However, even if, of all the conceivable Lorentz-invariant laws, one had accidentally guessed precisely the law which belongs to the wider group, one would still not yet be on the plane of insight achieved by the general principle of relativity. For, from the standpoint of the Lorentz-group two solutions would incorrectly have to be viewed as physically different from each other, if they can be transformed into each other by a non-linear transformation of co-ordinates, i.e., if they are, from the point of view of the wider field, only different representations of the same field.

One more general remark concerning field-structure and the group. It is clear that in general one will judge a theory to be the more nearly perfect the simpler a "structure" it postulates and the broader the group is concerning which the field-equations are invariant. One sees now that these two demands get in each other's way. For example: according to the special theory of relativity (Lorentz-Group) one can set up a covariant law for simplest structure imaginable (a scalar field), whereas in the general theory of relativity (wider group of the continuous transformations of co-ordinates) there is an invariant field-law only for the more complicated structure of the symmetric tensor. We have already given *physical* reasons for the fact that in physics invariance under the wider group has to be demanded:[1] from a purely mathematical standpoint I can see no necessity for sacrificing the simpler structure to the generality of the group.

The group of the general relativity is the first one which

[1] To remain with the narrower group and at the same time to base the relativity theory of gravitation upon the more complicated (tensor-) structure implies a naïve inconsequence. Sin remains sin, even if it is committed by otherwise ever so respectable men.

Male mit sich, dass das einfachste invariante Gesetz nicht linear und homogen in den Feldvariabeln und ihren Differentialquotienten ist. Dies ist aus folgendem Grunde von fundamentaler Wichtigkeit. Ist das Feldgesetz linear (und homogen), so ist die Summe zweier Lösungen wieder eine Lösung; so ist es z.B. bei den Maxwell'schen Feldgleichungen des leeren Raumes. In einer solchen Theorie kann aus dem Feldgesetz allein nicht auf eine Wechselwirkung von Gebilden geschlossen werden, die isoliert durch Lösungen des Systems dargestellt werden können. Daher bedurfte es in den bisherigen Theorien neben den Feldgesetzen besonderer Gesetze für die Bewegung der materiellen Gebilde unter dem Einfluss der Felder. In der relativistischen Gravitationstheorie wurde nun zwar ursprünglich neben dem Feldgesetz das Bewegungsgesetz (Geodätische Linie) unabhängig postuliert. Es hat sich aber nachträglich herausgestellt, dass das Bewegungsgesetz nicht unabhängig angenommen werden muss (und darf), sondern dass es in dem Gesetz des Gravitationsfeldes implicite enthalten ist.

Das Wesen dieser an sich komplizierten Sachlage kann man sich wie folgt veranschaulichen. Ein einziger ruhender materieller Punkt wird durch ein Gravitationsfeld repräsentiert, das überall endlich und regulär ist ausser an dem Orte, an dem der materielle Punkt sitzt; dort hat das Feld eine Singularität. Berechnet man aber durch Integration der Feldgleichungen das Feld, welches zu zwei ruhenden materiellen Punkten gehört, so hat dieses ausser den Singularitäten am Orte der materiellen Punkte noch eine aus singulären Punkten bestehende Linie, welche die beiden Punkte verbindet. Man kann aber eine Bewegung der materiellen Punkte in solcher Weise vorgeben, dass das durch sie bestimmte Gravitationsfeld ausserhalb der materiellen Punkte nirgends singulär wird. Es sind dies gerade jene Bewegungen, die in erster Näherung durch die Newton'schen Gesetze beschrieben werden. Man kann also sagen: Die Massen bewegen sich so, dass die Feldgleichung im Raume ausserhalb der Massen nirgends Singularitäten des Feldes bedingt. Diese Eigenschaft der Gravitationsgleichungen hängt unmittelbar zusammen mit ihrer Nicht-Linearität, und diese

demands that the simplest invariant law be no longer linear or homogeneous in the field-variables and in their differential quotients. This is of fundamental importance for the following reason. If the field-law is linear (and homogeneous), then the sum of two solutions is again a solution; as, for example: in Maxwell's field-equations for the vacuum. In such a theory it is impossible to deduce from the field equations alone an interaction between bodies, which can be described separately by means of solutions of the system. For this reason all theories up to now required, in addition to the field equations, special equations for the motion of material bodies under the influence of the fields. In the relativistic theory of gravitation, it is true, the law of motion (geodetic line) was originally postulated independently in addition to the field-law equations. Afterwards, however, it became apparent that the law of motion need not (and must not) be assumed independently, but that it is already implicitly contained within the law of the gravitational field.

The essence of this genuinely complicated situation can be visualized as follows: A single material point at rest will be represented by a gravitational field which is everywhere finite and regular, except at the position where the material point is located: there the field has a singularity. If, however, one computes by means of the integration of the field-equations the field which belongs to two material points at rest, then this field has, in addition to the singularities at the positions of the material points, a line consisting of singular points, which connects the two points. However, it is possible to stipulate a motion of the material points in such a way that the gravitational field which is determined by them does not become singular anywhere at all except at the material points. These are precisely those motions which are described in first approximation by Newton's laws. One may say, therefore: The masses move in such fashion that the solution of the field-equation is nowhere singular except in the mass points. This attribute of the gravitational equations is intimately connected with their non-linearity,

ihrerseits wird durch die weitere Transformationsgruppe bedingt.

Nun könnte man allerdings den Einwand machen: Wenn am Orte der materiellen Punkte Singularitäten zugelassen werden, was für eine Berechtigung besteht dann, das Auftreten von Singularitäten im übrigen Raume zu verbieten? Dieser Einwand wäre dann berechtigt, wenn die Gleichungen der Gravitation als Gleichungen des Gesamtfeldes anzusehen wären. So aber wird man sagen müssen, dass das Feld eines materiellen Teilchens desto weniger als *reines Gravitationsfeld* wird betrachtet werden dürfen, je näher man dem eigentlichen Ort des Teilchens kommt. Würde man die Feldgleichung des Gesamtfeldes haben, so müsste man verlangen, dass die Teilchen selbst als *überall* singularitätsfreie Lösungen der vollständigen Feldgleichungen sich darstellen lassen. Dann erst wäre die allgemeine Relativitätstheorie eine *vollständige* Theorie.

Bevor ich auf die Frage der Vollendung der allgemeinen Relativitätstheorie eingehe, muss ich Stellung nehmen zu der erfolgreichsten physikalischen Theorie unserer Zeit, der statistischen Quantentheorie, die vor etwa 25 Jahren eine konsistente logische Form angenommen hat (Schrödinger, Heisenberg, Dirac, Born). Es ist die einzige gegenwärtige Theorie, welche die Erfahrungen über den Quanten-Charakter der mikromechanischen Vorgänge einheitlich zu begreifen gestattet. Diese Theorie auf der einen Seite und die Relativitätstheorie auf der andern Seite werden beide in gewissem Sinne für richtig gehalten, obwohl ihre Verschmelzung allen bisherigen Bemühungen widerstanden hat. Damit hängt es wohl zusammen, dass unter den theoretischen Physikern der Gegenwart durchaus verschiedene Meinungen darüber bestehen, wie das theoretische Fundament der künftigen Physik aussehen wird. Ist es eine Feldtheorie; ist es eine im Wessentlichen statistische Theorie? Ich will hier kurz sagen, wie ich darüber denke.

Die Physik ist eine Bemühung das Seiende als etwas begrifflich zu erfassen, was unabhängig vom Wahrgenommen-Werden gedacht wird. In diesem Sinne spricht man vom "Physikalisch-Realen." In der Vor-Quantenphysik war kein Zweifel, wie dies zu verstehen sei. In Newtons Theorie war das Reale

and this is a consequence of the wider group of transformations.

Now it would of course be possible to object: If singularities are permitted at the positions of the material points, what justification is there for forbidding the occurrence of singularities in the rest of space? This objection would be justified if the equations of gravitation were to be considered as equations of the total field. [Since this is not the case], however, one will have to say that the field of a material particle may the less be viewed as a *pure gravitational field* the closer one comes to the position of the particle. If one had the field-equation of the total field, one would be compelled to demand that the particles themselves would *everywhere* be describable as singularity-free solutions of the completed field-equations. Only then would the general theory of relativity be a *complete* theory.

Before I enter upon the question of the completion of the general theory of relativity, I must take a stand with reference to the most successful physical theory of our period, viz., the statistical quantum theory which, about twenty-five years ago, took on a consistent logical form (Schrödinger, Heisenberg, Dirac, Born). This is the only theory at present which permits a unitary grasp of experiences concerning the quantum character of micro-mechanical events. This theory, on the one hand, and the theory of relativity on the other, are both considered correct in a certain sense, although their combination has resisted all efforts up to now. This is probably the reason why among contemporary theoretical physicists there exist entirely differing opinions concerning the question as to how the theoretical foundation of the physics of the future will appear. Will it be a field theory; will it be in essence a statistical theory? I shall briefly indicate my own thoughts on this point.

Physics is an attempt conceptually to grasp reality as it is thought independently of its being observed. In this sense one speaks of "physical reality." In pre-quantum physics there was no doubt as to how this was to be understood. In Newton's theory reality was determined by a material point in space and

durch materielle Punkte in Raum und Zeit, in der Maxwell'schen Theorie durch ein Feld in Raum und Zeit dargestellt. In der Quantenmechanik ist es weniger durchsichtig. Wenn man fragt: Stellt eine ψ-Funktion der Quantentheorie einen realen Sachverhalt in demselben Sinne dar wie ein materielles Punktsystem oder ein elektromagnetisches Feld, so zögert man mit der simpeln Antwort "ja" oder "nein"; warum? Was die ψ-Funktion (zu einer bestimmten Zeit) aussagt, das ist: Welches ist die Wahrscheinlichkeit dafür, eine bestimmte physikalische Grösse q (oder p) in einem bestimmten gegebenen Intervall vorzufinden, wenn ich sie zur Zeit t messe? Die Wahrscheinlichkeit ist hierbei als eine empirisch feststellbare, also gewiss "reale" Grösse anzusehen, die ich feststellen kann, wenn ich dieselbe ψ-Funktion sehr oft erzeuge und jedesmal eine q-Messung vornehme. Wie steht es nun aber mit dem einzelnen gemessenen Wert von q? Hatte das betreffende individuelle System diesen q-Wert schon vor der Messung? Auf diese Frage gibt es im Rahmen der Theorie keine bestimmte Antwort, weil ja die Messung ein Prozess ist, der einen endlichen äusseren Eingriff in das System bedeutet; es wäre daher denkbar, dass das System einen bestimmten Zahlwert für q (bezw. p) den gemessenen Zahlwert erst durch die Messung selbst erhält. Für die weitere Diskussion denke ich mir zwei Physiker A und B, die bezüglich des durch die ψ-Funktion beschriebenen realen Zustandes eine verschiedene Auffassung vertreten.

A. Das einzelne System hat (vor der Messung) einen bestimmten Wert von q (bezw. p) für alle Variabeln des Systems, und zwar *den* Wert, der bei einer Messung dieser Variabeln festgestellt wird. Ausgehend von dieser Auffassung wird er erklären: Die ψ-Funktion ist keine erschöpfende Darstellung des realen Zustandes des Systems, sondern eine unvollständige Darstellung; sie drückt nur dasjenige aus, was wir auf Grund früherer Messungen über das System wissen.

B. Das einzelne System hat (vor der Messung) keinen bestimmten Wert von q (bezw. p). Der Messwert kommt unter Mitwirkung der ihm vermöge der ψ-Funktion eigen-

time; in Maxwell's theory, by the field in space and time. In quantum mechanics it is not so easily seen. If one asks: does a ψ-function of the quantum theory represent a real factual situation in the same sense in which this is the case of a material system of points or of an electromagnetic field, one hesitates to reply with a simple "yes" or "no"; why? What the ψ-function (at a definite time) asserts, is this: What is the probability for finding a definite physical magnitude q (or p) in a definitely given interval, if I measure it at time t? The probability is here to be viewed as an empirically determinable, and therefore certainly as a "real" quantity which I may determine if I create the same ψ-function very often and perform a q-measurement each time. But what about the single measured value of q? Did the respective individual system have this q-value even before the measurement? To this question there is no definite answer within the framework of the [existing] theory, since the measurement is a process which implies a finite disturbance of the system from the outside; it would therefore be thinkable that the system obtains a definite numerical value for q (or p), i.e., the measured numerical value, only through the measurement itself. For the further discussion I shall assume two physicists, *A* and *B*, who represent a different conception with reference to the real situation as described by the ψ-function.

A. The individual system (before the measurement) has a definite value of q (i.e., p) for all variables of the system, and more specifically, *that* value which is determined by a measurement of this variable. Proceeding from this conception, he will state: The ψ-function is no exhaustive description of the real situation of the system but an incomplete description; it expresses only what we know on the basis of former measurements concerning the system.

B. The individual system (before the measurement) has no definite value of q (i.e., p). The value of the measurement only arises in cooperation with the unique probability which is given to it in view of the ψ-function only through the

tümlichen Wahrscheinlichkeit erst durch den Akt der Messung zustande. Ausgehend von dieser Auffassung wird (oder wenigstens darf) er erklären: Die ψ-Funktion ist eine erschöpfende Darstellung des realen Zustandes des Systems.

Nun präsentieren wir diesen beiden Physikern folgenden Fall. Es liege ein System vor das zu der Zeit t unserer Betrachtung aus zwei Teilsystemen S_1 und S_2 bestehe, die zu dieser Zeit räumlich getrennt und (im Sinne der klassischen Physik) ohne erhebliche Wechselwirkung sind. Das Gesamtsystem sei durch eine bekannte ψ-Funktion ψ_{12} im Sinne der Quantenmechanik vollständig beschrieben. Alle Quantentheoretiker stimmen nun im Folgenden überein. Wenn ich eine vollständige Messung an S_1 mache, so erhalte ich aus den Messresultaten und aus ψ_{12} eine völlig bestimmte ψ-Funktion ψ_2 des Systems S_2. Der Charakter von ψ_2 hängt dann davon ab, was *für eine Art* Messung ich an S_1 vornehme. Nun scheint es mir, dass man von dem realen Sachverhalt des Teilsystems S_2 sprechen kann. Von diesem realen Sachverhalt wissen wir vor der Messung an S_1 von vornherein noch weniger als bei einem durch die ψ-Funktion beschriebenen System. Aber an *einer* Annahme sollten wir nach meiner Ansicht unbedingt festhalten: Der reale Sachverhalt (Zustand) des Systems S_2 ist unabhängig davon, was mit dem von ihm räumlich getrennten System S_1 vorgenommen wird. Je nach der Art der Messung, welche ich an S_1 vornehme, bekomme ich aber ein andersartiges ψ_2 für das zweite Teilsystem. (ψ_2, ψ_2^1 . . .). Nun muss aber der Realzustand von S_2 unabhängig davon sein, was an S_1 geschieht. Für denselben Realzustand von S_2 können also (je nach Wahl der Messung an S_1) verschiedenartige ψ-Funktionen gefunden werden. (Diesem Schlusse kann man nur dadurch ausweichen, dass man entweder annimmt, dass die Messung an S_1 den Realzustand von S_2 (telepathisch) verändert, oder aber dass man Dingen, die räumlich voneinander getrennt sind, unabhängige Realzustände überhaupt abspricht. Beides scheint mir ganz inacceptabel.)

Wenn nun die Physiker A und B diese Ueberlegung als stichhaltig annehmen, so wird B seinen Standpunkt aufgeben

act of measurement itself. Proceeding from this conception, he will (or, at least, he may) state: the ψ-function is an exhaustive description of the real situation of the system.

We now present to these two physicists the following instance: There is to be a system which at the time t of our observation consists of two partial systems S_1 and S_2, which at this time are spatially separated and (in the sense of the classical physics) are without significant reciprocity. The total system is to be completely described through a known ψ-function ψ_{12} in the sense of quantum mechanics. All quantum theoreticians now agree upon the following: If I make a complete measurement of S_1, I get from the results of the measurement and from ψ_{12} an entirely definite ψ-function ψ_2 of the system S_2. The character of ψ_2 then depends upon *what kind* of measurement I undertake on S_1.

Now it appears to me that one may speak of the real factual situation of the partial system S_2. Of this real factual situation, we know to begin with, before the measurement of S_1, even less than we know of a system described by the ψ-function. But on one supposition we should, in my opinion, absolutely hold fast: the real factual situation of the system S_2 is independent of what is done with the system S_1, which is spatially separated from the former. According to the type of measurement which I make of S_1, I get, however, a very different ψ_2 for the second partial system ($\Psi_2, \Psi_2^1, \ldots$). Now, however, the real situation of S_2 must be independent of what happens to S_1. For the same real situation of S_2 it is possible therefore to find, according to one's choice, different types of ψ-function. (One can escape from this conclusion only by either assuming that the measurement of S_1 ((telepathically)) changes the real situation of S_2 or by denying independent real situations as such to things which are spatially separated from each other. Both alternatives appear to me entirely unacceptable.)

If now the physicists, A and B, accept this consideration as valid, then B will have to give up his position that the Ψ-func-

müssen, dass die ψ-Funktion eine vollständige Beschreibung eines realen Sachverhaltes sei. Denn es wäre in diesem Falle unmöglich, dass demselben Sachverhalt (von S_2) zwei verschiedenartige ψ-Funktionen zugeordnet werden könnten.

Der statistische Charakter der gegenwärtigen Theorie würde dann eine notwendige Folge der Unvollständigkeit der Beschreibung der Systeme in der Quantenmechanik sein, und es bestände kein Grund mehr für die Annahme, dass eine zukünftige Basis der Physik auf Statistik gegründet sein müsse. – – –

Meine Meinung ist die, dass die gegenwärtige Quantentheorie bei gewissen festgelegten Grundbegriffen, die im Wesentlichen der klassischen Mechanik entnommen sind, eine optimale Formulierung der Zusammenhänge darstellt. Ich glaube aber, dass diese Theorie keinen brauchbaren Ausgangspunkt für die künftige Entwicklung bietet. Dies ist der Punkt, in welchem meine Erwartung von derjenigen der meisten zeitgenössischen Physiker abweicht. Sie sind davon überzeugt, dass den wesentlichen Zügen der Quantenphänomene (scheinbar sprunghafte und zeitlich nicht determinierte Aenderungen des Zustandes eines Systems, gleichzeitig korpuskuläre und undulatorische Qualitäten der elementaren energetischen Gebilde) nicht Rechnung getragen werden kann durch eine Theorie, die den Realzustand der Dinge durch kontinuierliche Funktionen des Raumes beschreibt, für welche Differentialgleichungen gelten. Sie denken auch, dass man auf solchem Wege die atomistische Struktur der Materie und Strahlung nicht wird verstehen können. Sie erwarten, dass Systeme von Differentialgleichungen, wie sie für eine solche Theorie in Betracht kämen, überhaupt keine Lösungen haben, die überall im vierdimensionalen Raume regulär (singularitätsfrei) sind. Vor allem aber glauben sie, dass der anscheinend sprunghafte Charakter der Elementarvorgänge nur durch eine im Wesen statistische Theorie dargestellt werden kann, in welcher den sprunghaften Aenderungen der Systeme durch *kontinuierliche* Aenderungen von Wahrscheinlichkeiten der möglichen Zustände Rechnung getragen wird.

All diese Bemerkungen erscheinen mir recht eindrucksvoll. Die Frage, auf die es ankommt, scheint mir aber die zu sein:

tion constitutes a complete description of a real factual situation. For in this case it would be impossible that two different types of ψ-functions could be co-ordinated with the identical factual situation of S_2.

The statistical character of the present theory would then have to be a necessary consequence of the incompleteness of the description of the systems in quantum mechanics, and there would no longer exist any ground for the supposition that a future basis of physics must be based upon statistics. – – –

It is my opinion that the contemporary quantum theory by means of certain definitely laid down basic concepts, which on the whole have been taken over from classical mechanics, constitutes an optimum formulation of the connections. I believe, however, that this theory offers no useful point of departure for future development. This is the point at which my expectation departs most widely from that of contemporary physicists. They are convinced that it is impossible to account for the essential aspects of quantum phenomena (apparently discontinuous and temporally not determined changes of the situation of a system, and at the same time corpuscular and undulatory qualities of the elementary bodies of energy) by means of a theory which describes the real state of things [objects] by continuous functions of space for which differential equations are valid. They are also of the opinion that in this way one can not understand the atomic structure of matter and of radiation. They rather expect that systems of differential equations, which could come under consideration for such a theory, in any case would have no solutions which would be regular (free from singularity) everywhere in four-dimensional space. Above everything else, however, they believe that the apparently discontinuous character of elementary events can be described only by means of an essentially statistical theory, in which the discontinuous changes of the systems are taken into account by way of the continuous changes of the probabilities of the possible states.

All of these remarks seem to me to be quite impressive. However, the question which is really determinative appears to me

Was kann bei der heutigen Situation der Theorie mit einiger Aussicht auf Erfolg versucht werden? Da sind es die Erfahrungen in der Gravitationstheorie, die für meine Erwartungen richtung-gebend sind. Diese Gleichungen haben nach meiner Ansicht mehr Aussicht, etwas *Genaues* auszusagen als alle andern Gleichungen der Physik. Man ziehe etwa die Maxwell'schen Gleichungen des leeren Raumes zum Vergleich heran. Diese sind Formulierungen, die den Erfahrungen an unendlich schwachen elektromagnetischen Feldern entsprechen. Dieser empirische Ursprung bedingt schon ihre lineare Form; dass aber die wahren Gesetze nicht linear sein können, wurde schon früher betont. Solche Gesetze erfüllen das Superpositions-Prinzip für ihre Lösungen, enthalten also keine Aussagen über die Wechselwirkungen von Elementargebilden. Die wahren Gesetze können nicht linear sein und aus solchen auch nicht gewonnen werden. Noch etwas anderes habe ich aus der Gravitationstheorie gelernt: Eine noch so umfangreiche Sammlung empirischer Fakten kann nicht zur Aufstellung so verwickelter Gleichungen führen. Eine Theorie kann an der Erfahrung geprüft werden, aber es gibt keinen Weg von der Erfahrung zur Aufstellung einer Theorie. Gleichungen von solcher Kompliziertheit wie die Gleichungen des Gravitationsfeldes können nur dadurch gefunden werden, dass eine logisch einfache mathematische Bedingung gefunden wird, welche die Gleichungen völlig oder nahezu determiniert. Hat man aber jene hinreichend starken formalen Bedingungen, so braucht man nur wenig Tatsachen-Wissen für die Aufstellung der Theorie; bei den Gravitationsgleichungen ist es die Vierdimensionalität und der symmetrische Tensor als Ausdruck für die Raumstruktur, welche zusammen mit der Invarianz bezüglich der kontinuierlichen Transformationsgruppe die Gleichungen praktisch vollkommen determinieren.

Unsere Aufgabe ist es, die Feldgleichungen für das totale Feld zu finden. Die gesuchte Struktur muss eine Verallgemeinerung des symmetrischen Tensors sein. Die Gruppe darf nicht enger sein als die der kontinuierlichen Koordinaten-Transformationen. Wenn man nun eine reichere Struktur einführt, so wird die Gruppe die Gleichungen nicht mehr so stark

to be as follows: What can be attempted with some hope of success in view of the present situation of physical theory? At this point it is the experiences with the theory of gravitation which determine my expectations. These equations give, from my point of view, more warrant for the expectation to assert something *precise* than all other equations of physics. One may, for example, call on Maxwell's equations of empty space by way of comparison. These are formulations which coincide with the experiences of infinitely weak electro-magnetic fields. This empirical origin already determines their linear form; it has, however, already been emphasized above that the true laws can not be linear. Such linear laws fulfill the super-position-principle for their solutions, but contain no assertions concerning the interaction of elementary bodies. The true laws can not be linear nor can they be derived from such. I have learned something else from the theory of gravitation: No ever so inclusive collection of empirical facts can ever lead to the setting up of such complicated equations. A theory can be tested by experience, but there is no way from experience to the setting up of a theory. Equations of such complexity as are the equations of the gravitational field can be found only through the discovery of a logically simple mathematical condition which determines the equations completely or [at least] almost completely. Once one has those sufficiently strong formal conditions, one requires only little knowledge of facts for the setting up of a theory; in the case of the equations of gravitation it is the four-dimensionality and the symmetric tensor as expression for the structure of space which, together with the invariance concerning the continuous transformation-group, determine the equations almost completely.

Our problem is that of finding the field equations for the total field. The desired structure must be a generalization of the symmetric tensor. The group must not be any narrower than that of the continuous transformations of co-ordinates. If one introduces a richer structure, then the group will no longer determine the equations as strongly as in the case of the sym-

determinieren wie im Falle des symmetrischen Tensors als Struktur. Deshalb wäre es am schönsten, wenn es gelänge, die Gruppe abermals zu erweitern in Analogie zu dem Schritte, der von der speziellen Relativität zur allgemeinen Relativität geführt hat. Im Besonderen habe ich versucht, die Gruppe der komplexen Koordinaten-Transformationen heranzuziehen. Alle derartigen Bemühungen waren erfolglos. Eine offene oder verdeckte Erhöhung der Dimensionszahl des Raumes habe ich ebenfalls aufgegeben, eine Bemühung, die von Kaluza begründet wurde und in ihrer projektiven Variante noch heute ihre Anhänger hat. Wir beschränken uns auf den vierdimensionalen Raum und die Gruppe der kontinuierlichen reellen Koordinaten-Transformationen. Nach vielen Jahren vergeblichen Suchens halte ich die im Folgenden skizzierte Lösung für die logischerweise am meisten befriedigende.

Anstelle des symmetrischen g_{ik} $(g_{ik} = g_{ki})$ wird der nichtsymmetrische Tensor g_{ik} eingeführt. Diese Grösse setzt sich aus einem symmetrischen Teil s_{ik} und einem reellen oder gänzlich imaginären antisymmetrischen a_{ik} so zusammen:

$$g_{ik} = s_{ik} + a_{ik}.$$

Vom Standpunkte der Gruppe aus betrachtet ist diese Zusammenfügung von s und a willkürlich, weil die Tensoren s und a einzeln Tensor-Charakter haben. Es zeigt sich aber, dass diese g_{ik} (als Ganzes betrachtet) im Aufbau der neuen Theorie eine analoge Rolle spielen wie die symmetrischen g_{ik} in der Theorie des reinen Gravitationsfeldes.

Diese Verallgemeinerung der Raum-Struktur scheint auch vom Standpunkt unseres physikalischen Wissens natürlich, weil wir wissen, dass das elektromagnetische Feld mit einem schief symmetrischen Tensor zu tun hat.

Es ist ferner für die Gravitationstheorie wesentlich, dass aus den symmetrischen g_{ik} die skalare Dichte $\sqrt{|\,g_{ik}\,|}$ gebildet werden kann sowie der kontravariante Tensor g^{ik} gemäss der Definition

$$g_{ik}g^{il} = \delta_k^{\,l} \ (\delta_k^{\,l} = \text{Kronecker-Tensor}).$$

Diese Bildungen lassen sich genau entsprechend für die nichtsymmetrischen g_{ik} definieren, ebenso Tensor-Dichten.

metrical tensor as structure. Therefore it would be most beautiful, if one were to succeed in expanding the group once more, analogous to the step which led from special relativity to general relativity. More specifically I have attempted to draw upon the group of the complex transformations of the co-ordinates. All such endeavors were unsuccessful. I also gave up an open or concealed raising of the number of dimensions of space, an endeavor which was originally undertaken by Kaluza and which, with its projective variant, even today has its adherents. We shall limit ourselves to the four-dimensional space and to the group of the continuous real transformations of co-ordinates. After many years of fruitless searching I consider the solution sketched in what follows as the logically most satisfactory.

In place of the symmetrical g_{ik} $(g_{ik} = g_{ki})$, the non-symmetrical tensor g_{ik} is introduced. This magnitude is constituted by a symmetric part s_{ik} and by a real or purely imaginary anti-symmetric a_{ik}, thus:

$$g_{ik} = s_{ik} + a_{ik}.$$

Viewed from the standpoint of the group the combination of s and a is arbitrary, because the tensors s and a individually have tensor-character. It turns out, however, that these g_{ik} (viewed as a whole) play a quite analogous rôle in the construction of the new theory as the symmetric g_{ik} in the theory of the pure gravitational field.

This generalization of the space structure seems natural also from the standpoint of our physical knowledge, because we know that the electro-magnetic field has to do with an anti-symmetric tensor.

For the theory of gravitation it is furthermore essential that from the symmetric g_{ik} it is possible to form the scalar density $\sqrt{|g_{ik}|}$ as well as the contravariant tensor g^{ik} according to the definition

$$g_{ik}g^{il} = \delta_k^l \quad (\delta_k^l = \text{Kronecker-Tensor}).$$

These concepts can be defined in precisely corresponding manner for the non-symmetric g_{ik}, also for tensor-densities.

In der Gravitationstheorie ist es ferner wesentlich, dass sich zu einem gegebenen symmetrischen g_{ik}-Feld ein Feld Γ^l_{ik} definieren lässt, das in den unteren Indices symmetrisch ist und geometrisch betrachtet die Parallel-Verschiebung eines Vektors beherrscht. Analog lässt sich zu den nicht-symmetrischen g_{ik} ein nicht-symmetrisches Γ^l_{ik} definieren, gemäss der Formel

$$g_{ik,l} - g_{sk}\Gamma^s_{il} - g_{is}\Gamma^s_{lk} = 0, \ldots \qquad \text{(A)}$$

welche mit der betreffenden Beziehung der symmetrischen g übereinstimmt, nur dass hier natürlich auf die Stellung der unteren Indices in den g und Γ geachtet werden muss.

Wie in der reellen Theorie kann aus den Γ eine Krümmung $R^i{}_{klm}$ gebildet werden und aus dieser eine kontrahierte Krümmung R_{kl}. Endlich kann man unter Verwendung eines Variationsprinzips mit (A) zusammen kompatible Feldgleichungen finden:

$$\mathfrak{g}^{\underbrace{ik}} = \tfrac{1}{2}(g^{ik} - g^{ki})\sqrt{-|g_{ik}|} \qquad \text{(B}_1\text{)}$$

$$\Gamma_{\underbrace{is}}{}^s = 0 \left(\Gamma_{\underbrace{is}}{}^s = \tfrac{1}{2}(\Gamma_{is}{}^s - \Gamma_{si}{}^s)\right) \qquad \text{(B}_2\text{)}$$

$$R_{\underline{ik}} = 0 \qquad \text{(C}_1\text{)}$$

$$R_{\underbrace{kl},m} + R_{\underbrace{lm},k} + R_{\underbrace{mk},l} = 0 \qquad \text{(C}_2\text{)}$$

Hierbei ist jede der beiden Gleichungen (B_1), (B_2) eine Folge der andern, wenn (A) erfüllt ist. $R_{\underline{kl}}$ bedeutet den symmetrischen, $R_{\underbrace{kl}}$ den antisymmetrischen Teil von R_{kl}.

Im Falle des Verschwindens des antisymmetrischen Teils von g_{ik} reduzieren sich diese Formeln auf (A) und (C_1)—Fall des reinen Gravitationsfeldes.

Ich glaube, dass diese Gleichungen die natürlichste Verallgemeinerung der Gravitationsgleichungen darstellen.[2] Die Prüfung ihrer physikalischen Brauchbarkeit ist eine überaus schwierige Aufgabe, weil es mit Annäherungen nicht getan

[2] Die hier vorgeschlagene Theorie hat nach meiner Ansicht ziemliche Wahrscheinlichkeit der Bewährung, wenn sich der Weg einer erschöpfenden Darstellung der physischen Realität auf der Grundlage des Kontinuums überhaupt als gangbar erweisen wird.

In the theory of gravitation it is further essential that for a given symmetrical g_{ik}-field a field Γ^{l}_{ik} can be defined, which is symmetric in the lower indices and which, considered geometrically, governs the parallel displacement of a vector. Analogously for the non-symmetric g_{ik} a non-symmetric Γ^{l}_{ik} can be defined, according to the formula

$$g_{ik,l} - g_{sk}\Gamma^{s}_{il} - g_{is}\Gamma^{s} = 0, \ldots \qquad (A)$$

which coincides with the respective relation of the symmetrical g, only that it is, of course, necessary to pay attention here to the position of the lower indices in the g and Γ.

Just as in the theory of a symmetrical g_{ik}, it is possible to form a curvature R^{i}_{klm} out of the Γ and a contracted curvature R_{kl}. Finally, with the use of a variation principle, together with (A), it is possible to find compatible field-equations:

$$\mathfrak{g}^{\underset{\smile}{ik}} = \tfrac{1}{2}(g^{ik} - g^{ki})\sqrt{-|g_{ik}|)} \qquad (B_1)$$

$$\Gamma_{\underset{\smile}{is}}^{s} = 0(\Gamma_{is}^{s} = \tfrac{1}{2}(\Gamma_{is}^{s} - \Gamma_{si}^{s})) \qquad (B_2)$$

$$R_{\underline{ik}} = 0 \qquad (C_1)$$

$$R_{\underset{\smile}{kl},m} + R_{\underset{\smile}{lm},k} + R_{\underset{\smile}{mk},l} = 0 \qquad (C_2)$$

Each of the two equations (B_1), (B_2) is a consequence of the other, if (A) is satisfied. R_{kl} means the symmetric, R_{kl} the anti-symmetric part of R_{kl}.

If the anti-symmetric part of g_{ik} vanishes, these formulas reduce to (A) and (C_1)—the case of the pure gravitational field.

I believe that these equations constitute the most natural generalization of the equations of gravitation.[2] The proof of their physical usefulness is a tremendously difficult task, inasmuch as mere approximations will not suffice. The question is:

[2] The theory here proposed, according to my view, represents a fair probability of being found valid, if the way to an exhaustive description of physical reality on the basis of the continuum turns out to be possible at all.

ist. Die Frage ist: Was für im ganzen Raume singularitätsfreie Lösungen dieser Gleichungen gibt es? ---

Diese Darlegung hat ihren Zweck erfüllt, wenn sie dem Leser zeigen, wie die Bemühungen eines Lebens miteinander zusammenhängen und warum sie zu Erwartungen bestimmter Art geführt haben.

A. Einstein.

INSTITUTE FOR ADVANCED STUDY
PRINCETON, NEW JERSEY

AUTOBIOGRAPHICAL NOTES

What are the everywhere regular solutions of these equations? ---

This exposition has fulfilled its purpose if it shows the reader how the efforts of a life hang together and why they have led to expectations of a definite form.

A. Einstein.

INSTITUTE FOR ADVANCED STUDY
PRINCETON, NEW JERSEY

Dort hatte ich vortreffliche Lehrer (z. B. Hurwitz, Minkowski), so dass ich eigentlich eine tiefe mathematische Ausbildung hätte erlangen können. Ich aber arbeitete die meiste Zeit im physikalischen Laboratorium, fasziniert durch die direkte Berührung mit der Erfahrung. Die übrige Zeit benutzte ich hauptsächlich, um die Werke von Kirchhoff, Helmholtz, Hertz etc. zu Hause zu studieren. Dass ich die Mathematik bis zu einem gewissen Grade vernachlässigte, hatte nicht nur den Grund, dass das naturwissenschaftliche Interesse stärker war als das mathematische, sondern das folgende eigentümliche Erlebnis. Ich sah, dass die Mathematik in viele Spezialgebiete gespalten war, deren jedes diese kurze uns vergönnte Lebenszeit wegnehmen konnte. So sah ich mich in der Lage von Buridans Esel, der sich nicht für ein besonderes Bündel Heu entschliessen konnte. Dies lag offenbar daran, dass meine Intuition auf mathematischem Gebiete nicht stark genug war, um das Fundamental-Wichtige, Grundlegende

Facsimile of Part of a Page from Albert Einstein's Autobiography
Written Especially for This Volume (see p. 14 *supra*)

THE EDITOR WITH ALBERT EINSTEIN IN THE LATTER'S STUDY IN PRINCETON, NEW JERSEY, DECEMBER 28, 1947

1

Arnold Sommerfeld

TO ALBERT EINSTEIN'S SEVENTIETH BIRTHDAY

I

TO ALBERT EINSTEIN'S SEVENTIETH BIRTHDAY*

I AM TOLD that Adolf Harnack once said, in the conference-room of the University of Berlin: "People complain that our generation has no philosophers. Quite unjustly: it is merely that today's philosophers sit in another department, their names are Planck and Einstein." And it is indeed true that with the great work of Einstein of 1905 the mutual distrust, which existed during the last century between philosophy and physics, has disappeared. Einstein at this point touches upon the old epistemological basic questions of space and time, and, proceeding from the most general results of physics, gives them a new content. Be it noted that that essay does not bear the widely misunderstood and not very fortunate name of "theory of relativity," but the much more harmless yet at the same time more significant title, "On the Electrodynamics of Moving Bodies." It is the relation between material motion and the universal speed of light which has led Einstein to the new analysis of space and time, that is to say, to their indissoluble connection. Not the *relativizing* of the perceptions of length and duration are the chief point for him, but the *independence of natural laws,* particularly those of electrodynamics and optics, *of the standpoint of the observer.* The essay has, of course, absolutely nothing whatsoever to do with ethical relativism, with the "Beyond Good and Evil." This invariance of natural laws exists in that group of motions (the uniform translations),

* From the original German essay, "Zum Siebzigsten Geburtstag Albert Einsteins," which appeared in *Deutsche Beiträge* (Eine Zweimonatsschrift, Vol. III, No. 2, Nymphenburger Verlagshandlung, München, 1949), translated (with the permission of author and publisher) specifically for this volume by Paul Arthur Schilpp.

to which Einstein, after the prior work of the great Dutchman H. A. Lorentz, has given the name of "Lorentz-transformations," although their true nature was first really grasped only by Einstein himself. Since that time the so-called "special theory of relativity," which is based upon these [Lorentz transformations], forms the unshakable foundation of physics and astronomy.

Immediately after 1905 Einstein attacked the problem of Newtonian gravitation. How is this [latter] to be reconciled with the postulate of invariance? We know fictitious forces, which come into being as the result of the non-uniform motion of material bodies, for example the centrifugal force of rotation. One of the factors which appears here is the common mechanical mass, which we call "inert mass" because of its connection with the law of inertia. The same magnitude occurs also in the law of gravitation as "heavy mass." The equality of heavy and inert mass had already been emphasized by Newton, tested by Bessel, and confirmed with extreme precision by Roland Eötvös. This made Einstein wonder. For him there could be no doubt that the equality of the masses pointed to an equality of causes; that is to say, that gravitation also would have to be a kind of inertia effect. With this the problem of space and time assumed a new empirical aspect. The structure of space and time had to be determined by the spatially-temporally distributed masses (stated more generally, energies). Einstein wrestled with the program of this structural theory of the space-time continuum in the years 1905-1915. We shall let him speak for himself. In reply to several letters of mine he answered on November 28, 1915, as follows:

During the last month I experienced one of the most exciting and most exacting times of my life, true enough, also one of the most successful. [Letter-] Writing was out of the question.

For I realized that all of my field equations of gravitation up till now were entirely without support. Instead of that the following points of departure turned up....

After all confidence in the former theory has thus disappeared, I saw clearly that a satisfactory solution could be found only by means of a

connection with the universal theory of covariants of Riemann. . . . The final result is as follows: . . .

Now the marvellous thing which I experienced was the fact that not only did Newton's theory result as first approximation but also the perihelion motion of Mercury (43″ per century) as second approximation. For the deflection of light by the sun twice the former amount resulted.

Naturally I reacted somewhat incredulously. To this he remarked, on a postcard dated February 8th[, 1916]:

Of the general theory of relativity you will be convinced, once you have studied it. Therefore I am not going to defend it with a single word.

We may elaborate on Einstein's letter by saying: The marvellous thing which we experienced was that now the paths of the planets could be calculated as "shortest lines" in the structurally modified space, analogous to the straight lines in Euclidean space. The space-time continuum has become "non-Euclidean" in Riemann's most generalized sense, it has received a "curvature" which is impressed upon it by local energies.

The experimental verification was not to be long delayed. In the year 1918 a British solar eclipse expedition to the tropics had photographed the surroundings of the eclipsed sun and compared the positions of the fixed stars nearest to the sun with their normal positions. They showed deviations from these latter to the extent of the effect predicted by Einstein. The light-rays of these stars in passing close by the edge of the sun, go through an area of modified spatial structure and thereby are deflected, just as the rays of the sun are deflected in the inhomogeneous atmosphere of the earth and no longer follow a straight line. The great, now already deceased, British astronomer, Sir Arthur Eddington, became an inspired apostle of Einstein's doctrine and has worked it out in its manifold consequences.

From then on this doctrine entered into the publicity of home and foreign countries. When a representative of the *Kölnische Zeitung* asked me for further information about it in the year 1920, I told him that this was no matter for the general public, which lacked every prerequisite for the mathematical understanding of this theory. Nevertheless there began,

in Berlin's newspapers, the "relativity-rumpus" with a passionate pro and con Einstein. Einstein suffered greatly under this. He was not made to be a newspaper-celebrity; every form of vanity was foreign to him. He has always retained something of the "boy of nature" and of the "Bohemian." Even his golden humor, which often took the form of very drastic statements, was not able to help him surmount the discomforts and obligations of a famous celebrity.

At this point a few biographical notes may be inserted. Born in a small Swabian Jewish community, Einstein attended the Humanistische Gynmasium in Munich, where his father was temporarily a businessman. After graduation he first went with his family to Italy and then studied at the Federal Institute of Technology in Zürich. Strangely enough no personal contacts resulted between his teacher of mathematics, Hermann Minkowski, and Einstein. When, later on, Minkowski built up the special theory of relativity into his "world-geometry," Einstein said on one occasion: "Since the mathematicians have invaded the theory of relativity, I do not understand it myself any more." But soon thereafter, at the time of the conception of the general theory of relativity, he readily acknowledged the indispensability of the four-dimensional scheme of Minkowski. At the time when Einstein discovered his special theory of relativity, in 1905, he was working in the Federal Patent-Office in Bern. From there he was called to the University of Zürich as associate professor. Thereafter he was, in passing, active as full professor of theoretical physics in Prague and returned then to an identical position in the Federal Institute of Technology in Zürich. Nernst succeeded in getting him to accept a research professorship in Berlin. The lecture cycles, to which his Zürich position obligated him, were not to Einstein's taste. He never had any orderly lecture-manuscripts. By the time a certain lecture came around again, he had lost his former notes. In Berlin he could freely choose to give university-lectures, but he had no obligation whatsoever to do so. We owe the completion of his general theory of relativity to his leisure while in Berlin. When, at the beginning of the first world-war, I visited him in Berlin and we read a war-report concerning the use of gas-

bombs on the part of the enemies, Einstein remarked: "This is supposed to say that they stunk first, but we know better how to do it." This latter he knew from his friend, Fritz Haber. Politically he was, of course, definitely left of center, and possibly expected something good from the Russian revolution. During the "relativity-rumpus," which occasionally sank to the level of anti-Semitic mass-meetings, he had considered leaving Berlin. The decision came at the Nauheim Congress of Natural Scientists, in 1920: thanks to the efforts of Planck, he decided "to remain faithful to his friends in Berlin." I visited him for the last time in 1930 in Kaputh near Potsdam, where he pursued the sport of sailing. This was the only sport which he enjoyed; he had no use for physical exertion. Concerning the joy of intellectual work he once remarked: "Whoever knows it, does not go tearing after it." This means to say: His results did not fall into his lap, but had to be achieved by way of hard work and laborious mathematical investigations.

The battle over the theory of relativity had also slightly reached over into America, where youth was warned by a Boston Cardinal to beware of Einstein the atheist. Thereupon Rabbi Herbert S. Goldstein of New York cabled Einstein: "Do you believe in God?" Einstein cabled back: "I believe in Spinoza's God, who reveals himself in the harmony of all being, not in a God who concerns himself with the fate and actions of men." It would have been impossible for Einstein to give the rabbi a more pointed reply or one which came closer to his own innermost convictions. Many a time, when a new theory appeared to him arbitrary or forced, he remarked: "God doesn't do anything like that." I have often felt and occasionally also stated that Einstein stands in particularly intimate relation to the God of Spinoza.

Then came the shameful year 1933. Einstein was driven out of Berlin and robbed of his possessions.

A number of countries vied for his immigration. He chose America, where he found a worthy field of activity as a member of the Institute for Advanced Studies in Princeton. After Hahn's discovery of uranium fission he was the first to call President Roosevelt's attention to the possible military conse-

quences of this discovery. The interpretation of this discovery, after all, was based directly upon Einstein's law of the equivalence of mass and energy. He did not participate in the technical development of the atom-bomb; I presume that he belonged to that group of American physicists who advised against the aggressive use of the new weapon. As an active pacifist, Einstein is an exponent of the organization "One World or None."*

Last year the newspapers carried the announcement that Einstein would make a lecture-tour in the interests of this organization. When I asked him not to forget Munich on this occasion, he replied: "Now I am an old duck and am no longer travelling, after I have come to know men sufficiently from all angles. The newspaper report was of course false, as usual."

We must once more return to the year 1905. Besides the special theory of relativity Einstein published in this year a still far more revolutionary work: the discovery of light-quanta. The old question, whether light is undulatory or corpuscular, was being raised again. The photo-electric effect and the phenomena of fluorescence can be understood only from the latter point of view. This was Einstein's first step on the road of the quantum theory indicated by Planck, which was later followed by further important steps, for example his theory of specific heat, and the theory of the fluctuation-phenomena of the black body radiation. Today we know that light unites both characteristics, that, according to the type of experiment, it shows us either its undulatory or its corpuscular aspect. The logical dissonance which seems to lie in this dualism, we consider as a direct consequence of the existence of the quantum of action discovered by Planck.

Out of the year 1905 comes also Einstein's brief note on Brownian motion. It has nothing to do with quantum theory or with the atomism of action, but rests entirely upon the atomism

* EDITOR'S NOTE: There is no such organization. However, the Federation of American Scientists, of which Professor Einstein is honorary president, late in 1945 published a volume by this title, *One World or None*. This Federation of American Scientists, therefore, is undoubtedly the organization to which Geheimrat Sommerfeld refers here. It must be added, moreover, that this Federation is by no means pacifist. *Ed.*

of matter and upon the general principles of statistical thermodynamics. The old fighter against atomistics, Wilhelm Ostwald, told me once that he had been converted to atomistics by the complete explanation of the Brownian motion.

Boltzmann's idea to reduce thermodynamics to statistics and entropy to the enumeration of probabilities, Einstein brought to manifold application as the "Boltzmann principle." He also has improved the explanation of the blueness of the sky by his statistical calculation of the small scale fluctuations in the density of air. Einstein is therefore also a scientist of first rank in the field of atomic theory.

In spite of all this, in the old question "continuum versus discontinuity," he has taken his position most decisively on the side of the continuum. Everything of the nature of quanta—to which, in the final analysis, the material atoms and the elementary particles belong also—he would like to derive from a continuum-physics by means of methods which relate to his general theory of relativity and expand this theory. His unceasing efforts, since he resides in America, have been directed towards this end. Until now, however, they have led to no tangible success. Even his most recent note, written for the *Review of Modern Physics* on the occasion of Robert Millikan's 80th birthday, still contains a mathematical attack in this direction, which, in his opinion, has hope of success. By far the most of today's physicists consider Einstein's aim as unachievable and, consequently, aim to get along with the dualism: wave-corpuscle, which he himself first clearly uncovered. However, in view of the total work of Einstein we want to remind ourselves of the beautiful couplet, which Schiller dedicated to Columbus:

> With the genius nature remains in eternal union:
> What the one promises, the other certainly redeems.

ARNOLD SOMMERFELD

UNIVERSITÄT MÜNCHEN
GERMANY

2

Louis de Broglie

A GENERAL SURVEY OF THE SCIENTIFIC WORK OF ALBERT EINSTEIN

2

A GENERAL SURVEY OF THE SCIENTIFIC WORK OF ALBERT EINSTEIN*

FOR ANY educated man, whether or not a professional scientist, the name of Albert Einstein calls to mind the intellectual effort and genius which overturned the most traditional notions of physics and culminated in the establishment of the relativity of the notions of space and time, the inertia of energy, and an interpretation of gravitational forces which is in some sort purely geometrical. Therein lies a magnificent achievement comparable to the greatest that may be found in the history of the sciences; comparable, for example, to the achievements of Newton. This alone would have sufficed to assure its author imperishable fame. But, great as it was, this achievement must not cause us to forget that Albert Einstein also rendered decisive contributions to other important advances in contemporary physics. Even if we were to overlook his no less remarkable work on the Brownian movement, statistical thermodynamics, and equilibrium fluctuations, we could not fail to take note of the tremendous import of his research upon a developing quantum theory and, in particular, his conception of "light quanta" which, reintroducing the corpuscular notion into optics, was to send physicists in search of some kind of synthesis of Fresnel's wave theory of light and the old corpuscular theory. The latter, after having been held by such men as Newton, was, as we know, destined for oblivion. Thus, Einstein became the source of an entire movement of ideas which, as wave mechanics and quantum mechanics, was to cast so disturbing a light upon atomic phenomena twenty years later.

* Translated from the French manuscript by Forrest W. Williams.

Before attempting to describe briefly the principal ideas which Einstein introduced into the scientific thought of our time, I would like to isolate some of the essential traits of his work.

Albert Einstein wrote, especially during his youth, numerous papers, almost all of them brief. He wrote only a few comparatively comprehensive expositions, and even these were quite succinct. Generally, he left to the care of others the task of presenting in complete works the theories whose foundations were laid by his powerful mind. Nevertheless, if most of his articles were short, there was not one among them that did not contain marvelous new ideas destined to revolutionize science, or acute and profound remarks penetrating to the most obscure recesses of the problem under consideration and opening in a few words almost unlimited perspectives. The work of Einstein is above all a "work of quality" in which elaboration and detailed development are not to be found. His articles might be compared to blazing rockets which in the dark of the night suddenly cast a brief but powerful illumination over an immense unknown region.

In every inquiry which he undertook Einstein always was able—and this is the mark of his genius—to master all the questions which faced him and to envisage them in some novel aspect which had escaped his precursors. Thus, he saw in the transformation formulas of Lorentz, not a pure and simple mathematical artifice, as did those before him, but the very expression of the bond which exists physically between space and time. Again, he saw in the laws of the photoelectric effect, unforeseen and inexplicable by classical notions, the necessity for returning in some fashion to a corpuscular conception of light. Example after example could be cited: each would prove to us the originality and genius of a mind which can perceive in a single glance, through the complex maze of difficult questions, the new and simple idea which enabled him to elicit their true significance and suddenly to bring clarity and light where darkness had reigned.

It is not to the discredit of great inventors to say that a discovery always comes "in the fulness of time," having been, in

a sense, prepared by a number of previous investigations. The fruit was ripe, but no one as yet had been able to see it and pluck it.

When, in 1905, Albert Einstein with marvelous insight enunciated the principle of relativity and perceived its meaning and consequences, physicists had known for two decades that the old theories were beset with difficulties whose origin they were not able to comprehend. These older theories, in fact, admitted the existence of an ether, that is to say, a subtle medium filling all space, which served, so to speak, to materialize the classical conception of absolute space. This medium, support of all electrical and luminous phenomena, remained quite mysterious. A half-century of research had not enabled the successors of Fresnel to specify its physical properties in any plausible fashion. In the quite abstract theories of the electromagnetic field developed principally by Maxwell, Hertz, and Lorentz, the ether functioned as little more than a medium of reference; and, even in this modest rôle, it caused some discomfiture, for the assumption of its existence led to prediction of phenomena which, in fact, did not transpire. These phenomena would be extremely minute under any realizable conditions, and for a long time the impossibility of making them evident could be attributed to the lack of sufficiently precise instruments of measurement. But the great progress effected in the field of precision measurement by the technique of interferometric measures enabled physicists such as Michelson to assert, in respect to the earth's motion relative to the ether, the absence of any of the effects upon optic phenomena which had been predicted by the theories hitherto advanced. Stimulated by this discrepancy between observation and theoretical prediction, theorists examined the problem from all sides, subjecting the electromagnetic theory to all manner of critical study and reconstruction. H. A. Lorentz, the great specialist in this field who had gained the distinction of establishing a solid foundation for the electron theory and of deducing from his conclusions certain predictions thoroughly authenticated by the facts, notably the Zeeman effect, perceived an important fact. Examining the manner in which the Max-

well equations are transformed when one passes from one frame of reference to a second in a motion rectilinear and uniform relative to the first, he showed that these equations remain invariant when one utilizes certain variables, x', y', z', and t', bound to the initial variables by linear relations constituting what has since come to be known as the "Lorentz transformation." But, according to the ideas then prevailing in regard to the absolute character of space and time, the variables x', y', z', and t', of the Lorentz transformation could not coincide with the true co-ordinates of space-time in the new frame of reference. Consequently, Lorentz considered them to be merely kinds of fictitious variables facilitating certain calculations. Nevertheless, he came very close to the correct solution of the problem by defining a "local time" with the aid of the variable, t', whereas Fitzgerald, interpreting in his own fashion the Lorentz formulas, attributed the "failure" [*l'échec*] of the Michelson experiments to a flattening or longitudinal contraction suffered by every moving solid. The Lorentz transformation, local time, and the Fitzgerald contraction appeared to be artifices permitting one to account for certain aspects of the electromagnetic field without disclosing their profound significance.

Then came Albert Einstein.

With great vigor he attacked this formidable problem, which had already been the object of so much study, by resolutely adopting a new point of view. For him, the Lorentz transformation formulas were not simple mathematical relations defining a change of variables, convenient for studying the equations of electromagnetism; rather, they were the expression of the relations which *physically* exist between the spatial and temporal co-ordinates of two Galilean observers. A daring hypothesis indeed, before which the perspicacious mind of Lorentz recoiled! It carried in its wake, in fact, an abandonment of the ideas, traditional since Newton, regarding the absolute nature of space and time, and established between these two elements of the schema [*cadre*], in which all our perceptions are ordered, an unforeseen relation entirely contrary to the immediate data of our intuitions. It was the high

distinction of Albert Einstein to succeed in showing, by means of an extremely minute and subtle analysis of the manner in which the physicist is led by his measuring operations to constitute his own schema of space and time, that the co-ordinates of space and time of different Galilean observers are really interlocked by the Lorentz formulas. Revealing that the absence of signals which travel at infinite speed results in the impossibility of verifying the simultaneity of two events occurring at points distant from each other, he analyzed the manner in which observers related to the same Galilean system nevertheless are able, through synchronization of clocks by exchanges of signals, to define a simultaneity within their system of reference; however, this simultaneity would be valid only for them, and events which would seem to them to be thus simultaneous would not be so for observers in motion relative to them. Central to this reasoning is the fact that no signal can travel with a speed greater than that of light in a void.

It is not our intention to explain here in detail how the ideas of Einstein led to the development of a precise and subtle mathematical theory, the special theory of relativity, which reveals the manner in which space and time co-ordinates are transformed by a change of Galilean reference systems in rectilinear and uniform motion with respect to each other. We must be confined to enumerating later some of the chief consequences of this theory. But we must underscore the magnificent effort, having few precedents in the history of the sciences, by which Einstein succeeded in isolating the fundamental new conceptions which removed at a stroke all the obstacles which lay in the path of the electrodynamics of moving bodies.

The new ideas regarding space and time were represented by introducing space-time or the world of Minkowski. This four-dimensional continuum preserves the *a priori* character which accrued separately, according to thinkers before Einstein, to absolute space and absolute time. Distances and elements of volume have, in fact, an invariant value, that is to say, have the same value for all Galilean observers notwithstanding the diversity of space co-ordinates and time co-ordinates which they employ. Space and time cease to possess an absolute na-

ture, but the space-time which reunites them preserves this character. In space-time, each observer carves out in his own fashion his space and his time, and the Lorentz transformation formulas show us how the different portions are inter-related.

In space-time, everything which for each of us constitutes the past, the present, and the future is given in block, and the entire collection of events, successive for us, which form the existence of a material particle is represented by a line, the world-line of the particle. Moreover, this new conception defers to the principle of causality and in no way prejudices the determinism of phenomena. Each observer, as his time passes, discovers, so to speak, new slices of space-time which appear to him as successive aspects of the material world, though in reality the ensemble of events constituting space-time exist prior to his knowledge of them. Although overturning a large number of the notions held by classical physics, the special theory of relativity may in one sense be considered as the crown or culmination of that physics, for it maintains the possibility of each observer localizing and describing all the phenomena in the schema of space and time, as well as maintaining the rigorous determinism of those phenomena, from which it follows that the aggregate of past, present, and future phenomena are in some sense given *a priori.* Quantum physics, which issued from the study of atomic phenomena, led to quite different conceptions on these points, which were far from those of classical physics. We will not pursue this question, which would lead us too far astray, but will only say that, in any case, for all macroscopic phenomena investigated by classical physics, phenomena in which an enormous number of quantum processes intervene, the conceptions of the theory of relativity retain their validity throughout by virtue of the most exact statistical approximations.

As soon as Albert Einstein had laid the foundation of the special theory of relativity, innumerable consequences of great interest flowed from these unusual ideas. Some of the chief consequences were the Lorentz-Fitzgerald contraction, the apparent retardation of moving clocks, the variation of mass with velocity among high-speed particles, new formulas con-

taining second-order terms [*termes supplémentaires*] for aberration and the Doppler effect, and new formulas for the compounding of velocities, yielding as a simple consequence of relative kinematics the celebrated formula of Fresnel, verified by Fizeau, specifying the light-wave-trains [*l'entrainement des ondes lumineuses*] of refracting bodies in motion. And these are not merely theoretical notions: one can not insist sufficiently upon the fact that the special theory of relativity today rests upon innumerable experimental verifications, for we can regularly obtain particles of velocities approaching that of light in vacuum, particles in regard to which it is necessary to take account of corrections introduced by the special theory of relativity. To cite only two examples among many, let us recall that the variation of mass with velocity deduced by Einstein from relativistic dynamics, after having been firmly established by the experiments of Guye and Lavanchy, is verified daily by observation of the motion of the high-speed particles of which nuclear physics currently makes such extensive use; let us also recall that some of the beautiful experiments of Mr. Ives have made possible verification of the relativistic formulas of the Doppler effect, and thus, indirect verification of the existence of the retardation of clocks of which they are a consequence.

If the special theory of relativity was thus directly verified by experiment in a number of ways, it also indirectly demonstrated its full worth by serving as a point of departure for new and fruitful theories. It performed this function in regard to the theory of photons (quanta of light), and the Compton effect, obtaining experimental verifications from the study of the photoelectric effect and the diffraction of electrons in the presence of high-velocity particles for which the variation of mass to velocity is detectable. Consideration of the Bohr atomic theory in the light of relativity dynamics enabled Sommerfeld to derive for the first time a theory of the fine structure of spectral rays which, at the time, constituted considerable progress. The author of the present article cannot forget the rôle of relativity considerations in the reasoning which led him to the basic ideas of wave mechanics. Finally, the electron theory

of Dirac made possible a relativistic theory of "spin" and disclosed a slender, well-concealed link between relativistic ideas and the spin notion.

Today, even a summary analysis of the special theory of relativity requires mention of the inertia of energy. In relativity dynamics, the expression of the energy of a material particle reveals that in each Galilean system of reference the energy is equal to the product of the square of the velocity of light and the mass which the material particle under consideration possesses by virtue of its movement in the given system of reference. From this proposition Albert Einstein concluded by means of a momentous generalization that every mass necessarily corresponds to an energy equal to the product of the mass and the square of the velocity of light, and he showed by ingenious examples how this idea could be verified in particular cases. An enormous simplification of prevailing conceptions resulted from this single idea, since the two principles of conservation of mass and conservation of energy, hitherto considered to be absolutely distinct, became in a sense amalgamated. Since radiation transmits energy, it followed that a radiating body loses mass and that an absorbing body gains mass. These new ideas were, moreover, entirely in accord with the existence of a momentum of radiation which had been indicated by the work of Henri Poincaré and Max Abraham.

One of the most important consequences of this principle of inertial energy was that the least fragment of matter contains, in virtue of its mass, an enormous quantity of energy. Henceforth, matter was regarded as an immense reservoir of energy congealed, so to speak, in the form of mass, and nothing prevented one from imagining that some day man would succeed in liberating and using a portion of this hidden treasure. We know how, exactly forty years after the preliminary work of Einstein on relativity, this prediction received a dazzling, and sufficiently terrifying, verification.

The principle of the inertia of energy also explains why the exothermal formation of an atomic nucleus from its constituents yields a lesser mass than the sum of the masses of the constituents. Thus originated the explanation, as Paul

Langevin once observed, of the "mass-defects" of nuclei. Inertial energy thus enters significantly into energy-balances relative to nuclear reactions. The principle established by Einstein today plays a fundamental rôle in nuclear physics and chemistry and has found a wide range of application in this realm. It is one of the most magnificent conquests which we owe to the creator of the theory of relativity.

The special theory of relativity is a marvelous advance, but in itself, incomplete. For it deals only with the description of phenomena in Galilean systems of reference, that is to say, in systems of reference which are in rectilinear and uniform motion relative to the aggregate of fixed stars. Thus, on the one hand, it treats only of changes of variables corresponding to rectilinear and uniform relative motions, and on the other hand, it grants a kind of primacy to reference-systems in respect to the ensemble of fixed stars. It seemed necessary to break free of these restrictions in constructing a more general theory which would extend the principle of relativity to cases of any kind of accelerated motion and relate the apparently absolute character of velocities to the existence of the ensemble of stellar masses. Albert Einstein, keenly aware from the outset of his investigations of the necessity for such a generalization, arrived step by step at the solution sought. In this investigation he was guided by the ideas of certain precursors such as Mach, and by his extensive knowledge of tensor- and absolute differential-calculus, of which the special theory of relativity had already made some use; but, once again, it was the genius and originality of his mind which enabled him to attain the goal, which was definitively reached in 1916.

No attempt can be made here to analyze the general theory of relativity, which requires for its exposition extensive reference to difficult mathematical theories. Let us only say that it rests essentially upon the notion that all the laws of physics can be expressed by "covariant" equations, that is to say, equations which have the same mathematical form regardless of the system of reference selected or the space-time variables used. If this notion is applied to a reference system in rotation, it is evident that the centrifugal forces [*forces centrifuges et*

centrifuges composés] which are involved in the motion of a moving body in respect to this system may be considered as resulting from the metrical form of the space-time element and the variables used by the observer in rotation.

The new flash of Einstein's genius during this investigation was to perceive the possibility of deriving a geometrical interpretation of gravitational forces analogous to that of centrifugal forces. The centrifugal forces are proportional to the mass of the body, and this seems only natural. But, what is far more extraordinary, the same may be said of gravitational forces inasmuch as the gravitational force experienced by a body is likewise always proportional to its mass. This proportionality of "inertial mass" and "gravitational mass" was verified in precise experiments conducted by Eötvös and seems to hold rigorously. It follows that the trajectory of a material particle in a field of gravitation is independent of its mass. This analogy between centrifugal and gravitational forces suggests that they be similarly interpreted as resulting from the expression of the metrical form of space-time with the aid of the variables employed by the observer embedded in the gravitational field. Pursuing this line of thought, Einstein showed the "equivalence" of inertial force and gravitational force, and illustrated it by the famous example of a free-falling elevator: an observer inside an elevator could say that he maintains contact with the floor by his weight, but he could as well say that he has no weight at all and that the elevator is propelled upward by a velocity of motion equal to g.

However, the analogy between centrifugal and gravitational forces is not complete. One can, in fact, eliminate centrifugal forces by placing oneself in a Galilean system of co-ordinates; in which case one calls upon the formulas of special relativity. Yet one cannot, by any apposite choice of the system of reference, eliminate the gravitational forces. Einstein discovered the geometrical interpretation of this fact.

In the absence of gravitational force, space-time is Euclidean.[1] One can select Cartesian reference systems in which there are no centrifugal forces: these forces appear only if one adopts

[1] Or, more precisely, pseudo-Euclidean.

curvilinear co-ordinates, which amounts to placing oneself in an accelerated reference system, for example, in a rotating system. On the other hand, space-time is not Euclidean in the presence of a gravitational field; hence, as for a curved surface, it is impossible to adopt Cartesian co-ordinates. Gravitation is thus reduced to an effect of the curvature of space-time dependent upon the existence of masses scattered through the universe. It follows that the structure of the universe, and in particular its curvature in a geometrical sense, depends upon the masses contained in the universe. Relying upon the Riemannian theory of curved space, the general theory of relativity develops, by means of tensor-calculus, an interpretation of gravitational phenomena whose elegance and beauty is incontestable. This will remain one of the finest monuments of mathematical physics of the twentieth century.

Verifications of the general theory of relativity are few in number and still rather inaccurate. The rotation of the perihelion of Mercury, whose exact value had not been predictable by classical celestial mechanics, appears to conform to the predictions of the relativistic theory of gravitation. But since there subsists a residual effect after one has taken into account the perturbations due to other bodies of the solar system, and precise calculations are long and difficult and have not been verified often, this verification of relativity theory calls for further examination and debate. The deviation of light rays passing through a strong field of gravitation, predicted by Einstein's theory, was sought by studying the light rays of a distant star as they passed near the edge of the sun during a total solar eclipse. The results were encouraging, but further measurements would be desirable. As for the red-shift of rays emitted by a source located in a strong gravitational field, this has been the subject of much debate. It seems that this phenomenon has been observed at the surface of the sun, but the very minute displacements detected could perhaps be due to other causes (pressure, magnetic fields, etc. . . .). A more significant displacement was foreseen in regard to the "white dwarfs," very small stars of extremely high density whose surfaces have a very intense gravitational field. A very great displacement of

rays has actually been observed in the spectrum of the Companion of Sirius, and this appears to be one of the best experimental verifications of the relativity theory of gravitation.

The assimilation of space-time to a four-dimensional curved surface leads necessarily to the question of whether the universe is infinite, or partially—or totally—bent back upon itself like a cylinder or a sphere. One arrives, in pursuing this question, at cosmological theories, naturally of a rather conjectural character, concerning the structure of the whole universe. Einstein himself led the way by introducing into the theory of gravitation a cosmological constant related to the dimensions of a universe considered as finite, and by developing the hypothesis of a cylindrical universe; whereas the Dutch astronomer, de Sitter, studied the hypothesis of a spherical universe. These bold theories led to predictions for which the actual state of astronomy permitted no verification, and they would have remained somewhat sterile if Abbé Lemaître had not succeeded, by slightly modifying them, in extracting an explanation of that most curious phenomenon, the recession of distant nebulae, and of the linear law of Hubble. Lemaître conceived the universe, not as a static sphere in the style of de Sitter, but as a sphere whose dimensions increase (the expanding universe), and demonstrated that the hypothesis may logically be introduced into the framework of the general theory of relativity. No one can say at present with any certainty whether the explanation thus derived of the apparent recession of nebulae is appropriate, but it seems that no other valid explanation has yet been proposed. Without wishing to pass upon questions which only a study of the limits of the sky by the most powerful instruments of contemporary astronomy might succeed in resolving, we might note the extent to which Einstein's theory was fecund with new conceptions of all kinds and how, beginning in pure physics, it came to exercise a stimulating influence upon the highest of astronomical research.

The general theory of relativity advances a geometrical interpretation of the notion of "force." It succeeds satisfactorily in regard to gravitational forces. Its goal, therefore, would be entirely achieved if it were to succeed also in interpreting elec-

tromagnetic forces; for it certainly seems that all forces existing in nature are either gravitational or electromagnetic in character. But electromagnetic forces are proportional to the charge, and not to the mass, of the body upon which they act. It follows that the trajectory of a charged particle in an electromagnetic field depends upon the relation between its charge and its mass and varies according to the nature of the particle. Therein lies a fundamental difference between gravitational and electromagnetic fields which does not allow an extension to the latter of the geometrical interpretation which succeeded in respect to the former. Innumerable attempts have been made in the past thirty years to complete the general theory of relativity on this point and transform it into a "unified theory" capable of interpreting at once the existence of gravitational forces and electromagnetic forces. The theories of Weyl, Eddington, Kaluza, etc., are well known, but none appears to have had complete success. Naturally, Einstein also applied himself to the solution of this problem, and for twenty years or more has published, sometimes as sole author, sometimes in collaboration, a number of papers on new forms of unified theories. Einstein's efforts in this direction, ever characterized by the salient originality of his thought, will not be examined here. Despite their indisputable interest, they have not, to the best of our knowledge, attained any decisive success, and form, rather, landmarks placed on a road as yet uncleared. Moreover, the nature of the electromagnetic field is so intimately bound to the existence of quantum phenomena that any non-quantum unified theory is necessarily incomplete. These are problems of redoubtable complexity whose solution is still "in the lap of the gods."

The work of Albert Einstein on fluctuations, on the Brownian movement, on statistical thermodynamics, doubtless possesses less general significance than his trail-blazing research on the theory of relativity. However, the former alone would suffice to make the reputation of a great physicist. Accomplished during the years 1905-1912 and paralleling in its development the remarkable theoretical studies of Mr. Smoluchovski on the same subject, it was most timely, for during this period direct

or indirect proofs of the reality of molecules were being sought on all sides. A great number of first-rate experimenters, including Jean Perrin and Mr. The. Svedberg, were supplying the decisive proofs desired for the existence of molecules, by their observations of the equilibrium of emulsions, the Brownian movement, fluctuations of density, critical opalescence, etc. All of these studies were guided and clarified by Einstein's calculations. And the conceptions or methods which Einstein, with his customary acuity, had introduced in the course of his theoretical studies, brought new light to certain aspects of the statistical interpretation of thermodynamics.

If, for the sake of brevity, I must pass rapidly over this portion, however important, of the work of Albert Einstein, I must in contrast dwell at greater length upon the capital contribution which he made to the development of quantum theory. It should not be forgotten that it was particularly for his photoelectric research that Einstein received the Nobel prize for physics in 1921.

At the time that Einstein was undertaking his first investigations, Planck was introducing into physics the startling hypothesis regarding quanta and revealing that they enabled one to find the experimental laws of the spectral distribution of the radiation of thermal equilibrium, of which the classical theories had been unable to give any account. Planck had assumed, in disturbing contradiction to the most inveterate conceptions of the old physics, that the electron oscillators within matter which are responsible for the emission and absorption of radiation could emit radiant energy only as finite quantities, by quanta, whose value was proportional to the frequency emitted. Thus, he was led to introduce as the factor of proportionality the famous Planck constant whose importance on the atomic scale has never ceased to be reconfirmed to an increasing degree. Planck thus obtained as well the correct law of black-body radiation and, comparing his formula with experimental results, ascertained the value of the constant, h. Moreover, the introduction of the quantum hypothesis proved necessary to obtain a correct representation of the properties of black-body radiation. The work of Lord Rayleigh, Jeans, Planck him-

self, and somewhat later that of Henri Poincaré, proved that the old conceptions must lead to inexact laws and that the introduction of the element of discontinuity represented by the quantum of action was inevitable.

In his first works on this subject, Planck held that radiation was emitted *and absorbed* in quanta: this was the first version of the quantum theory. But, if radiation is always absorbed in quanta, it seemed necessary to admit that radiant energy arrived in quanta, that is to say, that electromagnetic waves, instead of being homogeneous (as had always been supposed), must consist of local concentrations of energy, packets of energy. Such a constitution of electromagnetic waves and, in particular, of light waves seemed, however, difficult to reconcile with the known properties of radiation, notably the phenomena of interference and diffraction so precisely described by the theory of homogeneous waves advanced by Fresnel and Maxwell. Since one could, strictly speaking, grant that the emission of radiation is accomplished in quanta without therefore postulating a corpuscular structure of radiation, the prudent mind of Planck, accustomed to the methods of classical physics, preferred to revise his theory of black-body radiation by the hypothesis that emission, but not absorption, proceeds in quantum fashion: this was the second, somewhat hybrid, version of the quantum theory.

The young Einstein reflected deeply upon this difficult subject and, in 1905, at the age of twenty-six, when he was laying the foundations of the theory of relativity, he proposed to adopt quite frankly the more radical point of view by granting the hypothesis of a corpuscular structure of radiation; and derived therefrom an interpretation of the mysterious laws of the photoelectric effect. Thus, with the vigor of an exceptional mind, Einstein, in the same year, founded *one* of the two great theories (relativity and quantum) which today reign supreme over the whole of contemporary physics, and made a capital contribution to the progress of the *other*.

The photoelectric effect, discovered by Hertz in 1887, obeys laws which long seemed incomprehensible. A metal subjected to an irradiation ejects electrons if the frequency of incident

radiation lies above a certain threshold: the kinetic energy of the ejected electrons increasing in linear fashion as a function of the difference between the excitatory frequency and the threshold frequency. Thus the elementary phenomenon of the ejection of an electron by the metal depends uniquely upon the frequency of incident radiation and in no way upon its amplitude, only the number of these elementary phenomena increasing with the intensity of the excitatory radiation. The classical theories of the constitution of light could not predict anything of the sort and the laws of the photoelectric effect remained inexplicable. Einstein, abandoning the prudent attitude of Planck, perceived in these laws the proof that the radiation possesses a corpuscular structure, the energy in a wave of frequency ν being concentrated in a corpuscle of energy content equal to $h\nu$. He derived with admirable simplicity an interpretation of photoelectric laws. If an electron, in order to be ejected from matter, must spend an amount of energy ω equal to $h\nu_0$, it could not, after having absorbed a quantum equal to $h\nu$, be ejected unless ν is greater than ν_0; hence the existence of a threshold frequency. If ν is greater than ν_0, the electron will be ejected with a kinetic energy equal to $h(\nu - \nu_0)$; hence the linear growth of this energy as a function of $\nu - \nu_0$. This theory of such great simplicity has since been verified by Millikan for ordinary light, by Maurice de Broglie for X-rays, and by Jean Thibaud and Ellis for γ-rays. Their experiments furnished a new means of measuring the value of the constant, h. Thus did precise experiments directly require a return in some fashion to a corpuscular conception of light, already maintained by Newton and other thinkers before the success of the wave theory, as a consequence of the fine work of Fresnel, almost led to its abandonment by all physicists. In order to signify its quantum origin, Einstein called this new corpuscular theory of light "the theory of light-quanta" (*Licht-Quanta*). Today, we call it the "photon theory."

During the succeeding years, Einstein did not cease to reflect upon this new conception of light. Assisted by arguments drawn from the theory of relativity, studies of the equilibrium between radiation and matter, and research into the fluctuations

of energy in black-body radiation, he showed that photons must not only have an energy equal to $h\nu$, but a momentum equal to $h\nu/c$. This conclusion was later verified by the discovery and study of the Compton effect. To be sure, Einstein's conceptions immediately encountered strong opposition. Masters of science such as Lorentz and Planck were not slow to point out that a purely corpuscular theory of light could not account for the phenomena of diffraction and coherence of wave-trains, for which the wave theory offered a ready interpretation. Einstein did not deny these difficulties, yet insisted upon the need for introducing into light waves an element of discontinuity, supporting his contentions by some penetrating observations. He inclined toward a "mixed theory" which would admit the existence of packets of radiant energy, but would link their movement and their localization to the propagation of a homogeneous wave of the Maxwell-Fresnel type. Later, the author of the present article was to attempt, at the outset of the development of wave mechanics, to develop an analogous idea for interpreting the general relation between the corpuscles and their associated waves. These attempts were unsuccessful, and it was necessary to find a very different interpretation connected with the indeterminacy relations of Heisenberg: we shall speak of this later. But it is certain that the ideas of Einstein on the constitution of light played a decisive rôle in the evolution of quantum theory and the growth of wave mechanics.

Pursuing his study of the applications of Planck's hypothesis, Albert Einstein demonstrated that it furnished a new theory of specific heats and removed the difficulties which had beset this domain. The Einsteinian formula for specific heats, though based upon hypotheses which were too simple to be truly applicable to real cases, clearly revealed the rôle of the quantum of action in these phenomena and served as a model for the more detailed research subsequently undertaken by Lindeman, Debye, Born, and Karman. . . .

However, the theory of quanta was elsewhere making enormous progress. In 1913 Bohr published his quantum theory of the atom, the immense repercussion of which upon the whole

field of physics is well known. In 1916 Sommerfeld perfected Bohr's theory by introducing the corrections of relativity and accounted, at least in part, for the fine structures observed in spectra. Einstein followed all these investigations with great interest. In a paper he formulated the method of quantization employed by Sommerfeld and, when Bohr enunciated his "correspondence principle," Einstein published a celebrated work in which, studying the thermodynamic equilibrium between black-body radiation and a gas, he revealed the connection between Planck's formula and Bohr's law of frequencies. In accord with the correspondence principle, he gave expression to the probability of quantum transitions which may be undergone by an atom in a field of incident radiation. Thus, once again, he made a capital contribution to the development of quantum theory.

When the author of the present article expounded in his Doctoral thesis in 1924 the ideas which remained at the foundation of wave mechanics, Einstein learned of them through Paul Langevin. Realizing their interest, he published in January of 1925 in the *Proceedings* of the Berlin Academy a note in which, drawing upon these new ideas and upon a then-recent work by the Indian physicist Bose, he formulated the statistics applicable to a group of particles indistinguishable one from another. This statistics, which is applicable to photons, α-particles, and more generally to any complex particle containing an even number of elementary corpuscles, today goes by the name of the "Bose-Einstein statistics." As we now know, electrons, protons, neutrons, and complex particles composed of an odd number of elementary corpuscles fall under the Pauli principle of exclusion, and groups of them obey a different statistics, that of Fermi-Dirac. By calling attention to the new ideas of wave mechanics, Einstein's paper certainly contributed greatly toward hastening this development.

Between 1924 and 1928 the new quantum theories, wave mechanics and quantum mechanics, rapidly gained great momentum, largely due to the work of Heisenberg, Born, Schrödinger, and Dirac. In 1927 Heisenberg made public his indeterminacy relations. His work, together with Bohr's penetrating analyses, led to a physical interpretation of the new mechanics in which the notion of probability plays a primordial rôle and

which, abandoning the ideas dearest to classical physics, ceases to attribute simultaneously a position and a velocity to particles on the atomic scale and refuses to impose a rigorous determinism upon the succession of their observable manifestations. Einstein, along with certain physicists of his generation or of preceding generations (Langevin, Planck), never granted, it seems, the new ideas of Bohr and Heisenberg. At the Solvay Conference of October, 1927, he was already raising serious objections. A few years later, in a paper written with Podolsky and Rosen, he expounded the difficulties which the actual interpretation of quantum mechanics appeared to him to raise. To Einstein's objections various physicists, and notably Mr. Bohr, composed acute replies, and it rather seems today that the physicists of the younger generation are almost unanimously in favor of granting the Bohr-Heisenberg interpretation, which seems to be the only one compatible with the totality of the known facts. Nevertheless, Einstein's objections, which bear the imprint of his profound mind, were surely useful because they forced the champions of the new conceptions to clarify subtle points. Even if one considers it possible to circumvent them, it is useful to have studied and reflected upon them at length.

The first half of the twentieth century was marked by an extraordinary impetus to physics which will remain one of the most brilliant chapters in the history of science. In these few years, human science raised two monuments which will stand in future centuries: the theory of relativity and the quantum theory. The first emerged wholly from the creative brain of Albert Einstein. The second, whose first stones were laid by Planck, owes to the mind of Einstein some of its most noteworthy advances.

One could not contemplate a work at once so profound and so powerfully original, accomplished in a few years, without astonishment and admiration. The name of Albert Einstein will be forever joined to two of the most magnificent achievements in which the human mind may take pride.

Louis de Broglie

Institut de France
Académie des Sciences

3

Ilse Rosenthal-Schneider

PRESUPPOSITIONS AND ANTICIPATIONS IN EINSTEIN'S PHYSICS

3

PRESUPPOSITIONS AND ANTICIPATIONS IN EINSTEIN'S PHYSICS

THE PRESUPPOSITIONS in Einstein's physics which I am discussing here are not the well known and often explicitly stated fundamental hypotheses of the theory of relativity; nor are the "anticipations" those consequences of the theory which provided the possibilities of testing the relativity theory's theoretical results and of verifying them. My remarks are concerned with some fundamental ideas which, I think, are determining principles of Einstein's work, and with his anticipations as to the possibilities of future developments in theoretical physics. The evidence will be drawn from his own methods in his scientific work and from his epistemological statements in publications as well as in personal discussions and correspondence.

Einstein's views on the comprehensibility of the world of our sense-experiences will be contrasted with Planck's, and some other problems, as for instance the significance of the constants of nature, will be touched upon.

Einstein's contention that "the axiomatic basis of theoretical physics cannot be an inference from experience," but is a "free invention" of the human mind, has been reasserted by him again and again.[1] This contention represents the starting point

[1] "On the Methods of Theoretical Physics," Herbert Spencer Lecture (Oxford, 1933, Clarendon Press). (Afterwards referred to as M.T.P.)

"Physik und Realität," *J. Franklin Inst.*, v. 221 (1933), n. 3. (Afterwards referred to as P.R.)

"Russell's Theory of Knowledge," *The Library of Living Philosophers*, v. 5 (1944). (Afterwards referred to as R.T.K.)

Translations from the German of all quotations except those from R.T.K. are mine.

of a much debated problem. The most debatable point is "the gulf—logically unbridgeable—which separates the world of sensory experiences from the world of concepts and propositions."[2] Taking the existence of sense-experiences as "given" and "knowable," Einstein states, that the concept of the "real external world" of our everyday thinking rests exclusively on sense-impressions, and that physics . . . deals with sense-experiences and with "comprehending" connections between them. The notions of bodily objects are formed by assigning concepts to repeatedly occurring complexes of sense-impressions "arbitrarily" selected from the multitude of sensory experiences. Logically viewed the concepts of bodily objects are "free creations of the human (or animal) mind,"[3] but they owe their meaning and their "justification" exclusively to the totality of sense-impressions to which they are co-ordinated and with which they are directly and intuitively connected. We attribute to the concept of the object real existence, i.e., a meaning which is largely independent of the sense-impressions to which the concept was assigned. We are justified in setting up "real objects" only because, by means of these concepts and their mutual relations (also set up by us), we are in a position to find our way in the "labyrinth of sense-impressions." Just like these "primary" concepts of everyday thinking, the "secondary" concepts and the basic laws connecting them, which form the foundation of scientific theory, are "free inventions."

To the question whether any principle can be established in accordance with which a co-ordinating selection is performed (or, as Eddington would have said, must be performed), Einstein's answer would be a definite "no." He emphasizes that concepts do not originate from experience by way of abstraction, a conception which he regards as "fateful." In order to illustrate that concepts are not abstracted from, but logically independent of sense-experiences, he refers to the series of integers as an invention of the human mind, and he states that "there is no way in which this concept could be made to grow, as it

[2] R.T.K., 287.
[3] P.R., 314.

were, directly out of sense-experiences."[4] This illustration, seen from a different angle, represents the same complications as the still unsolved—and perhaps insoluble—μέθεξις-problem which, ever since it impeded the unity of Plato's philosophy and eluded attempts at its solution by Aristotle's theory of substance, has constituted a stumbling-block for metaphysicians and epistemologists.

For Einstein the concepts are to the sense-experiences "not like the soup to the beef, but more like the cloakroom number to the coat."[5] However, I think, we should not forget that there are *complexes* of sense-experiences: to the coat there belongs a hat and gloves, etc.; we have to select them as a complex, and they, as a complex, must be suitable to be designated by the *one* cloakroom number.

It may be argued that the arbitrary selection of complexes of sense-experiences represents a sort of interference with the given totality of sense-impressions. We should be conscious that such interference, implied in the formation of primary concepts, is of still greater significance when secondary concepts and the laws of their interrelations, basic to physical theory, are concerned.

Eddington's presentation of the scientist's interference with the things he studies refers not only to this selection (representing interference at the "early" stage, where concepts are co-ordinated to sense-experiences) but also to interference at "later" stages. "It makes no difference whether we create or whether we select the conditions we study,"[6] may be an overstatement, but it is by no means a commonplace. The truth it contains had rarely been admitted by scientists. Poincaré, one of the few who did admit it, drew attention to interference by selection; the problem, however, came to the fore with the growth of quantum ideas—especially those of complementarity. The interference to which the scientist is compelled by the intrinsic nature of objects represents a type of "physical"

[4] R.T.K., 287.

[5] P.R., 317.

[6] A. Eddington, *The Philosophy of Physical Science* (Cambridge, 1939, University Press), 110.

interference which has far reaching philosophical implications, some of which will be touched upon in connection with Einstein's anticipations.

Eddington, in his "selective subjectivism," or "structuralism," sees the "Procrustean method" not only in the physical violence but also in the interference through selection brought about by our "sensory and intellectual equipment,"[7] the framework into which the observationally acquired knowledge is fitted. Eddington's framework is by no means identical with Kant's, to which it may be compared; but the basic idea of looking for a frame of thought originated from similar considerations, i.e., to find the conditions of the possibility of experience. In Kant's epistemology, too, we find some Procrustean methods; they form an integral part of his transcendental deduction. Our understanding "imposes laws on nature,"[8] but —to prevent misunderstanding—only universal principles (like the principles of causality and of substantiality), not laws concerning special facts which can only be ascertained by "experience," or, we may say, by the special sciences. Eddington, however, goes much further than Kant; he regards also special laws, and even the constants of nature, as deducible from epistemological considerations only, so that we can have *a priori* knowledge of them. This point is of interest when compared with Einstein's anticipations concerning the universal constants.

A few more lines on Kant's epistemology may help in elucidating Einstein's views on the comprehensibility of the external world, in contradistinction to Planck's, whose philosophical attitude is largely based on that of Kant—though of a Kant slightly distorted by Helmholtz. Kant did not stop at subjectivism, as Eddington did, but tried to find a "bridge," as I may call it, from the human mind to the phenomena of the external world which we perceive and judge. This bridge is to be found in his critical or transcendental idealism. The laws of nature are, for Kant, the laws of the experience of nature.

[7] *Ibid.*, 16.

[8] I. Kant, *Critik der reinen Vernunft*, 2. Aufl. (Riga, 1787), J. F. Hartknoch, 163.

He saw the harmony between laws of thinking and nature in the principle of the synthetic unity of thinking. Our intellectual equipment (to use Eddington's term, though I am fully conscious of its being completely un-Kantian) contains the forms of intuition, space and time,—which Einstein once jokingly compared to the emperor's new clothes in Andersen's story—as well as the principles of pure understanding. Both are elements of "knowledge restricted to objects of experience, though not wholly borrowed from experience."[9] These elements are *a priori;* but Kant's *a priori* is not a temporal—previous to experience—it is a logical *a priori:* independent of experience. For him, just as for Locke, there are only acquired, no innate, ideas.

Einstein writes: "That the totality of our sense-experiences is such that they can be arranged in an order by means of thinking . . . is a fact which strikes us with amazement, but which we shall never be able to comprehend."[10] There is no *a priori* framework, and apparently nothing—even *a posteriori* —that can be established about the co-ordination of concepts to sense-experiences or amongst each other. His statements that they are "somehow" (*irgendwie*)[11] connected, or "that enough propositions of the conceptual system be firmly enough connected with sensory experiences"[12] appear to be, perhaps deliberately, somewhat vague formulations. But he thinks it necessary that rules are fixed for building up a "system," like rules of a game, the fixation of which rules, though arbitrary, makes the game possible. He also stresses that this fixation of rules will never be a final one but will be valid only for a particular field of application, and that "there are no final categories in the sense of Kant." Any set of rules for the game is permissible as long as it leads to the desired result.

The question is whether the game can be played at all unless certain fundamental rules of thinking, or at least a scheme for their fixation, are established to which all players of all games

[9] *Ibid.*, 166.
[10] P.R., 315.
[11] P.R., 315.
[12] R.T.K., 289.

have to conform. Einstein agrees with Kant that "in thinking we use, with a certain 'right,' concepts to which there is no access from the materials of sensory experience, if the situation is viewed from the logical point of view."[13] This "right," just as Poincaré's *"conventions justifiées"*[14] (conventions justified on the grounds of intuition), seems to be very similar to Kant's *a priori* correctly interpreted as "logical independence of experience," though Einstein stresses that neither its certainty nor its inherent necessity can be upheld.

At this juncture we are in a position to compare Einstein's with Planck's views on the comprehensibility of the external world—certainly the most essential presupposition of science. Planck's standpoint may briefly be sketched as follows: We believe in the real external world, but we have no possibility of investigating it. The symbols we use in physics are constituents of the world picture and to a certain extent arbitrary; there are no observables in the world picture. Observables belong to the world of sense-experiences, and behind this, there is the real world which we can perceive only by means of the world of our sense-experiences. It is this real world which Planck presupposes as the "absolute," and it is this absolute which he tried to establish in physics: in the absolute value of the energy and of the entropy, or even in the space-time metric.

Whoever discussed such problems with Planck will have felt the powerful impact of his basic philosophical ideas on his scientific work. His attitude towards the problem of the comprehensibility of the external world is revealed in the beginning of his autobiography:

> The fact which led me to my science and filled me with enthusiasm for it, from my youth onwards, and which is by no means self-evident, is that our laws of thinking coincide with the lawfulness in the course of impressions which we receive from the external world, so that man is enabled to obtain enlightenment on this lawfulness by means of pure thinking. In this it is of essential significance that the external world represents something independent of ourselves, something absolute that we are

[13] R.T.K., 287.

[14] H. Poincaré, *Dernières Pensées* (Paris, Flamarion), 94.

facing, and the search for the laws that hold for this absolute seem to me the most satisfying task for the life's work of a scientist.[15]

Unlike Einstein, Planck does not see an "unbridgeable gulf" separating the world of sense-experiences from the world of concepts. For him there *is* a bridge, i.e., the Kantian solution. When Planck says that our laws of thinking coincide with[16] the lawfulness in the course of sense-impressions, it is obvious that he thinks of Kant's forms of intuition and concepts of pure understanding as bridging the gulf, and therewith guaranteeing the comprehensibility of the external world. The reality of the external world is presupposed as absolute and independent of ourselves.

This is very different from the views of Einstein, who in all his writings starts his fundamental considerations not with the "reality of the external world," whose existence is a problem he does not discuss, but with our sense-experiences. Nevertheless, Einstein's statement: "All knowledge about reality begins with experience and terminates in it," is exactly in agreement with Planck's philosophy (and with Kant's), viz., with the idea of a logically formed coherent physical theory based on experience, which theory has to stand the test of verification when its results are confronted by the facts of experience.

Very important in Einstein's presuppositions is the notion of simplicity, imposed as a condition on the formation of a basis, and, on the deduction from this basis, of a logical theory of physics. This simplicity is to be understood as including the reduction in number of the logically independent basic elements, i.e., concepts and fundamental hypotheses, and is generally agreed upon as a goal of all scientific theory. The logically simpler is not always the mathematically simpler. The essential point is that for a physical theory a type of mathematics be chosen which allows of the description of a coherent theory consistent as a whole. It sometimes appears as if Einstein were identifying a purely logical with a purely mathematical derivation. I do not think that he does so in the sense Leibniz did—or did at least in theory. Leibniz's theory of pure logic as *ars*

[15] M. Planck, *Wissenschaftliche Selbstbiographie* (Leipzig, 1948, J. A. Barth).
[16] Or: are identical with (*stimmen überein*).

demonstrandi et ars inveniendi, being capable of embracing the whole of mathematics and providing the means for mathematical progress by logical analytical methods only, excludes all synthetic, all intuitional aspects, and was not practised by himself, as can easily be shown, e.g., in his "synthetic" approach to the problem which led him to his invention of the differential calculus.

In contrast to this, Einstein's achievements seem to have been attained by means of exactly those methods which he described as the appropriate methods of theoretical physics: the physical world is represented as a four-dimensional continuum, a Riemannian metric is adopted, and, in looking for the "simplest" laws which such a metric can satisfy, he arrives at his relativistic theory of gravitation of empty space. Adopting in this space a vector field, or the antisymmetrical tensor field derived from it, and looking again for the "simplest" laws which such a field can satisfy he arrives at the Maxwell equations for free space. He also states that in the paucity of the mathematically existent field types, and of the relations between them, lies the hope of comprehending "reality in its depth."[17]

Simplicity and comprehensiveness are actualized in the theory of relativity in a most impressive way: the general theory includes the special theory for the special limiting case of $g_{\mu\nu}$ = const. The form of the laws of nature must be covariant with respect to arbitrary transformations, and the tensor analysis makes such a formulation possible. The immense heuristic value embodied in this postulate of general covariance is obvious; it restricts the possible laws of nature to those that satisfy the covariance condition.[18]

[17] M.T.P., 14.

[18] Theoretically, it is possible to express all laws of nature in covariant form (cf. E. Kretschmann, *Ann. Phys.*, v. 53, 1917, n. 16, and A. Einstein, *Ann. Phys.*, v. 55, 1918, n. 4). Therefore covariance in itself provides no sufficient criterion for the admissibility of an equation as expression of a law of nature. Combined, however, with the conditions of simplicity and, of course, of compatibility with experience, the principle of covariance has its great heuristic value, as Einstein's derivation of the gravitation law demonstrated clearly enough. In case there were two theoretical systems "possible," i.e., both compatible with experience, the selec-

Also, the unity built on the paucity of independent assumptions is reached in relativity theory as never before. After having discarded the inconsistent concept of a stationary ether, and after having replaced Lorentz's *ad hoc* invented hypothesis of contraction by the relativistic interpretation, Einstein was, as shown above, guided throughout by the ideal of mathematical simplicity and of an epistemologically satisfying unification. He felt, for instance, not satisfied with having to introduce into the equations the cosmological constant λ, which seemed to disturb the logical coherence and homogeneity of the system. That is why he welcomed every suggestion[19] which promised a way out of the dilemma, as, e.g., Friedmann's assumption of a spherical space with a radius varying with time, avoiding the unsatisfactory λ.

The fundamental assumptions of physical theory and the consequences of such theory to be tested by experiment are separated by a gap widening progressively with the unification of the logical structure. This drifting away from phenomenological physics, this loss of closeness to experience for the sake of greater comprehensiveness and unity, can be seen in the whole development of modern physics. In general relativity, for instance, the four co-ordinates by themselves had no longer any direct physical meaning, they were only mathematical symbols, and the theory obtained its physical foundation by the introduction of the invariant infinitesimal distance $ds^2 = \sum_{\mu,\nu 1}^{4} g_{\mu\nu} dx_\mu dx_\nu$ The remoteness from experience, however, of the theory, which in its unity and comprehensiveness has surpassed the fondest

tion would have to be guided by the covariance principle, in preferring the system which is simpler (from the viewpoint of the absolute differential calculus). "Someone should just try to formulate the Newtonian mechanics of gravitation in the form of absolutely covariant equations (four-dimensional), and he will certainly be convinced, that the principle (of covariance) excludes this theory practically, even if not theoretically!" (Einstein, *loc. cit.*) From the epistemological point of view, the covariant form is natural for a law of nature, because it expresses its independence of any frame of reference, and excludes all laws that appear simple only when a special co-ordinate system is used. In contrast to P. W. Bridgman (*The Nature of Physical Theory*, 81), I feel that the principle of covariance is very important.

[19] *Berl. Preuss. Akad. Wiss., Berlin*, 16.4.1931; and *The Meaning of Relativity*, 3 ed. (London, 1946, Methuen & Co.), 106-107.

expectations of physicists, has not impeded its verifiability.

Planck, too, like Einstein, pointed to the remarkable, and at first sight paradoxical, fact that the physical world picture is becoming more and more perfect, in spite of its continuously growing distance from the world of senses. But Planck insisted that the only reasonable interpretation of this fact was that: "The increasing distance of the physical world picture from the world of senses means nothing but a progressive approach to the real world." He added that there was no possibility of proving this opinion by logic, since not even the existence of the real world could be logically proved.[20] The difference in Einstein's and Planck's attitudes is obvious, although as physicists they are in complete agreement, so that a logically unified theory, and its significance to the world of senses, have the same meaning for both of them.

The axiomatic basis of such a theory, i.e., the fundamental concepts and the relations between them, should be as narrow as possible, freely selected, but with a view to parsimony. The freedom, however,

> is not much of a freedom, it is not like the freedom of a fiction writer, but rather like that of a person who has to solve a cleverly-designed word-puzzle. He may suggest any word as a solution, but there is probably only *one* which really solves the puzzle in all its parts. That nature . . . has the character of such a well designed puzzle is a faith which is, however, to a certain extent encouraged by the successes of science up to date.[21]

If we were to assume Planck's viewpoint, we should say: a condition of finding a solution at all is that the person who tries to solve the puzzle uses the same laws of thinking in accordance with which the puzzle was designed.

Einstein's analogy suggests that he sees the final aim of physics in an approach to the unique solution, that of a unified and most comprehensive theory, and one which, we know, should be of the greatest possible logical simplicity. Einstein feels that "experience will guide us aright" and that "there is a correct path and, moreover, that it is in our power to find

[20] M. Planck, *Wege zur physikalischen Erkenntnis*, 2. Aufl. (Leipzig, 1934, S. Hirzel), 184.

[21] P.R., 318.

it;" he also speaks of feeling sure that "in nature is actualized the ideal of mathematical simplicity," and that "pure mathematical construction enables us to discover the concepts and the laws connecting them which give us the key to the understanding of the phenomena of nature." He stresses that an agreement with experience remains "the sole criterion of the serviceability of a mathematical construction for physics," a view generally agreed upon; and—perhaps not so unanimously agreed upon—that "the truly creative principle resides in mathematics," so that he can say: "In a certain sense, therefore, I hold it to be true that pure thought is competent to comprehend the real, as the ancients dreamed."[22] These words are almost identical with Planck's;[23] but, whereas "pure thinking" for Planck includes the Kantian solution and its *a priori* with its necessity and universality, the same words have a different meaning for Einstein. The "pure thought" to which he refers is to be understood as "mathematical thinking;" and the understanding of the phenomena of nature, viz., comprehending the real, refers to nature in which the ideal of mathematical simplicity is actualized. However, Einstein emphasizes that mathematical concepts contain "nothing of the certainty, of the inherent necessity, which Kant had attributed to them."[24]

Einstein's ideas of a complete and unified theory have led to an exciting controversy on the significance of the physical world picture provided by quantum mechanics, a controversy which, I am sure, will be discussed by other contributors to this volume. I shall, therefore, only briefly mention a few points in so far as they reveal Einstein's anticipations concerning the future development of physics.

His criterion for the reality of a physical quantity is "the possibility of predicting it with certainty without disturbing the system."[25] In quantum mechanics, there is no possibility of such prediction of complementary quantities. Quite apart from this "incompleteness" and from the statistical character

[22] M.T.P., 13.
[23] Cf. fn. 15 above.
[24] R.T.K., 285.
[25] A. Einstein, B. Podolsky, N. Rosen, *Phys. Rev.* (v. 47, 1935), 777.

of the laws, quite apart from the influence of the measuring process on the measured system, Einstein feels that quantum mechanics is *not* likely to furnish the *basis* of a complete theory for the whole of physics,—though it may be deducible from this basis—, because of the fact that the ψ-function does not describe the happenings in a single system, but relates to an ensemble of systems only. He also stresses the point that the relative independence of spatially distant things should be maintained, if possible, in all its consequences (without admitting action-at-a-distance), as it is carried out most consistently in the field theory, otherwise "the existence of (quasi-)closed systems, and therewith the setting up of laws to be tested empirically in the usual sense, would be made impossible."[26]

In contrast to Bohr, who claims that quantum theory—seen from the viewpoint of complementarity—appears as "a completely rational description of physical phenomena," and thinks that "a radical revision of our attitude as regards physical reality"[27] is needed, Einstein regards this description as incomplete, and anticipates that a comprehensive unified field theory may finally include a satisfactory explanation of quantum phenomena. His aim is a theory which represents "events themselves and not merely the probability of their occurrence,"[28] and he expressed[29] the opinion that there may be a chance of solving the quantum puzzle without having to renounce the representation of "reality."

The existence of empirically observed and calculated constants of nature, and the numerical agreement between the results of observations and calculations of such constants,—even if arrived at by widely diverging methods—, provides a strong support for the belief in the lawfulness of nature, and therewith for the hope of its comprehensibility. The endeavour to form the basis and the methods of physical theories in conformity with the law of parsimony may lead us to expect the same tendency with respect to the universal constants of na-

[26] "Quantenmechanik und Wirklichkeit," *Dialectica*, v. 2 (1948), n. 3/4, 322.
[27] N. Bohr, *Phys. Rev.*, v. 48 (1935), 702; also: *Dialectica, loc. cit.*, 313.
[28] M.T.P., 15.
[29] In a letter to the author, March 1944.

ture; attempts to follow up this line of thought have actually been made. Very important problems are linked up with the nature and the significance of these constants.

Planck, in accordance with his ideas of reality, regarded the universal constants, e.g., the gravitational constant, the velocity of light, the masses and charges of protons and electrons, as "the most tangible signs of a real world," which also keep their significance as "foundation stones," (together with the conservation laws of energy and impulse, the second principle of thermodynamics, and the principle of relativity) in the new world picture into which the new universal constant, his elementary quantum of action, entered as "a mysterious messenger from the real world."[30] Planck's opinion concerning the possibility of finding connections between the universal constants was: "it is without doubt an attractive idea to link them up as closely as possible, by reducing them to a single one. I myself, however, doubt that this endeavour will be successful. But I may be mistaken."[31]

The idea of deducing the constants of nature in a purely epistemological way had been expressed by Eddington in his earlier writings and was mathematically treated in his *Fundamental Theory*.[32] I do not feel competent to judge whether his efforts to carry out his certainly fascinating, though somewhat fantastic, plans were successful.

Einstein's anticipations as to the constants of nature and the rôle they may play in the structure of a unified theory are very different indeed. In reply to some questions, he expressed his views. I should like to emphasize, however, that the communications I am here permitted [by Einstein] to use should by no means be taken as categorical statements, but only as conjectures based merely on intuition.

Einstein begins with the elimination of conventional units; in order to arrive at dimensionless constants he proceeds in the following way: Let there be a *complete* theory of physics in whose fundamental equations the "universal" constants

[30] Cf. fn. 20 above, 187.
[31] Letter from Planck to the author, dated: 30.3.1947.
[32] Cambridge, 1946, University Press.

$c_1 \ldots . c_n$ appear. The quantities shall somehow be reduced to gr.cm.sec. The choice of these three units is evidently completely a matter of convention. Each of the $c_1 \ldots$ (which Einstein, in another letter, called "apparent" constants) has a dimension in these units. We now will choose conditions so that c_1, c_2, c_3 have such dimensions that it is not possible to build from these c_1, c_2, c_3 a dimensionless product c_1^{α}, c_2^{β}, c_3^{γ}. Then we can multiply c_4, c_5, etc., in such a way, by factors built from powers of c_1, c_2, c_3, that these new symbols c_4^*, c_5^*, c_6^* are pure numbers. These are the genuine (*eigentlichen*) universal constants of the theoretical system, which have nothing to do with conventional units.

Einstein now expects that these constants c_4^*, etc. must be rational (*rationelle*) numbers whose values are established by the logical foundation of the whole theory. As rational (*rationell*) he regards such numbers

> which appear in some sense with necessity in the logical evolution of mathematics as unique individual formations, as e.g.,
>
> $$e = 1 + 1 + \tfrac{1}{2!} + \tfrac{1}{3!} + \cdots$$
>
> It is the same with π, which indeed is closely connected with e. In contrast to such rational numbers are the remaining numbers which are not derived from 1 by means of a clear construction.

There follow more remarks about such rational numbers, as far as they are "simple," resp. "natural" formations. Einstein characterizes these remarks as not fundamental; they may, however, be taken as further proof of his desire for simplicity in physical theory.

He expressed his anticipations concerning the true universal constants $c_4^* \ldots$, also in the following way: "In a reasonable theory, there are no (dimensionless) numbers whose values are only empirically determinable." He stressed again, however, that he, naturally, has no proof for this, but that he could not imagine a unified and reasonable theory explicitly to contain a number which the mood of the creator could just as well have chosen differently, whereby a world of a qualitatively

different lawfulness would have resulted.[33] Or, in other words: a theory which in its fundamental equations would explicitly contain a non-rational constant would have to be built up from logically independent bits and pieces. But Einstein is confident that "this world is not such as to make such an 'ugly' construction necessary for its theoretical comprehension. Of course, up to now there is no consistent theoretical foundation for the whole of physics, and still less a foundation satisfying such a radical postulation." Einstein's main concern is not merely that of overcoming the mathematical difficulties in finding the field equations for such a comprehensive theory, but—true to his whole scientific attitude—it is his desire to arrive at verifiable consequences.

From all that has been stated it may be gathered that Einstein regards the significance of the constants of nature as fundamental; and I think I have understood him correctly when I assume that a really complete unified field theory would have to provide the possibility of finding these constants mathematically. In such a generalized general theory of relativity a definite solution of the field equations would have to give information about all details of the atomic arrangement in a space lattice; and again, a solution would have to correspond to the frequency in an H-atom. In that way it should be possible to derive, for instance, the velocity of light mathematically from the field equations.

Presuppositions and anticipations in science are not—in the first instance, certainly—open to experimental or logical proof. The faith, the endeavour, and the expectations, as they manifest themselves in the basis, the methods, and the aim of physical science, are grounded in a personal philosophy which transcends the sphere of science itself. The deep satisfaction found in scientific work, akin to the delight derived from

[33] Einstein letter to the author, dated: 13.10.1945. The last sentence refers probably to Kant's remarks that God could have chosen a different law of gravitation, with, e.g., inverse proportionality to the third power, and that from such a law a space of different properties and dimensions would have resulted. Details about this first hint at a connection between physics and geometry, cf. Ilse Schneider, *Das Raum-Zeit-Problem bei Kant und Einstein* (Berlin, 1921, J. Springer), 69.

genuine art, is one of the fundamental human emotions which is highly intensified by personal contact with the creative mind.

I feel extremely grateful, therefore, for having been privileged not only to attend Einstein's regular lectures, but also to have had the opportunity very frequently of discussing scientific problems with him. He was at all times ready to listen patiently to questions and to answer them in detail. I shall never forget the animating hours when, together, we were reading a book full of objections to his theory, or the humorous remarks with which he had adorned the book. I am conscious that, like so many others, I shall never be able to express my gratitude in an adequate way; but I hope that my small contribution to this volume will show my great indebtedness to him.

Ilse Rosenthal-Schneider

The University of Sydney
Sydney, Australia

4

Wolfgang Pauli

EINSTEIN'S CONTRIBUTIONS TO QUANTUM THEORY

4

EINSTEIN'S CONTRIBUTIONS TO QUANTUM THEORY

IF NEW features of the phenomena of nature are discovered that are incompatible with the system of theories assumed at that time, the question arises, which of the known principles used in the description of nature are general enough to comprehend the new situation and which have to be modified or abandoned. The attitude of different physicists on a problem of this kind, which makes strong demands on the intuition and tact of a scientist, depends to some extent on the personal temperament of the investigator. In the case of Planck's discovery in 1900 of the quantum of action during the course of his famous investigations of the law of the black-body radiation, it was clear that Boltzmann's principle connecting entropy and probability, and the law of the conservation of energy and momentum were two pillars sufficiently strong to stand unshaken by the development resulting from the new discovery. It was indeed the faithfulness to these principles which enabled Planck to introduce the new constant h, the quantum of action, into his statistical theory of the thermodynamic equilibrium of radiation.

The earlier work of Planck, however, had treated only with a certain discretion the question whether the new "quantum-hypothesis" implied the necessity of changing the laws of microscopic phenomena themselves independent of statistical applications, or whether one had to use only an improvement of the statistical method to enumerate equally probable states. In any case, the tendency towards a compromise between the older ideas of physics, now called the "classical" ones, and the quantum theory was always favored by Planck, both in his earlier and later work on the subject, although such a pos-

sibility had diminished considerably the significance of his own discovery.

This was the background of Einstein's first paper* on quantum theory [1], which was preceded by his papers on the fundamentals of statistical mechanics[1] and accompanied, in the same year 1905, by his other fundamental papers on the theory of the Brownian movement[2] and the theory of relativity.[3] In this and subsequent papers [2, 3, 4b], Einstein clarified and strengthened the thermodynamical arguments underlying Planck's theory so much that he was able to draw definite conclusions on the microscopic phenomena themselves. He gave to Boltzmann's equation between entropy S and "probability" W

$$S = k \log W + \text{constant} \tag{1}$$

a definite physical meaning by defining W for a given state, as the relative duration in which this state (which may deviate more or less from the state of thermodynamical equilibrium) is realized in a closed system with a given value of its energy (time-ensemble). Hence, Boltzmann's relation is not only a definition of W, but also gives a connection between quantities which are in principle observable. For instance, one obtains for the mean value of the square of the energy-fluctuation ε of a small partial volume of a closed system, as a consequence of (1), the expression

$$\overline{\epsilon^2} = k\left[-\left(\frac{\partial^2 S}{\partial E^2}\right)_{T,V}\right]^{-1} = kT^2\left(\frac{\partial E}{\partial T}\right)_V \tag{2}$$

where T is the temperature and E the average energy (we disregard here the complication of the formula due to density fluctuations, because it is absent in the case of radiation). This relation must hold independent of the theoretical model of

* Editor's Note: All numerals appearing in brackets [ ] in this paper refer to Einstein's papers, dealing with the quantum theory, appearing under equivalent numbers at the close of this paper. *Ed.*

[1] Ann. Phys. (4) *9*, 417 (1902); *11*, 170 (1903); *14*, 354 (1904).

[2] Ann. Phys. (4) *17*, 549 (1905).

[3] Ann. Phys. (4) *17*, 891 (1905).

the system. If the energy of a system as a function of the temperature is empirically known, the model has to be in accordance with the fluctuation computed with help of equation (2) and inversely, the assumption of such a theoretical model prescribes the choice of states supposed to be equally probable in Boltzmann's relation (1). For the mean square of the energy fluctuation of the part of the radiation within the frequency interval (ν, $\nu + d\nu$), in the small partial volume V of a hole filled with radiation in thermodynamical equilibrium, Planck's radiation formula gives, according to (2), the expression, first derived by Einstein [4b]

$$\overline{\epsilon^2} = h\nu E + \frac{c^3}{8\pi\nu^2 d\nu}\frac{E^2}{V} \tag{3}$$

if E is the mean energy of the radiation in V of the frequency interval in question. Whereas the second term can easily be interpreted with help of the classical wave theory as due to the interferences between the partial waves,[4] the first term is in obvious contradiction to classical electrodynamics. It can, however, be interpreted by analogy to the fluctuations of the number of molecules in ideal gases with the help of the picture that the energy of radiation stays concentrated in limited regions of space in energy amounts $h\nu$, which behave like independent particles, called "light-quanta" or "photons."

As one was reluctant to apply statistical methods to the radiation itself, Einstein also considered the Brownian motion of a mirror which perfectly reflects radiation in the frequency interval (ν, $\nu + d\nu$), but transmits for all other frequencies, [4b]. If Pv is the frictional force corresponding to the velocity v of the mirror normal to its surface, Einstein's general theory of the Brownian movement gives, for the irregular change of the momentum of the mirror in the normal direction during the time interval τ, the statistical relation.

$$\overline{\Delta^2} = 2Pm\overline{v^2}\tau = 2PkT\tau \tag{4}$$

[4] For a quantitative computation, see H. A. Lorentz "Théories statistiques en thermodynamiques," Leipzig 1916, Appendix No. IX.

since $m\overline{v^2} = kT$ (m is the mass of the mirror). One first computes P according to the usual wave theory as given by

$$P = \frac{3}{2c}\left(\rho - \frac{1}{3}\nu\frac{\partial\rho}{\partial\nu}\right)d\nu\cdot f \tag{5}$$

where $\rho d\nu$ is the radiative energy in the unit of volume of the frequency interval, $(\nu, \nu + d\nu)$ considered, and f the surface of the mirror. Inserting (5) into (4), and using Planck's formula, one obtains

$$\frac{\overline{\Delta^2}}{\tau} = \frac{1}{c}\left[h\nu\rho + \frac{c^3}{8\pi\nu^2}\rho^2\right]d\nu\cdot f \tag{6}$$

This formula is very closely connected with (3), since using $E = \rho d\nu V$ one has

$$\frac{\overline{\Delta^2}}{\tau} = \frac{1}{c}f\frac{\overline{\epsilon^2}}{V} \tag{6a}$$

Just as in (3), it is only the last term in (6) which can be explained by the classical wave theory, whereas the first term can be interpreted with the picture of corpuscular light-quanta of the energy $h\nu$ and the momentum $h\nu/c$ in the direction of their propagation.

We have to add two remarks. 1°) If one starts with the simplified law of Wien for the black-body radiation, which holds for $h\nu \gg kT$, only the first term in (3) is obtained. 2°) In his first paper [1], Einstein computed for the region of validity of Wien's law, with help of a direct application of equation (1), the probability of the rare state in which the entire radiation energy is contained in a certain partial volume (instead of considering the mean square of the energy fluctuation). Also in this case he could interpret the results with the help of the above mentioned picture of corpuscular "light-quanta."

In this way Einstein was led to his famous "light-quantum hypothesis," which he immediately applied to the photoelectric effect and to Stockes' law for fluorescence [1], later also to the generation of secondary cathode rays by X-rays [5] and to the prediction of the high frequency limit in the *Bremsstrah-*

lung [9]. All this is so well known today that it is hardly necessary to go into a detailed discussion of these consequences. We are only briefly recalling that, by this earlier work of Einstein, it became clear that the existence of the quantum of action implies a radical change in the laws governing microphenomena. In the case of radiation, this change is expressed in the contrast between the use of the particle picture and the wave picture for different phenomena.

The consequences of Planck's theory, that material harmonic oscillators with the *eigen*frequency ν can only have discrete energy values, given by integral multiples of $h\nu$ [2], was also successfully applied by Einstein to the theory of the specific heat of solids [3]. Methodically it has to be pointed out that on this occasion Einstein for the first time applied the simpler method of the canonical ensemble to the derivation of the free energy and the mean energy of such oscillators as a function of the temperature, whereas in the earlier papers of Planck the entropy as a function of the energy was calculated with aid of Boltzmann's method in which the microcanonic ensemble is used. Regarding the physical content of the theory, it was obvious that the assumption of only a single value of the frequency of the oscillators in the solid body could not be correct. In connection with Madelung[5] and Sutherland's[6] discovery of a relation between the assumed value of this frequency and the elastic properties of the solid, this problem was discussed in several subsequent papers of Einstein [7, 8, 9], among which Einstein's report at the Solvay Congress in 1911 is most interesting, since it was given after the establishment of the empirical formula of Nernst and Lindemann for the thermal energy of solids and just before the problem was solved theoretically by Born and Karman[7] and independently, by Debye.[8] It may be considered as rather strange today that these later theories were not found much earlier, all the more since the method of *eigen*vibrations was applied to the black-body radiation from the standpoint of the classical theory much

[5] J. Madelung, Phys. ZS. *11*, 898 (1910).
[6] W. Sutherland, Phil. Mag. (6) *20*, 657 (1910).
[7] M. Born and Th. van Karman, Phys. ZS. *13*, 297 (1912).
[8] P. Debye, Ann. Phys. (4) *39*, 789 (1912).

earlier by Rayleigh and Jeans. One has to bear in mind, however, that until then no general rule for determining the discrete energy values of states had been found and also that physicists wre rather hesitant to apply quantum laws to objects so widely extended in space as a proper vibration.

Einstein's report on the constitution of radiation at the physics meeting in Salzburg [5] in 1909, where he appeared before a larger audience for the first time, can be considered as one of the landmarks in the development of theoretical physics. It deals with both special relativity and quantum theory and contains the important conclusion that the elementary process must be directed (needle radiation) not only for absorption, but also for emission of radiation, although this postulate was in open conflict with the classical idea of emission in a spherical wave, which is indispensable for the understanding of the coherence properties of radiation, as they appear in interference experiments. Einstein's postulate of a directed emission process has been further supported by strong thermodynamical arguments in his subsequent work. In papers published with L. Hopf [6] (which later also caused an interesting discussion with von Laue [12] on the degree of disorder in the "black" radiation) he could extend the earlier work on the fluctuations of momentum of a mirror under the influence of a radiation field to the corresponding momentum fluctuations of a harmonic oscillator. In this way, it was possible, at least for this particular system which played such an important rôle in Planck's original theory, to compute the translatory motion in equilibrium with the surrounding radiation, besides their oscillating motion which had been treated much earlier by Planck. The result was disappointing for those who still had the vain hope of deriving Planck's radiation formula by merely changing the statistical assumption rather than by a fundamental break with the classical ideas regarding the elementary microphenomena themselves: The classical computation of the fluctuation of momentum of an harmonic oscillator in its interaction with a radiation field is only compatible with the well-known value $3/2\ kT$ for its kinetic energy in thermodynamic equilibrium, if the radiation field fulfills the classical law of

Rayleigh-Jeans instead of the law of Planck. If inversely the latter law is assumed, the fluctuation of momentum of the oscillators must be due to irregularities in the radiation field, which have to be much larger than the classical ones for a small density of the radiation energy.

With Bohr's successful application of quantum theory to the explanation of the line spectra of the elements with help of his well-known two "fundamental postulates of quantum theory" (1913), a rapid development started, in the course of which the quantum theory was liberated from the restriction to such particular systems as Planck's oscillators.

Therefore the problem arose of deriving Planck's radiation formula using general assumptions holding for all atomic systems in accordance with Bohr's postulates. This problem was solved by Einstein in 1917 in a famous paper [13] which can be considered as the peak of one stage of Einstein's achievements in quantum theory (see also [10] and [11]) and as the ripe fruit of his earlier work on the Brownian movement. With the help of general statistical laws for the spantaneous and induced emission processes and for the absorption processes which are the inverse of the former, he could derive Planck's formula under the assumption of the validity of two general relations between the three co-efficients which determine the frequency of these processes and which, if one of these co-efficients is given, permits the computation of the other two. As these results of Einstein are today contained in all textbooks of quantum theory, it is hardly necessary to discuss here the details of this theory and its later generalization to more complicated radiation processes [15]. Besides this derivation of Planck's formula, the same paper discusses also the exchange of momentum between the atomic system and the radiation in a definite and very general way, using again equation (4) of the theory of the Brownian movement, which connects the mean square of the exchange of momentum in a certain time interval and the friction force Pv. The latter can be computed, using the general assumption indicated by both experience and classical electrodynamics that the absorption or emission of light induced from pencils with different directions are inde-

pendent of each other.[9] The condition (4) is then fulfilled in Planck's radiation field, only if the spontaneous emission is assumed to be directed in such a way that for every elementary process of radiation an amount $h\nu/c$ of momentum is emitted in a random direction and that the atomic system suffers a corresponding recoil in the opposite direction. The latter consequence was later confirmed experimentally by Frisch.[10]

Insufficient attention has been paid, according to the author's opinion, to Einstein's own critical judgement of the fundamental rôle ascribed to "chance" in this description of the radiation processes by statistical laws. We are therefore quoting the following passage from the end of his paper of 1917:

> Die Schwäche der Theorie liegt einerseits darin, dass sie uns dem Anschluss an die Undulationstheorie nicht näher bringt, andererseits darin, dass sie Zeit und Richtung der Elementarprozesse dem „Zufall" überlässt; trotzdem hege ich das volle Vertrauen in die Zuverlässigkeit des eingeschlagenen Weges.[11]

The contrast between the interference properties of radiation, for the description of which the superposition principle of the wave theory is indispensable, and the properties of exchange of energy and momentum between radiation and matter, which can only be described with the help of the corpuscular picture, was undiminished and seemed at first to be irreconcilable. As is well known, de Broglie later quantitatively formulated the idea that a similar contrast will appear again with matter. Einstein was very much in favour of this new idea; the author remembers that, in a discussion at the physics meeting in Innsbruck in the autumn of 1924, Einstein proposed to search for interference and diffraction phenomena with molecular beams.[12]

[9] Compare to this point the discussion between Einstein and Jordan [16].

[10] R. Frisch, ZS. f. Phys. *86*, 42 (1933).

[11] "The weakness of the theory lies, on the one hand, in the fact that it does not bring us any closer to a merger with the undulatory theory, and, on the other hand, in the fact that it leaves the time and direction of elementary processes to 'chance'; in spite of this I harbor full confidence in the trustworthiness of the path entered upon." (Tr. by the editor.)

[12] Compare in this connection also the earlier discussion by Einstein and Ehrenfest [14] of questions regarding molecular beams.

At the same time, in a paper of S.N. Bose, a derivation of Planck's formula was given, in which only the corpuscular picture, but no wave mechanical concept was used. This inspired Einstein to give an analogous application to the theory of the so-called degeneration of ideal gases [17], now known to describe the thermodynamical properties of a system of particles with symmetrical wave functions (Einstein-Bose statistics). It is interesting that later an attempt was made to apply this theory to liquid helium. The fundamental difference between the statistical properties of like and unlike particles, which is also discussed in the cited papers of Einstein, is connected, according to wave mechanics, with the circumstance that due to Heisenberg's principle of indeterminacy, which belongs to the foundation of the new theory, the possibility of distinguishing between different like particles, with help of the continuity of their motion in space and time, is getting lost. Shortly after Einstein's paper appeared, the thermodynamical consequence of the other alternative of particles with antisymmetric wave functions, which applies to electrons, was discussed in literature ("Fermi-Dirac statistics").

The formulation of quantum mechanics which soon followed the publication of de Broglie's paper was not only decisive, for the first time since Planck's discovery, in establishing again a self-consistent theoretical description of such phenomena in which the quantum of action plays an essential rôle, but it made also possible the achievement of a deeper insight into the general epistemological situation of atomic physics in connection with the point of view termed by Bohr "complementarity."[13] The writer belongs to those physicists who believe that the new epistemological situation underlying quantum mechanics is satisfactory, both from the standpoint of physics and from the broader standpoint of the conditions of human knowledge in general. He regrets that Einstein seems to have a different opinion on this situation; and this all the more, because the new aspect of the description of nature, in contrast to the ideas underlying classical physics, seems to open up hopes for a fu-

[13] An account of Einstein's position during this development is given in the subsequent article of N. Bohr.

ture development of different branches of science towards a greater unity.

Inside physics in the proper sense we are well aware that the present form of quantum mechanics is far from anything final, but, on the contrary, leaves problems open which Einstein considered long ago. In his previously cited paper of 1909 [4b], he stresses the importance of Jeans' remark that the elementary electric charge e, with the help of the velocity of light c, determines the constant e^2/c of the same dimension as the quantum of action h (thus aiming at the now well known fine structure constant $2\pi e^2/hc$). He recalled "that the elementary quantum of electricity e is a stranger in Maxwell-Lorentz' electrodynamics" and expressed the hope that "the same modification of the theory which will contain the elementary quantum e as a consequence, will also have as a consequence the quantum theory of radiation." The reverse certainly turned out to be not true, since the new quantum theory of radiation and matter does not have the value of the elementary electric charge as a consequence, which is still a stranger in quantum mechanics, too.

The theoretical determination of the fine structure constant is certainly the most important of the unsolved problems of modern physics. We believe that any regression to the ideas of classical physics (as, for instance, to the use of the classical field concept) cannot bring us nearer to this goal. To reach it, we shall, presumably, have to pay with further revolutionary changes of the fundamental concepts of physics with a still farther digression from the concepts of the classical theories.

Wolfgang Pauli

Zürich, Switzerland

List of Einstein's Papers on Quantum Theory Referred to:

1 *Ann. Phys.*, Lpz. (4) *17*, 132 (1905): "Über einen die Erzeugung und Verwandlung des Lichtes betreffenden heuristischen Gesichtspunkt."

2. *Ann. Phys.*, Lpz. (4) *20*, 199 (1906): "Zur Theorie der Lichterzeugung und Lichtabsorption."

3. *Ann. Phys.*, Lpz. (4) *22*, 180 and 800 (1907): "Die Planck'sche Theorie der Strahlung und die Theorie der spezifischen Wärme."

4. Discussion with W. Ritz: a) W. Ritz, *Phys. ZS. 9*, 903, (1908) and *10*, 224, (1908); b) A. Einstein, *Phys. ZS. 10*, 185, (1909) "Zum gegenwärtigen Stand des Strahlungsproblems." c) W. Ritz and A. Einstein, *Phys. ZS. 10*, 323, (1909) "Zur Aufklärung."

5. *Phys. ZS. 10*, 817, (1909): "Über die Entwicklung unserer Anschauungen über das Wesen und die Konstitution der Strahlung." (Report given at the physics meeting in Salzburg, September 1909).

6. a) A. Einstein and L. Hopf, *Ann. Phys.*, Lpz. *33*, 1096, (1910) "Über einen Satz der Wahrscheinlichkeitsrechnung und seine Anwendung in der Quantentheorie" (compare also below, reference 12).

   b) A. Einstein and L. Hopf, *Ann. Phys.*, Lpz. *33*, 1105, (1910): "Statistische Untersuchung der Bewegung eines Resonators in einem Strahlungsfeld."

7. *Ann. Phys.*, Lpz. *34*, 170 and 590, (1911): "Eine Beziehung zwischen dem elastischen Verhalten und der spezifischen Wärme bei festen Körpern mit einatomigem Molekül."

8. *Ann. Phys.*, Lpz. *35*, 679, (1911): "Elementare Betrachtungen über die thermische Molekularbewegung in festen Körpern."

9. *Rapport et discussions de la Réunion Solvay*, 1911: "La théorie du Rayonnement et les Quanta," Paris, 1912. Report by Einstein: "L'état actuel du problème des chaleurs spécifiques."

10. *Ann. Phys.*, Lpz. *37*, 832, (1912) and *38*, 881 (1912): "Thermodynamische Begründung des photochemischen Aequivalentgesetzes."

11. A. Einstein and O. Stern, *Ann Phys.*, Lpz. *40*, 551, (1913): "Einige Argumente für die Annahme einer molekularen Agitation beim absoluten Nullpunkt."

12. Discussion Einstein and v. Laue: a) M. v. Laue, *Ann. Phys.*, Lpz. *47*, 853, (1915); b) A. Einstein, *Ann. Phys.*, Lpz. *47*, 879, (1915); c) M. v. Laue, *Ann. Phys.*, Lpz. *48*, 668, (1915).

13. *Phys. ZS. 18*, 121, (1917) (compare also *Verhandlungen der deutschen physikalischen Gesellschaft*, No. 13/14, 1916): "Zur Quantentheorie der Strahlung."

14. A. Einstein and P. Ehrenfest, *Z. Phys. 11*, 326, (1922): "Quan-

tentheoretische Bemerkungen zum Experiment von Stern und Gerlach."

15. A. Einstein and P. Ehrenfest, Z. *Phys.* *19*, 301, (1923): "Zur Quantentheorie des Strahlungsgleichgewichtes." (See also: W. Pauli, Z. *Phys.* *18*, 272, 1923).
16. Discussion Jordan-Einstein: a) P. Jordan, Z. *Phys.* *30*, 297, (1924). b) A. Einstein, Z. *Phys.* *31*, 784, (1925).
17. *Berl. Ber.* (1924), p. 261 and (1925), p. 3 and 18: "Zur Quantumtheorie des einatomigen idealen Gases." (See also: S. N. Bose, Z. *Phys.* *26*, 178, 1924 and *27*, 384, 1924).

5

Max Born

EINSTEIN'S STATISTICAL THEORIES

5

EINSTEIN'S STATISTICAL THEORIES

ONE of the most remarkable volumes in the whole of scientific literature seems to me Vol. 17 (4th series) of *Annalen der Physik*, 1905. It contains three papers by Einstein, each dealing with a different subject, and each to-day acknowledged to be a masterpiece, the source of a new branch of physics. These three subjects, in order of pages, are: theory of photons, Brownian motion, and relativity.

Relativity is the last one, and this shows that Einstein's mind at that time was not completely absorbed by his ideas on space and time, simultaneity and electro-dynamics. In my opinion he would be one of the greatest theoretical physicists of all times even if he had not written a single line on relativity—an assumption for which I have to apologise, as it is rather absurd. For Einstein's conception of the physical world cannot be divided into watertight compartments, and it is impossible to imagine that he should have by-passed one of the fundamental problems of the time.

Here I propose to discuss Einstein's contributions to statistical methods in physics. His publications on this subject can be divided into two groups: an early set of papers deals with classical statistical mechanics, whereas the rest is connected with quantum theory. Both groups are intimately connected with Einstein's philosophy of science. He has seen more clearly than anyone before him the statistical background of the laws of physics, and he was a pioneer in the struggle for conquering the wilderness of quantum phenomena. Yet later, when out of his own work a synthesis of statistical and quantum principles emerged which seemed to be acceptable to almost all physicists, he kept himself aloof and sceptical. Many of us regard this as a tragedy—for him, as he gropes his way in loneliness, and for

us who miss our leader and standard-bearer. I shall not try to suggest a resolution of this discord. We have to accept the fact that even in physics fundamental convictions are prior to reasoning, as in all other human activities. It is my task to give an account of Einstein's work and to discuss it from my own philosophical standpoint.

Einstein's first paper of 1902, "Kinetische Theorie des Wärmegleichgewichtes und des zweiten Hauptsatzes der Thermodynamik"[1] is a remarkable example of the fact that when the time is ripe important ideas are developed almost simultaneously by different men at distant places. Einstein says in his introduction that nobody has yet succeeded in deriving the conditions of thermal equilibrium and of the second law of thermodynamics from probability considerations, although Maxwell and Boltzmann came near to it. Willard Gibbs is not mentioned. In fact, Einstein's paper is a re-discovery of all essential features of statistical mechanics and obviously written in total ignorance of the fact that the whole matter had been thoroughly treated by Gibbs a year before (1901). The similarity is quite amazing. Like Gibbs, Einstein investigates the statistical behaviour of a virtual assembly of equal mechanical systems of a very general type. A state of the single system is described by a set of generalised co-ordinates and velocities, which can be represented as a point in a $2n$-dimensional "phase-space;" the energy is given as function of these variables. The only consequence of the dynamical laws used is the theorem of Liouville according to which any domain in the $2n$-dimensional phase-space of all co-ordinates and momenta preserves its volume in time. This law makes it possible to define regions of equal weight and to apply the laws of probability. In fact, Einstein's method is essentially identical with Gibb's theory of canonical assemblies. In a second paper, of the following year, entitled "Eine Theorie der Grundlagen der Thermodynamik,"[2] Einstein builds the theory on another basis not used by Gibbs, namely on the consideration of a single system in course of time (later called *"Zeit-Gesammtheit,"* time

[1] *Annalen der Physik* (4), *9*, p. 477, (1902).
[2] *Annalen der Physik* (4), *11*, p. 170, (1903).

assembly), and proves that this is equivalent to a certain virtual assembly of many systems, Gibb's micro-canonical assembly. Finally, he shows that the canonical and micro-canonical distribution lead to the same physical consequences.

Einstein's approach to the subject seems to me slightly less abstract than that of Gibbs. This is also confirmed by the fact that Gibbs made no striking application of his new method, while Einstein at once proceeded to apply his theorems to a case of utmost importance, namely to systems of a size suited for demonstrating the reality of molecules and the correctness of the kinetic theory of matter.

This was the theory of Brownian movement. Einstein's papers on this subject are now easily accessible in a little volume edited and supplied with notes by R. Fürth, and translated into English by A. D. Cowper.[3] In the first paper (1905) he sets out to show "that, according to the molecular-kinetic theory of heat, bodies of microscopically visible size suspended in a liquid will perform movements of such magnitude that they can be easily observed in a microscope, on account of the molecular motion of heat," and he adds that these movements are possibly identical with the "Brownian motion" though his information about the latter is too vague to form a definite judgment.

The fundamental step taken by Einstein was the idea of raising the kinetic theory of matter from a possible, plausible, useful hypothesis to a matter of observation, by pointing out cases where the molecular motion and its statistical character can be made visible. It was the first example of a phenomenon of thermal fluctuations, and his method is the classical paradigma for the treatment of all of them. He regards the movement of the suspended particles as a process of diffusion under the action of osmotic pressure and other forces, among which friction due to the viscosity of the liquid is the most important one. The logical clue to the understanding of the phenomenon consists in the statement that the actual velocity of the suspended particle, produced by the impacts of the molecules of the liquid on it, is unobservable; the visible effect in a finite interval of

[3] *Investigations on the Theory of the Brownian Movement;* Methuen & Co., London, (1926).

time τ consists of irregular displacements, the probability of which satisfies a differential equation of the same type as the equation of diffusion. The diffusion coefficient is nothing but the mean square of the displacement divided by 2τ. In this way Einstein obtained his celebrated law expressing the mean square displacement for τ in terms of measurable quantities (temperature, radius of the particle, viscosity of the liquid) and of the number of molecules in a gramme-molecule (Avogadro's number N). By its simplicity and clarity this paper is a classic of our science.

In the second paper (1906) Einstein refers to the work of Siedentopf (Jena) and Gouy (Lyons) who convinced themselves by observations that the Brownian motion was in fact caused by the thermal agitation of the molecules of the liquid, and from this moment on he takes it for granted that the "irregular motion of suspended particles" predicted by him is identical with the Brownian motion. This and the following publications are devoted to the working out of details (e.g., rotatory Brownian motion) and presenting the theory in other forms; but they contain nothing essentially new.

I think that these investigations of Einstein have done more than any other work to convince physicists of the reality of atoms and molecules, of the kinetic theory of heat, and of the fundamental part of probability in the natural laws. Reading these papers one is inclined to believe that at that time the statistical aspect of physics was preponderant in Einstein's mind; yet at the same time he worked on relativity where rigorous causality reigns. His conviction seems always to have been, and still is to-day, that the ultimate laws of nature are causal and deterministic, that probability is used to cover our ignorance if we have to do with numerous particles, and that only the vastness of this ignorance pushes statistics into the fore-front.

Most physicists do not share this view to-day, and the reason for this is the development of quantum theory. Einstein's contribution to this development is great. His first paper of 1905, mentioned already, is usually quoted for the interpretation of the photo-electric effect and similar phenomena (Stokes law

of photo-luminescence, photo-ionisation) in terms of light-quanta (light-darts, photons). As a matter of fact, the main argument of Einstein is again of a statistical nature, and the phenomena just mentioned are used in the end for confirmation. This statistical reasoning is very characteristic of Einstein, and produces the impression that for him the laws of probability are central and by far more important than any other law. He starts with the fundamental difference between an ideal gas and a cavity filled with radiation: the gas consists of a finite number of particles, while radiation is described by a set of functions in space, hence by an infinite number of variables. This is the root of the difficulty of explaining the law of black body radiation; the monochromatic density of radiation turns out to be proportional to the absolute temperature (later known as the law of Rayleigh-Jeans) with a factor independent of frequency, and therefore the total density becomes infinite. In order to avoid this, Planck (1900) had introduced the hypothesis that radiation consists of quanta of finite size. Einstein, however, does not use Planck's radiation law, but the simpler law of Wien, which is the limiting case for low radiation density, expecting rightly that here the corpuscular character of the radiation will be more evident. He shows how one can obtain the entropy S of black body radiation from a given radiation law (monochromatic density as function of frequency) and applies then Boltzmann's fundamental relation between entropy S and thermodynamic probability W

$$S = k \log W$$

where k is the gas constant per molecule, for determining W. This formula was certainly meant by Boltzmann to express the physical quantity S in terms of the combinatory quantity W, obtained by counting all possible configurations of the atomistic elements of the statistical ensemble. Einstein inverts this process: he starts from the known function S in order to obtain an expression for the probability which can be used as a clue to the interpretation of the statistical elements. (The same trick has been applied by him later in his work on fluctuations;[4] although this is of considerable practical importance,

[4] *Annalen der Physik* (4), *19*, p. 373, (1906).

I shall only mention it, since it introduces no new fundamental concept apart from that "inversion.")

Substituting the entropy derived from Wien's law into Boltzmann's formula, Einstein obtains for the probability of finding the total energy E by chance compressed in a fraction αV of the total volume V

$$W = \alpha^{E/h\nu}$$

that means, the radiation behaves as if it consisted of independent quanta of energy of size and number $n = E/h\nu$. It is obvious from the text of the paper that this result had an overwhelming power of conviction for Einstein, and that it led him to search for confirmation of a more direct kind. This he found in the physical phenomena mentioned above (e.g., photoelectric effect) whose common feature is the exchange of energy between an electron and light. The impression produced on the experimentalists by these discoveries was very great. For the facts were known to many, but not correlated. At that time Einstein's gift for intuiting such correlations was almost uncanny. It was based on a thorough knowledge of experimental facts combined with a profound understanding of the present state of theory, which enabled him to see at once where something strange was happening. His work at that period was essentially empirical in method, though directed to building up a consistent theory—in contrast to his later work when he was more and more led by philosophical and mathematical ideas.

A second example of the application of this method is the work on specific heat.[5] It started again with a theoretical consideration of that type which provided the strongest evidence in Einstein's mind, namely on statistics. He remarks that Planck's radiation formula can be understood by giving up the continuous distribution of statistical weight in the phase-space which is a consequence of Liouville's theorem of dynamics; instead, for vibrating systems of the kind used as absorbers and emitters in the theory of radiation most states have a vanishing statistical weight and only a selected number (whose energies are multiples of a quantum) have finite weights.

[5] "Die Planck'sche Theorie der Strahlung und die Theorie der specifischen Wärme," *Annalen der Physik* (4), 22, p. 180, (1907).

Now if this is so, the quantum is not a feature of radiation but of general physical statistics, and should therefore appear in other phenomena where vibrators are involved. This argument was obviously the moving force in Einstein's mind, and it became fertile by his knowledge of facts and his unfailing judgment of their bearing on the problem. I wonder whether he knew that there were solid elements for which the specific heat per mole was lower than its normal value 5.94 calories, given by the law of Dulong-Petit, or whether he first had the theory and then scanned the tables to find examples. The law of Dulong-Petit is a direct consequence of the law of equipartition of classical statistical mechanics, which states that each co-ordinate or momentum contributing a quadratic term to the energy should carry the same average energy, namely $\frac{1}{2}RT$ per mole where R is the gas constant; as R is a little less than 2 calories per degree and an oscillator has 3 co-ordinates and 3 momenta, the energy of one mole of a solid element per degree of temperature should be $6 \times \frac{1}{2}RT$, or 5.94 calories. If there are substances for which the experimental value is essentially lower, as it actually is for carbon (diamond), boron, silicon, one has a contradiction between facts and classical theory. Another such contradiction is provided by some substances with poly-atomic molecules. Drude had proved by optical experiments that the atoms in these molecules were performing oscillations about each other; hence the number of vibrating units per molecule should be higher than 6 and therefore the specific heat higher than the Dulong-Petit value—but that is not always the case. Moreover Einstein could not help wondering about the contribution of the electrons to the specific heat. At that time vibrating electrons in the atom were assumed for explaining the ultra-violet absorption; they did apparently not contribute to the specific heat, in contradiction to the equipartition law.

All these difficulties were at once swept away by Einstein's suggestion that the atomic oscillators do not follow the equipartition law, but the same law which leads to Planck's radiation formula. Then the mean energy would not be proportional to the absolute temperature but decrease more quickly with falling temperature in a way which still depends on the fre-

quencies of the oscillators. High frequency oscillators like the electrons would at ordinary temperature contribute nothing to the specific heat, atoms only if they were not too light and not too strongly bound. Einstein confirmed that these conditions were satisfied for the cases of poly-atomic molecules for which Drude had estimated the frequencies, and he showed that the measurements of the specific heat of diamond agreed fairly well with his calculation.

But this is not the place to enter into a discussion of the physical details of Einstein's discovery. The consequences with regard to the principles of scientific knowledge were far reaching. It was now proved that the quantum effects were not a specific property of radiation but a general feature of physical systems. The old rule "*natura non facit saltus*" was disproved: there are fundamental discontinuities, quanta of energy, not only in radiation but in ordinary matter.

In Einstein's model of a molecule or a solid these quanta are still closely connected with the motion of single vibrating particles. But soon it became clear that a considerable generalisation was necessary. The atoms in molecules and crystals are not independent but coupled by strong forces. Therefore the motion of an individual particle is not that of a single harmonic oscillator, but the superposition of many harmonic vibrations. The carrier of a simple harmonic motion is nothing material at all; it is the abstract "normal mode," well known from ordinary mechanics. For crystals in particular each normal mode is a standing wave. The introduction of this idea opened the way to a quantitative theory of thermodynamics of molecules and crystals and demonstrated the abstract character of the new quantum physics which began to emerge from this work. It became clear that the laws of micro-physics differed fundamentally from those of matter in bulk. Nobody has done more to elucidate this than Einstein. I cannot report all his contributions, but shall confine myself to two outstanding investigations which paved the way for the new micro-mechanics which physics at large has accepted to-day—while Einstein himself stands aloof, critical, sceptical, and hoping that this episode may pass by and physics return to classical principles.

The first of these two investigations has again to do with the law of radiation and statistics.[6] There are two ways of tackling problems of statistical equilibrium. The first is a direct one, which one may call the combinatory method: After having established the weights of elementary cases one calculates the number of combinations of these elements which correspond to an observable state; this number is the statistical probability W, from which all physical properties can be obtained (e.g. the entropy by Boltzmann's formula). The second method consists in determining the rates of all competing elementary processes, which lead to the equilibrium in question. This is, of course, much more difficult; for it demands not only the counting of equally probable cases but a real knowledge of the mechanism involved. But, on the other hand, it carries much further, providing not only the conditions of equilibrium but also of the time-rate of processes starting from non-equilibrium configurations. A classical example of this second method is Boltzmann's and Maxwell's formulation of the kinetic theory of gases; here the elementary mechanism is given by binary encounters of molecules, the rate of which is proportional to the number-density of both partners. From the "collision equation" the distribution function of the molecules can be determined not only in statistical equilibrium, but also for the case of motion in bulk, flow of heat, diffusion etc. Another example is the law of mass-action in chemistry, established by Guldberg and Waage; here again the elementary mechanism is provided by multiple collisions of groups of molecules which combine, split, or exchange atoms at a rate proportional to the number-density of the partners. A special case of these elementary processes is the monatomic reaction, where the molecules of one type spontaneously explode with a rate proportional to their number-density. This case has a tremendous importance in nuclear physics: it is the law of radio-active decay. Whereas in the few examples of ordinary chemistry, where monatomic reaction has been observed, a dependence of reaction velocity on the physical conditions (e.g. temperature) could be assumed or even observed, this was not the case for radio-activity:

[6] "Zur Quantentheorie der Strahlung," *Phys. Z. 18*, p. 121, (1917).

The decay constant seemed to be an invariable property of the nucleus, unchangeable by any external influences. Each individual nucleus explodes at an unpredictable moment; yet if a great number of nuclei are observed, the average rate of disintegration is proportional to the total number present. It looks as if the law of causality is put out of action for these processes.

Now what Einstein did was to show that Planck's law of radiation can just be reduced to processes of a similar type, of a more or less non-causal character. Consider two stationary states of an atom, say the lowest state 1 and an excited state 2. Einstein assumes that if an atom is found to be in the state 2 it has a certain probability of returning to the ground state 1, emitting a photon of a frequency which, according to the quantum law, corresponds to the energy difference between the two states; i.e. in a big assembly of such atoms the number of atoms in state 2 returning to the ground state 1 per unit time is proportional to their initial number—exactly as for radio-active disintegration. The radiation, on the other hand, produces a certain probability for the reverse process $1 \rightarrow 2$ which represents absorption of a photon of frequency ν_{12} and is proportional to the radiation density for the frequency.

Now these two processes alone balancing one another would not lead to Planck's formula; Einstein is compelled to introduce a third one, namely an influence of the radiation on the emission process $2 \rightarrow 1$, "induced emission," which again has a probability proportional to the radiation density for ν_{12}.

This extremely simple argument together with the most elementary principle of Boltzmann's statistics leads at once to Planck's formula without any specification of the magnitude of the transition probabilities. Einstein has connected it with a consideration of the transfer of momentum between atom and radiation, showing that the mechanism proposed by him is not consistent with the classical idea of spherical waves but only with a dart-like behaviour of the quanta. Here we are not concerned with this side of Einstein's work, but with its bearing on his attitude to the fundamental question of causal and statistical laws in physics. From this point of view this paper is of particular interest. For it meant a decisive step in the direction of non-

causal, indeterministic reasoning. Of course, I am sure that Einstein himself was—and is still—convinced that there are structural properties in the excited atom which determine the exact moment of emission, and that probability is called in only because of our incomplete knowledge of the pre-history of the atom. Yet the fact remains that he has initiated the spreading of indeterministic statistical reasoning from its original source, radio-activity, into other domains of physics.

Still another feature of Einstein's work must be mentioned which was also of considerable assistance to the formulation of indeterministic physics in quantum mechanics. It is the fact that it follows from the validity of Planck's law of radiation that the probabilities of absorption ($1 \rightarrow 2$) and induced emission ($2 \rightarrow 1$) are equal. This was the first indication that interaction of atomic systems always involves two states in a symmetrical way. In classical mechanics an external agent like radiation acts on one definite state, and the result of the action can be calculated from the properties of this state and the external agent. In quantum mechanics each process is a transition between two states which enter symmetrically into the laws of interaction with an external agent. This symmetrical property was one of the deciding clues which led to the formulation of matrix mechanics, the earliest form of modern quantum mechanics. The first indication of this symmetry was provided by Einstein's discovery of the equality of up- and down-ward transition probabilities.

The last of Einstein's investigations which I wish to discuss in this report is his work on the quantum theory of monatomic ideal gases.[7] In this case the original idea was not his but came from an Indian physicist, S. N. Bose; his paper appeared in a translation by Einstein[8] himself who added a remark that he regarded this work as an important progress. The essential point in Bose's procedure is that he treats photons like particles of a gas with the method of statistical mechanics but with the difference that these particles are not distinguishable. He does not distribute individual particles over a set of states, but counts

[7] *Berl. Ber.* 1924, p. 261, 1925, p. 318.

[8] S. N. Bose, *Zeitschrift für Physik*, 26, 178, (1924).

the number of states which contain a given number of particles. This combinatory process together with the physical conditions (given number of states and total energy) leads at once to Planck's radiation law. Einstein added to this idea the suggestion that the same process ought to be applied to material atoms in order to obtain the quantum theory of a monatomic gas. The deviation from the ordinary gas laws derived from this theory is called "gas degeneracy." Einstein's papers appeared just a year before the discovery of quantum mechanics; one of them contains moreover (p. 9 of the second paper) a reference to de Broglie's celebrated thesis, and the remark that a scalar wave field can be associated with a gas. These papers of de Broglie and Einstein stimulated Schroedinger to develop his wave mechanics, as he himself confessed at the end of his famous paper.[9] It was the same remark of Einstein's which a year or two later formed the link between de Broglie's theory and the experimental discovery of electron diffraction; for, when Davisson sent me his results on the strange maxima found in the reflexion of electrons by crystals, I remembered Einstein's hint and directed Elsasser to investigate whether those maxima could be interpreted as interference fringes of de Broglie waves. Einstein is therefore clearly involved in the foundation of wave mechanics, and no alibi can disprove it.

I cannot see how the Bose-Einstein counting of equally probable cases can be justified without the conceptions of quantum mechanics. There a state of equal particles is described not by noting their individual positions and momenta, but by a symmetric wave function containing the co-ordinates as arguments; this represents clearly only one state and has to be counted once. A group of equal particles, even if they are perfectly alike, can still be distributed between two boxes in many ways—you may not be able to distinguish them individually but that does not affect their being individuals. Although arguments of this kind are more metaphysical than physical, the use of a symmetric wave function as representation of a state seems to me preferable. This way of thinking has morover led to the other case of

[9] "Quantisierung als Eigenwertproblem," *Annalen der Physik* (4), 70, p. 361, (1926); s. p. 373.

gas degeneracy, discovered by Fermi and Dirac, where the wave function is skew, and to a host of physical consequences confirmed by experiment.

The Bose-Einstein statistics was, to my knowledge, Einstein's last decisive positive contribution to physical statistics. His following work in this line, though of great importance by stimulating thought and discussion, was essentially critical. He refused to acknowledge the claim of quantum mechanics to have reconciled the particle and wave aspects of radiation. This claim is based on a complete re-orientation of physical principles: causal laws are replaced by statistical ones, determinism by indeterminism. I have tried to show that Einstein himself has paved the way for this attitude. Yet some principle of his philosophy forbids him to follow it to the end. What is this principle?

Einstein's philosophy is not a system which you can read in a book; you have to take the trouble to abstract it from his papers on physics and from a few more general articles and pamphlets. I have found no definite statement of his about the question "What is Probability?"; nor has he taken part in the discussions going on about von Mises' definition and other such endeavours. I suppose he would have dismissed them as metaphysical speculation, or even joked about them. From the beginning he has used probability as a tool for dealing with nature just like any scientific device. He has certainly very strong convictions about the value of these tools. His attitude toward philosophy and epistemology is well described in his obituary article on Ernst Mach:[10]

> Nobody who devotes himself to science from other reasons than superficial ones, like ambition, money making, or the pleasure of brain-sport, can neglect the questions, what are the aims of science, how far are its general results true, what is essential and what based on accidental features of the development?

Later in the same article he formulates *his empirical creed* in these words:

> Concepts which have been proved to be useful in ordering things easily acquire such an authority over us that we forget their human origin

[10] *Phys. Zeitschr.* 17, p. 101, (1916).

and accept them as invariable. Then they become "necessities of thought," "given *a priori,*" etc. The path of scientific progress is then, by such errors, barred for a long time. It is therefore no useless game if we are practising to analyse current notions and to point out on what conditions their justification and usefulness depends, how they have grown especially from the data of experience. In this way their exaggerated authority is broken. They are removed, if they cannot properly legitimate themselves; corrected, if their correspondence to the given things was too negligently established; replaced by others, if a new system can be developed that we prefer for good reasons.

That is the core of the young Einstein, thirty years ago. I am sure the principles of probability were then for him of the same kind as all other concepts used for describing nature, so impressively formulated in the lines above. The Einstein of to-day is changed. I translate here a passage of a letter from him which I received about four years ago (7th November, 1944): "In our scientific expectation we have grown antipodes. You believe in God playing dice and I in perfect laws in the world of things existing as real objects, which I try to grasp in a wildly speculative way." These speculations distinguish indeed his present work from his earlier writing. But if any man has the right to speculate it is he whose fundamental results stand like rock. What he is aiming at is a general field-theory which preserves the rigid causality of classical physics and restricts probability to masking our ignorance of the initial conditions or, if you prefer, of the pre-history, of all details of the system considered. This is not the place to argue about the possibility of achieving this. Yet I wish to make one remark, using Einstein's own picturesque language: If God has made the world a perfect mechanism, he has at least conceded so much to our imperfect intellect that, in order to predict little parts of it, we need not solve innumerable differential equations but can use dice with fair success. That this is so I have learned, with many of my contemporaries, from Einstein himself. I think, this situation has not changed much by the introduction of quantum statistics; it is still we mortals who are playing dice for our little purposes of prognosis—God's actions are as mysterious in classical Brownian motion as in radio-activity and quantum radiation, or in life at large.

Einstein's dislike of modern physics has not only been expressed in general terms, which can be answered in a similarly general and vague way, but also in very substantial papers in which he has formulated objections against definite statements of wave mechanics. The best known paper of this kind is one published in collaboration with Podolsky and Rosen.[11] That it goes very deep into the logical foundations of quantum mechanics is apparent from the reactions it has evoked. Niels Bohr has answered in detail; Schroedinger has published his own sceptical views on the interpretation of quantum mechanics; Reichenbach deals with this problem in the last chapter of his excellent book, *Philosophic Foundations of Quantum Mechanics*, and shows that a complete treatment of the difficulties pointed out by Einstein, Podolsky, and Rosen needs an overhaul of logic itself. He introduces a three-valued logic, in which apart from the truth-values "true" and "false," there is an intermediate one, called "indeterminate," or, in other words, he rejects the old principle of "*tertium non datur*," as has been proposed long before, from purely mathematical reasons, by Brouwer and other mathematicians. I am not a logician, and in such disputes always trust that expert who last talked to me. My attitude to statistics in quantum mechanics is hardly affected by formal logics, and I venture to say that the same holds for Einstein. That his opinion in this matter differs from mine is regrettable, but it is no object of logical dispute between us. It is based on different experience in our work and life. But in spite of this, he remains my beloved master.

MAX BORN

DEPARTMENT OF MATHEMATICAL PHYSICS
UNIVERSITY OF EDINBURGH
EDINBURGH, SCOTLAND

[11] A. Einstein, B. Podolsky, N. Rosen: "Can Quantum Mechanical Description of Physical Reality be Considered Complete?" *Phys. Rev.* 47, p. 777, (1935).

6

Walter Heitler

THE DEPARTURE FROM CLASSICAL THOUGHT IN MODERN PHYSICS

6

THE DEPARTURE FROM CLASSICAL THOUGHT IN MODERN PHYSICS

THE beginning of the twentieth century is the milestone of a marked change in the direction of scientific thought as far as the science of the inanimate world, i.e., physics, is concerned. What is now termed classical physics is an unbroken line of continuous development lasting roughly 300 years, which began in earnest with Galileo, Newton and others and culminated in the completion of analytical dynamics, Maxwell's theory of the electromagnetic field and the inclusion of optics as a consequence of the latter by Hertz. If we also include Boltzmann's statistical interpretation of the second law of thermodynamics, the list of what constitutes the major parts of classical physics will be fairly complete.

The logical structure of all these theories is roughly as follows: The happenings in the outside world (always confined to dead nature) follow a strictly causal development, governed by strict laws in space and time. The space and time in which these events occur is the absolute space-time of Newton and identical with what we are used to in daily life. The term "outside world" presupposes a sharp distinction between an "objective" outside reality, of which we have knowledge ultimately through sense perception, but which is completely independent of us, and "us," the onlookers, and ultimately those who think about the results of our observations. The term "causal development" is meant in the following, rather narrow, sense: Given at any time the complete[1] knowledge of the state of a physical object (which may be a mechanical system, an

[1] What "complete knowledge" means is defined in each part of physics, as the knowledge of a well defined set of initial conditions.

electromagnetic field, etc.), the future development of the object (or for that matter, its previous development until it has reached the state in question) follows then with mathematical certainty from the laws of nature, and is exactly predictable.

It was Einstein who, in 1905, made the first inroad into this logical structure. The greatness and courage of this step can only be measured by the fact that it was a departure from a 300 years old, and exceedingly successful, tradition. The change which our concepts of space and time have since undergone, through his special and general theories of relativity, are well known and adequately dealt with in other parts of this book. In this essay I want to deal with the second great departure from the classical program, namely quantum theory. It was also Einstein who has taken here some of the most decisive steps and who has paved the way short till the completion of quantum mechanics.

As far as the theory of relativity is concerned, that part of the classical structure which is concerned with the causal development of events (in the above sense) and with the relation of object and observer remained intact, or very nearly so. It is true that in the theory of relativity, the simultaneity of two events depends on the state of motion of the "observer," but it is equally true that nothing is changed in the happenings of the outside world if no observer is there at all, or if he is replaced by some lifeless mechanism, and the events follow in the same causal chain as in classical physics.

It is in the microscopical world and in quantum mechanics, which describes it, that a change in these concepts has come about.

In 1900 Planck discovered, through his analysis of the radiation emitted by a hot black body, that light of a given frequency ν could not be emitted in any arbitrary intensity, but that the emitted energy must be an integral multiple of a certain smallest unit $h\nu$ where h is a universal constant—Planck's constant—whose value is fixed once and for always. Consequently, when light is emitted by matter, this does not happen evenly or continuously, but must happen in jumps, a whole quantum $h\nu$ being emitted at a time. No doubt this picture

contains traces of an atomic structure of light and is quite at variance with the classical picture according to which all changes in the world occur continuously. However, Planck still supposed that light, once it is emitted, followed the laws of the Maxwell-Hertz theory. The discontinuity of the emission and absorption act were attributed to the material body rather than to the structure of light.

Planck's ideas were carried further, and to the extreme, by Einstein in 1905, when he gave us an understanding of the photoelectric phenomena. Here, Einstein, almost going back to the old ideas of Newton which had long been discarded, supposed an atomistic structure of light. The logical consequence of Planck's idea is evidently that light, of a given frequency ν, cannot itself exist with an arbitrary intensity. Quite independently of the way in which it is emitted or absorbed by material bodies, it consists of quanta (hardly anything else but another word for light-atoms) each containing an energy $h\nu$ and having quite a number of other characteristics (for instance momentum) of material corpuscles. Naturally, this hypothesis was now in flat contradiction to the Maxwell-Hertz theory of light, which was thought to be well established at the time and supported by innumerable facts. Moreover, it was felt that the picture of a discontinuous emission or absorption process, connected with a discontinuous change in the number of light-quanta, is rather difficult to reconcile with the general frame work of the classical theory. It is true, discontinuous happenings, or jumps, need not necessarily contradict what we have described above as the general structure of classical physics: It may be that the jumps are "caused" by some outside influence, and knowing the cause can be predicted exactly as regards the time and other characteristics of their occurrence. Many physicists hoped it would turn out to be so. Yet, the more sensitive of the physicists felt the very profound changes in the classical picture required by the introduction of jumps, and no one was more sensitive to this necessity than Einstein.

In fact it became quite clear that the jumps were not predictable as to the exact time of their occurence nor that they were caused by an outside influence taking place at the time

when they did occur, when Niels Bohr, in 1913, developed the quantum theory of the hydrogen atom. The essence of Planck's hypothesis found its more precise formulation in Bohr's statement: An atom can only exist in a discrete series of stationary states with various energies E_n, say, n = 0, 1, 2. . . . A change from the state E_n, say, to another E_m ($E_m < E_n$) takes place discontinuously with emission of one light-quantum whose frequency is determined by the change of energy $E_n - E_m = h\nu$. There exists a lowest state, the normal state of the atom, with energy E_0. This state is stable and the atom is incapable of emitting light. It followed further from the very fact that the black-body radiation had to be accounted for by these emission processes (Einstein 1917) that the jumps occurred *spontaneously*, and were not caused by any outside influence which happened to occur at the very time when the jump took place. Moreover, it was assumed from the start that the time which the atom spent in the higher state —supposing it had been brought to the higher state at a time $t = O$—was not a fixed interval of time which for all the atoms in the same excited state was the same, but that the life times of individual atoms followed the distribution law of *chance*. Only the average life time, taken for a large number of like atoms in the same excited state, was determined and a characteristic quantity for the atom and the excited state in question. It was here for the first time that statistical and probability considerations entered into the laws governing individual physical objects. Before, statistics was by definition to be applied only to an assembly of a large number of objects, in whose individual behaviour one was not interested, but who individually followed the strictly causal laws of classical physics. If one might have entertained any doubts as to whether the life time of an excited atom was not perhaps a fixed interval of time, which alone would have conformed with the classical idea of exact predictability (I am not aware that anyone thought that this might be the case), such doubts must have been dispelled by innumerable physical facts, such as the decay of radioactive bodies where the statistical nature of the jumps was proved by experiments.

As far as the nature of light was concerned, the situation was one—so it seemed—of flat contradictions. On the one hand the wave nature of light was used, and with complete success, to describe the phenomena of diffraction and countless other phenomena. On the other hand the light quanta of Planck and Einstein, equally indispensable to describe the phenomena of light emission and absorption and an ever increasing number of similar facts, had all or nearly all the characteristics of material particles. The two natures of light seemed quite irreconcilable.

The dynamics of material particles, atoms and electrons, was brought into an equally confusing state by the introduction of Planck's and Bohr's quantum ideas. Not only was it impossible to understand that in the lowest state of an atom an electron, i.e., a negatively charged particle, could forever rotate about a positively charged nucleus in an orbit of finite dimensions without radiating light and ultimately falling into the nucleus, but also the very nature of the quantum jumps seemed to escape any detailed description on the lines of classical dynamics or otherwise.

The next step which Einstein took was one that was likely to aggravate the situation by carrying the contradictions yet a step further, but in a way—as it turned out later—which contained many of the elements for the final clarification.

In 1924 Bose published a paper in which he treated light quanta like a gas of material particles rather than considering them as energy quanta of the electromagnetic waves as which Planck had conceived them. In order not to be at variance with Planck's formula for the black-body radiation, Bose was forced to apply a statistical treatment which was somewhat different from that usually applied to a gas of material particles. Attracted by the similarity of light quanta and a gas of material particles, Einstein turned round (1924/25) and applied Bose's statistical methods to a gas of atoms. That differences in the gas laws arose then was not surprising. Particular attention was paid by Einstein to the density fluctuations of such a gas. The energy fluctuations of the electromagnetic radiation was previously known to consist of two parts of which one was attributed

to the interference of the waves; the other part was due to the existence of the quanta and would not be there if the classical (i.e., not quantum-) theory of light had been used. On the other hand, the density fluctuations of a gas, treated according to the older statistical methods were quite analogous to the second part (thus stressing the similarity of light quanta and material particles), the first part being absent. Now when Einstein applied the new statistical methods to a gas of atoms, the first contribution to the fluctuations also appeared which in the case of radiation was due to the interference of waves. Upon this Einstein remarked:

One can interpret it (i.e., this part of the fluctuations) *in an analogous way by attributing to a gas some kind of radiation in a suitable way, and by calculating its interference-fluctuations. I go into further details because I believe that this is more than an analogy.*

Mr. E. de Broglie has shown, in a very remarkable thesis, how one can attribute a wave field to a material particle, or to a system of particles. To a material particle of mass m *first a frequency is attributed. . . . Relative to a system in which the particle moves with a velocity* v *a wave exists. Frequency and phase velocity are given by . . . whilst* v *is at the same time—as Mr. de Broglie has shown—the group velocity of this wave.*

A formula is given which expresses the phase velocity of the wave by the velocity of the particle v. If v is small compared with the velocity of light, the formula boils down to one for the *wave length* λ of the wave "accompanying" the particle, namely $\lambda = h/mv$. (m = mass of particle). Here Planck's constant h appears again. It always appears as a connecting link between concepts relating to a particle (v, energy E) and concepts relating to a wave (λ, ν).

In 1905 Einstein had put forward and stressed the "opposite nature" of light—its particle nature. Twenty years later, his considerations led him to draw attention to de Broglie's work, and put forward the "opposite nature" of what was always thought to be corpuscles—their wave nature. In this way he created the same paradoxical situation, that existed for light, also for material particles, putting the two on—so to speak—the same level.

Here Einstein's contribution to the development of quantum mechanics ends. He had given it two major impulses. Their strength can be measured by the fact that two or three years after the publication of the last mentioned work the problem was clarified and the structure of quantum mechanics was complete in its major outline. In particular the contrasting of the wave and particle natures of all physical objects has proved to be very fruitful, and it will be seen that it is just this contrast which leads most easily to an understanding of the typical features of quantum mechanics.

Following de Broglie and Einstein, Schrödinger developed the wave picture of an electron into a consistent mathematical theory, in which each electron was described by a wave field. At the same time and independently, a different more abstract line was pursued by Heisenberg, Born, and Jordan, and it soon turned out that both lines were in reality partly identical and partly supplemented each other. In particular the existence of a discrete set of energy levels of an atom appeared as a mathematical consequence of this theory. In 1927 Davisson and Germer verified the wave nature of the electron by proving experimentally that a beam of electrons showed much the same diffraction phenomena as a beam of light. Finally, and this gave the final solution of the apparent contradictions in the two pictures, Born (1926) gave his statistical interpretation of the wave field.

At first sight, Schrödinger's wave equation had much in common with other classical field theories. The wave field attributed to an electron develops in space and time in the same causal manner as an electromagnetic field, and the wave equation allows one to predict its future values at any point (in space) if the field is known at the present. Yet there were some marked differences, from the very beginning. In the first place, it turned out that the wave function was, in some cases, not real but necessarily complex. In the second place, when the problem of several (say n) electrons was considered, it turned out that the wave function was necessarily in a $3n$-dimensional space. These are not features which are shared by the electromagnetic field (or gravitational field) and make it unlikely

that the wave field of an electron could be a measurable physical object (as the other known fields are). The statistical interpretation by Born has finally decided against this idea.

What is now the logical structure of the new quantum mechanics, how are the double rôles of all physical objects as particles and waves to be reconciled, and how does the new theory differ from the classical ideas of space, time, and causality? The simplest way to explain this is to consider an example. In the following we shall give preference to the case of of the electron for the following reason: Although historically quantum theory originated from the idea of light quanta, the electron case is now the one better understood. In fact light quanta belong to the realm of relativistic quantum mechanics (they move always with the velocity of light) and the latter presents us still with very deep unsolved problems. However, as far as the following considerations go, not much would be changed if we substitute a beam of light for a beam of electrons and a light quantum for an electron.

Let us consider a beam of electrons and an experiment by which its wave nature is put into evidence. For this purpose we let the beam pass through a slit. On a screen behind the slit we observe the intensity of the electron beam arriving there. We make sure that the beam is monochromatic and that all electrons have the same wave length, or, by the wave length-velocity relation, the same velocity. We find then a characteristic diffraction pattern, maxima and minima of intensity in alternation, as would be the case if a monochromatic beam of light or X-rays had passed. The intensity distribution on the screen is exactly predictable from the wave equation, as would be the case for a classical field. So far the wave picture is successful and all the theoretical predictions were found to be true. In particular the relation between wave length and velocity could be verified.

On the other hand it is clear that the beam of electrons consists of a large number of individual particles. The atomistic structure of electricity had long ago been established beyond doubt, and we know in fact exactly how many electrons there are in a beam of given intensity. The contrast between the two

pictures we have formed of the electron is brought to a head, if we now ask: What will happen, if we use a beam of very weak intensity so that we can observe individual electrons one by one passing through the slit and arriving on the screen? If the wave picture were still correct in the more classical sense, we could at once predict that the diffraction pattern on the screen would be left intact and would appear with exactly the same distribution of maxima and minima, only with very much smaller overall intensity. All maxima and minima would have decreased in intensity in the same proportion. The absurdity of this proposition is clear. The diffraction pattern on the screen has an extension in space of several centimeters and this would mean that an individual electron would in fact have this extension! This is not indeed what has been found.[2] What is observed is this: Each individual electron arrives on the screen on one point, but each on a different point. When a sufficiently large number of electrons has passed (say a few dozens) it becomes more and more clear that the points at which the particles arrive are not distributed at random on the screen but lie *preferably* in the regions where in the former experiment with an intense beam the *maxima* of the diffraction pattern were found. Very few electrons arrive in the minima regions. This evidently means: The intensity distribution of the diffraction pattern is the *probability distribution* for the arrival (i.e., the position) of each individual electron. Now the diffraction pattern is nothing but the square of the amplitude of the wave function derived from the wave picture. We are therefore led to interpret the wave function not as the amplitude of some physical field analogous to the electromagnetic field, but as the *probability* (amplitude) *for finding the electron*, pictured as a particle, *at a given position.* This is Born's statistical interpretation.

From the very use of the world "probability" it is inferred that the *orbit of the electron* is *no longer precisely predictable.*

[2] The above experiment with individual particles has in fact been performed, although in a somewhat different way. The above description is, of course, an idealization, which, however, differs from the actual experiment in no essential point.

What can be predicted is only the probability of finding the electron at some point. This will amount to a certainty in general only if we have an assembly of a very *large number* of particles. Here then a drastic departure is made from the classical idea of strict determinism. The behaviour of atomistic particles no longer conforms with that idea. The departure is forced upon us by the necessity of reconciling the otherwise contradictory pictures of an electron behaving sometimes like a particle and sometimes like a wave. Through the statistical interpretation a first step is taken in reconciling the two "natures," but we must examine the situation more thoroughly. When the electron passes through the slit its wave function has a large extension in space and this means the probability distribution of its position extends also over a large area. We say then that the position of the electron is "not sharp." We then observe its position on the screen and find it, say, at some point x. Supposing now we can make the screen exceedingly thin so that the electron can pass through the screen. And supposing we place a second screen immediately behind the first one and observe the position of the electron again on the second screen. Where would we expect to find the particle? If the probability distribution for the position of the electron is the same as before we have no reason whatsoever to expect that we should find it at the same point (rather at the projection of x on the second screen). It would be just as probable to find it elsewhere at x', a few centimetres away, where, according to the probability distribution, the probability is just as great as in x. This again is absurd. It would mean that having observed the particle at a point x, we still know nothing about its position, and we could find it just as well at x', a moment afterwards. This cannot be so. On the second screen, the electron will, of course, appear at precisely the same position as on the first screen, i.e., on the projection of x. But then it follows that through the appearance of the electron on the first screen, the probability distribution for the position must have changed and *contracted into one of certainty*, i.e., into a distribution which is zero everywhere except in x where it is one. The wave function of the electron has, therefore, suddenly changed. This

sudden change of the probability distribution must have been effected by the *observation* on the first screen. It is indeed the outcome of an observation which changes a situation of "probability" into one of certainty. By this observation the *position* of the electron has suddenly become *sharp or certain.* It is here, for the first time in physics, that a measurement or observation has a decisive influence on the course of events and cannot be separated, as was the case in classical physics, from the physical picture. We come back to this point below.

There is now one further question to be answered before we can obtain a logically consistent picture. When the electron is observed on the screen, its position has become certain. Why can we then not work from the start with electrons with sharp positions and observe their positions before they pass the slit and thus return to a situation in which their orbits would be predictable? The answer is this: In order that the diffraction experiment works we had to use a monochromatic beam, which, as we have seen, means that all electrons have the same velocity, and hence wave length. Now a wave track with a given wave length has necessarily a long extension in space and therefore leads to a great uncertainty of the position of the electron. On the other hand, if the position is sharp, the wave function is such that it is different from zero only in a very small region of space. There is no trace of what we usually call a wave. As is well known, from Fourier analysis, such a "wave packet," as it is called, can be built up by a superposition of many monochromatic waves with many very different wave lengths. It follows then that we cannot assign a given wave length or, by the relation $\lambda = h/mv$, a given velocity, to such an electron. In other words: *the velocity is not sharp.* (Quantum mechanics allows us then to calculate a probability distribution for the various values of the velocity.) We see therefore that we have the *choice of either having the position* OR *the velocity sharp, but* WE CANNOT HAVE BOTH. (This is essentially Heisenberg's uncertainty principle.) Whereas in classical physics it is taken for granted that a body has a clearly defined position in space, as well as an equally clearly defined velocity, this is not the case in quantum mechanics. Only one of the two

quantities can have a sharp value, whereas the other is very uncertain. There are, of course, also intermediate cases, where both position and velocity are to some extent sharp,—say within a certain range of values,—and to some extent unsharp.

It is important to note that it is not possible to determine position and velocity of a particle at the same time, thus refuting the uncertainty principle by measurements. The measuring instrument exerts a non-negligible influence on the object to be measured, and since the instrument is also subjected to the quantum mechanical uncertainty relation, this influence is to some extent uncertain. Following this up in detail one finds that a measurement of the position changes the velocity of the object in an uncertain way (and vice versa), whereas it does not change the position of the object. A measure for the uncertainties with which we have to reckon is Planck's constant. In fact the uncertainty relation is $\Delta x \, \Delta v = h/m$ where Δx is the uncertainty of position, Δv that of velocity. Which of the two quantities, x or v, has a sharp value is determined solely by an observation. When beginning our diffraction experiment we had to make sure that the electrons had a sharp velocity (monochromatic beam). This meant: We have made an observation of their velocity somehow beforehand. In this way we have forced them into a state of sharp velocity, sacrificing any definite knowledge of their position. Afterwards we observe the position on the screen. From what was said above, it is clear that henceforth our *previous knowledge of the velocity is destroyed,* the electron has no longer a sharp velocity. Any further diffraction experiment would not show a clear diffraction pattern.

It is clear now why the orbit of the electron is not exactly predictable. For this purpose we would have to know, according to classical physics, the initial position *and* velocity. But the knowledge of both is contradictory to the uncertainty relation. With only half the knowledge sharp, the orbit is naturally not determined.

In the sudden change of the probability distribution (or the wave function) caused by an observation we have the prototype of a quantum jump. Supposing we have an atom which we

know to be in an excited state at the time $t = 0$. If we solve the wave equation for this case we find the following result: The wave function changes *gradually* and in course of time from that of the excited state into that of the ground state, owing to the very possibility of light emission. It allows us to predict a probability to find the atom either in the excited or in the ground state, at any later time. If we later make an observation of the state of the atom, we may find it, with a certain probability, in the ground state (and in that case we *always* find that also a light quantum has been emitted) and we say then for short: The atom has jumped down. The probability for the atom to be in the ground state changes steadily. We enforce a sudden change into certainty, by making the observation.

We have stated above that the wave function of an electron develops in space and time much in the same way as a classical field does, i.e., its future course is predictable when it is given at a time, say, $t = 0$. But its very nature and its physical interpretation (as a probability distribution) makes it clear that it is not itself the physical object we investigate (in contrast to the electromagnetic field of the classical theory, which *is* a physical object which we may consider, observe, and measure), although it is inseparable from the object under consideration (the electron, for instance). Its predictable course of development—causal development in the narrow sense of the introduction—continues so long as and until an observation is made. Then the chain of causal development is interrupted, the wave function changes suddenly, giving the quantity observed a sharp value. From here onwards a new, steady, causal development begins allowing us to predict probabilities for future observations, until the next observation is made, and so on. It appears that we are dealing with different aspects of the object: One is the world of observations in space and time, in which the objects under consideration have measurable positions, velocities, etc. Only one of these quantities has a sharply defined value at a time. The future values of these quantities are not precisely or entirely predictable. The other aspect from which we can consider the object is the one of the wave function. It escapes our immediate observation by apparatus or (ultimately) sense per-

ception entirely. It can be grasped by us only through our thinking, our spirit, not through our senses. It is in this world where the development is causal (in the sense used above). It casts its projection into the world of happenings in space and time, allowing us to predict probabilities for the results of any observations we choose to make (in some cases also their exact results). It is futile to argue which of the two aspects is the "real" one. Both are.[3] For both are but two *different projections of one and the same reality,* both are inseparable from each other, and both together only give the complete description of the object we consider.

The relationship that exists between position and velocity and between the causal development of the wave functions and the observations, namely that of mutual exclusiveness, which is so characteristic for quantum mechanics, is called by Bohr "complementarity."

The word "observation" used above requires perhaps still a more precise explanation. One may ask if it is sufficient to carry out a measurement by a self-registering apparatus or whether the presence of an observer is required. The above example of a position measurement by two screens may elucidate the situation. Supposing the first screen is a kind of thin photographic plate which retains an image of the point where the electron has passed through. Supposing we develop this plate only some time after the observation on the second screen has been made. It is then evidently impossible to predict with certainty the result of this observation. We shall, in fact, only be able to predict the probability distribution for the results of the observation on the second screen, and this is the same as that found before on the first screen. When we develop the first screen, it can, however, be said with certainty that the image will appear at the same point where it has been found on the second screen. The self-registering first screen does not itself make future observations certain, unless the result is acknowledged by a *conscious being.* We see, therefore, that here the *observer* appears, as a *necessary* part of the whole structure, and in his full capacity as a conscious being. The separation of the world into an "objective out-

[3] What we call "real" requires a clear statement.

side reality," and "us," the self-conscious onlookers, can no longer be maintained. Object and subject have become inseparable from each other. Their separation is an idealization which holds—approximately—where classical physics holds. The approximation is an exceedingly good one—as we shall presently see—in the macroscopical world, when we deal with bodies of our daily life.

It has often been argued whether the indeterminacy of quantum mechanics, with its profound consequences, may not be the result of an insufficient description, and whether it might not be possible that there is an underlying mechanism which has not been found yet, but which, when it is found, would allow us to return to the perfect determinism of classical physics. I believe it has been proved that quantum mechanics, when put on an axiomatic basis, is *logically complete* and permits therefore no such underlying mechanism. The following remark may also help to explain that this can hardly be expected. Classical mechanics (for instance the laws of motion of a heavy body) is certainly complete, in the sense that no unknown mechanism or so is omitted. Now classical mechanics is contained in quantum mechanics as a *special case.* If we consider the behaviour of particles with heavier and heavier masses according to quantum mechanics, it turns out that, owing to the small value of Planck's constant, all probability distributions contract into almost certainty. It is then possible to assign to both position and velocity almost sharp values and the behaviour of such bodies is one of near determinism. This amounts to practically complete determinism when the masses are as big as say those of a dust particle.

This being so, it is hardly conceivable that there could be any incompleteness in quantum mechanics, as the latter contains a complete theory as a special case. The lack of complete determinism does, of course, not mean that quantum mechanics is any less rich in precise predictions than classical physics. The complete mastering of the atomic world which it has given us should suffice to refute any such suggestions.

We summarize: What has been achieved in quantum mechanics is a new category of thinking, which, as far as I am aware, has not been thought of either by scientists or philosophers be-

fore. Apparently contradictory pictures of the structure of an object have been reconciled by this new mode of thinking. The happenings in the world of our sense perceptions supported by physical instruments are no longer strictly deterministic in the old sense. Instead, the full reality contains features which escape our senses (or their supporting instruments) and can only be grasped by our thought. No sharp line can be drawn between an outside world and the self-conscious observer who plays a vital rôle in the whole structure, and cannot be separated from it.

The departure from the classical idealization cannot fail to have, in course of time, its profound influences on other domains of human thought. It seems to be in the nature of the human spirit to give way to easy generalizations. When classical physics had its triumphs in the past, in particular in the nineteenth century, its logical structure was, consciously or unconsciously, taken over to almost all parts of human thought. Some have taken it for granted that a living organism is nothing more than a complicated mechanical and chemical system that is entirely subjected to the laws of classical physics and therefore itself deterministic in the same sense. Functions of the mind can, in such a picture, only be regarded as by-products of a deterministic mechanism, and must therefore be precisely predictable themselves. Clearly such views would destroy entirely the concepts of free will and ethical behaviour, and indeed, of "life" itself. And perhaps they have gone some way to destroy both. In the decline of ethical standards which the history of the past fifteen years has exhibited, it is not difficult to trace the influence of mechanistic and deterministic concepts which have unconsciously, but deeply, crept into human minds. That this would be the consequence of the nineteenth century scientific thought, with its subsequent visible destruction, was predicted by Dostojevski eighty years ago.

Of course, there is nothing, even in classical physics, which warrants such generalizations. What is true for a stone, a steam engine, or a water wave, need not hold for a tree and even less so for a mouse. The generalization is not much more logical than the argument: The sky is blue; clouds are in the sky; therefore clouds are blue.

Physics has now taken the first step towards a different atti-

tude. The new way of thinking opens up prospects also for an entirely different approach to problems which are outside the domain of physics. We mention, as an example, briefly some considerations of Niels Bohr concerning the borderline between lifeless matter and a living organism. We may enquire whether in the latter the same laws of physics are valid or not which hold for dead matter. If the answer would be in the affirmative (and even if the laws of physics are those of quantum mechanics) then a living organism would differ in no essential point from inanimate matter and no room would be left for the very concept of life. Now it is known that some of the most important life functions have their material seat in very small units of living matter which are indeed of almost molecular size. In order to answer our question we would therefore have to go into a detailed investigation of the atomic and molecular structure of the organism and then to ask whether the probability and other predictions of quantum mechanics are true or not. These observations must be made with physical instruments (X-rays, etc.) and cannot fail to have a profound influence on the object under consideration, i.e., the living organism. It may be now—and this is what Bohr assumes—that these detailed investigations with instruments would *destroy the life of the organism* and be therefore *incompatible with the very existence of life.* After having made our measurements we would be dealing with the dead body of the organism. It would therefore be impossible to verify or refute the validity of physics in the organism, as long as the latter is alive. In short, Bohr assumes that a similar relation of complementarity exists between life-matter and life-less matter as exists in quantum mechanics between the position and velocity of a particle. The very fact that an organism is living may be incompatible with too detailed a knowledge of its atomic and molecular structure, just as the knowledge of the position of a particle is incompatible with the knowledge of its momentum.

All this may or may not be so. But what is clear is that the new situation, with which we are confronted in quantum mechanics, has *created room* for an approach to the problem of life, (and other domains of human thought) which is no longer chained to the deterministic views of classical physics.

Finally, we return once more to the problems of physics. Quantum mechanics, for which Einstein has done so much to pave the way, is as yet essentially a non-relativistic theory, i.e., it applies to particles which move slowly and for which all gravitational effects can be neglected. It is as yet not reconciled with the great work of Einstein's, the theory of relativity. The two great theories, relativity and quantum mechanics, both creations of the twentieth century, and both departing profoundly from the classical picture, stand as yet apart from each other. A great deal of work has been done to bring about their unification,—and no doubt a certain amount of insight has been gained—, but the final solution is still in abeyance. We are concerned with the behaviour of fast moving atomistic particles, with the structure of the fundamental particles themselves, electrons, protons, the newly discovered mesons, etc., their creation and annihilation; with an understanding of the elementary unit of the electric charge, and with the understanding of such important dimensionless numbers as the universal constant hc/e^2 ($e =$ elementary charge, $h =$ Planck's constant, $c =$ velocity of light), which has the curious value 137. This is the domain of quantum-electrodynamics.

We are as yet far away from a solution of these problems. But when the solution is found, may we expect that it will bring us nearer to the classical ideal again? This can certainly not be the case. The non-quantum-mechanics theory of relativity, and the non-relativistic quantum mechanics must both be contained as specializations of the more general quantum electrodynamics. A generalization can hardly mean a return to the views of a still more special theory, classical physics. Instead we must be prepared for a further departure from the classical ideas. Further limitations will be imposed on the applicability of our present concepts. Perhaps some change will have to be made in our ideas of the continuity of space and time (atomistic structure of space?) or some other change in well established concepts, of which we have as yet not been able to think.

Walter Heitler

Dublin Institute for Advanced Studies
Dublin, Ireland

7

Niels Bohr

DISCUSSION WITH EINSTEIN ON EPISTEMOLOGICAL PROBLEMS IN ATOMIC PHYSICS

7

DISCUSSION WITH EINSTEIN ON EPISTEMOLOGICAL PROBLEMS IN ATOMIC PHYSICS

WHEN invited by the Editor of the series, "Living Philosophers," to write an article for this volume in which contemporary scientists are honouring the epoch-making contributions of Albert Einstein to the progress of natural philosophy and are acknowledging the indebtedness of our whole generation for the guidance his genius has given us, I thought much of the best way of explaining how much I owe to him for inspiration. In this connection, the many occasions through the years on which I had the privilege to discuss with Einstein epistemological problems raised by the modern development of atomic physics have come back vividly to my mind and I have felt that I could hardly attempt anything better than to give an account of these discussions which, even if no complete concord has so far been obtained, have been of greatest value and stimulus to me. I hope also that the account may convey to wider circles an impression of how essential the open-minded exchange of ideas has been for the progress in a field where new experience has time after time demanded a reconsideration of our views.

From the very beginning the main point under debate has been the attitude to take to the departure from customary principles of natural philosophy characteristic of the novel development of physics which was initiated in the first year of this century by Planck's discovery of the universal quantum of action. This discovery, which revealed a feature of atomicity in the laws of nature going far beyond the old doctrine of the limited divisibility of matter, has indeed taught us that the classical theories

of physics are idealizations which can be unambiguously applied only in the limit where all actions involved are large compared with the quantum. The question at issue has been whether the renunciation of a causal mode of description of atomic processes involved in the endeavours to cope with the situation should be regarded as a temporary departure from ideals to be ultimately revived or whether we are faced with an irrevocable step towards obtaining the proper harmony between analysis and synthesis of physical phenomena. To describe the background of our discussions and to bring out as clearly as possible the arguments for the contrasting viewpoints, I have felt it necessary to go to a certain length in recalling some main features of the development to which Einstein himself has contributed so decisively.

As is well known, it was the intimate relation, elucidated primarily by Boltzmann, between the laws of thermodynamics and the statistical regularities exhibited by mechanical systems with many degrees of freedom, which guided Planck in his ingenious treatment of the problem of thermal radiation, leading him to his fundamental discovery. While, in his work, Planck was principally concerned with considerations of essentially statistical character and with great caution refrained from definite conclusions as to the extent to which the existence of the quantum implied a departure from the foundations of mechanics and electrodynamics, Einstein's great original contribution to quantum theory (1905) was just the recognition of how physical phenomena like the photo-effect may depend directly on individual quantum effects.[1] In these very same years when, in developing his theory of relativity, Einstein laid a new foundation for physical science, he explored with a most daring spirit the novel features of atomicity which pointed beyond the whole framework of classical physics.

With unfailing intuition Einstein thus was led step by step to the conclusion that any radiation process involves the emission or absorption of individual light quanta or "photons" with energy and momentum

$$E = h\nu \quad \text{and} \quad P = h\sigma \tag{1}$$

[1] A. Einstein, *Ann. d. Phys.*, 17, 132, (1905).

respectively, where h is Planck's constant, while ν and σ are the number of vibrations per unit time and the number of waves per unit length, respectively. Notwithstanding its fertility, the idea of the photon implied a quite unforeseen dilemma, since any simple corpuscular picture of radiation would obviously be irreconcilable with interference effects, which present so essential an aspect of radiative phenomena, and which can be described only in terms of a wave picture. The acuteness of the dilemma is stressed by the fact that the interference effects offer our only means of defining the concepts of frequency and wavelength entering into the very expressions for the energy and momentum of the photon.

In this situation, there could be no question of attempting a causal analysis of radiative phenomena, but only, by a combined use of the contrasting pictures, to estimate probabilities for the occurrence of the individual radiation processes. However, it is most important to realize that the recourse to probability laws under such circumstances is essentially different in aim from the familiar application of statistical considerations as practical means of accounting for the properties of mechanical systems of great structural complexity. In fact, in quantum physics we are presented not with intricacies of this kind, but with the inability of the classical frame of concepts to comprise the peculiar feature of indivisibility, or "individuality," characterizing the elementary processes.

The failure of the theories of classical physics in accounting for atomic phenomena was further accentuated by the progress of our knowledge of the structure of atoms. Above all, Rutherford's discovery of the atomic nucleus (1911) revealed at once the inadequacy of classical mechanical and electromagnetic concepts to explain the inherent stability of the atom. Here again the quantum theory offered a clue for the elucidation of the situation and especially it was found possible to account for the atomic stability, as well as for the empirical laws governing the spectra of the elements, by assuming that any reaction of the atom resulting in a change of its energy involved a complete transition between two so-called stationary quantum states and that, in particular, the spectra were emitted by a step-like pro-

cess in which each transition is accompanied by the emission of a monochromatic light quantum of an energy just equal to that of an Einstein photon.

These ideas, which were soon confirmed by the experiments of Franck and Hertz (1914) on the excitation of spectra by impact of electrons on atoms, involved a further renunciation of the causal mode of description, since evidently the interpretation of the spectral laws implies that an atom in an excited state in general will have the possibility of transitions with photon emission to one or another of its lower energy states. In fact, the very idea of stationary states is incompatible with any directive for the choice between such transitions and leaves room only for the notion of the relative probabilities of the individual transition processes. The only guide in estimating such probabilities was the so-called correspondence principle which originated in the search for the closest possible connection between the statistical account of atomic processes and the consequences to be expected from classical theory, which should be valid in the limit where the actions involved in all stages of the analysis of the phenomena are large compared with the universal quantum.

At that time, no general self-consistent quantum theory was yet in sight, but the prevailing attitude may perhaps be illustrated by the following passage from a lecture by the writer from 1913:[2]

> I hope that I have expressed myself sufficiently clearly so that you may appreciate the extent to which these considerations conflict with the admirably consistent scheme of conceptions which has been rightly termed the classical theory of electrodynamics. On the other hand, I have tried to convey to you the impression that—just by emphasizing so strongly this conflict—it may also be possible in course of time to establish a certain coherence in the new ideas.

Important progress in the development of quantum theory was made by Einstein himself in his famous article on radiative equilibrium in 1917,[3] where he showed that Planck's law for thermal radiation could be simply deduced from assumptions

[2] N. Bohr, *Fysisk Tidsskrift, 12,* 97, (1914). (English version in *The Theory of Spectra and Atomic Constitution,* Cambridge, University Press, 1922).

[3] A. Einstein, *Phys. Zs., 18,* 121, (1917).

conforming with the basic ideas of the quantum theory of atomic constitution. To this purpose, Einstein formulated general statistical rules regarding the occurrence of radiative transitions between stationary states, assuming not only that, when the atom is exposed to a radiation field, absorption as well as emission processes will occur with a probability per unit time proportional to the intensity of the irradiation, but that even in the absence of external disturbances spontaneous emission processes will take place with a rate corresponding to a certain *a priori* probability. Regarding the latter point, Einstein emphasized the fundamental character of the statistical description in a most suggestive way by drawing attention to the analogy between the assumptions regarding the occurrence of the spontaneous radiative transitions and the well-known laws governing transformations of radioactive substances.

In connection with a thorough examination of the exigencies of thermodynamics as regards radiation problems, Einstein stressed the dilemma still further by pointing out that the argumentation implied that any radiation process was "unidirected" in the sense that not only is a momentum corresponding to a photon with the direction of propagation transferred to an atom in the absorption process, but that also the emitting atom will receive an equivalent impulse in the opposite direction, although there can on the wave picture be no question of a preference for a single direction in an emission process. Einstein's own attitude to such startling conclusions is expressed in a passage at the end of the article (*loc. cit.*, p. 127 f.), which may be translated as follows:

> These features of the elementary processes would seem to make the development of a proper quantum treatment of radiation almost unavoidable. The weakness of the theory lies in the fact that, on the one hand, no closer connection with the wave concepts is obtainable and that, on the other hand, it leaves to chance (*Zufall*) the time and the direction of the elementary processes; nevertheless, I have full confidence in the reliability of the way entered upon.

When I had the great experience of meeting Einstein for the first time during a visit to Berlin in 1920, these fundamental

questions formed the theme of our conversations. The discussions, to which I have often reverted in my thoughts, added to all my admiration for Einstein a deep impression of his detached attitude. Certainly, his favoured use of such picturesque phrases as "ghost waves (*Gespensterfelder*) guiding the photons" implied no tendency to mysticism, but illuminated rather a profound humour behind his piercing remarks. Yet, a certain difference in attitude and outlook remained, since, with his mastery for co-ordinating apparently contrasting experience without abandoning continuity and causality, Einstein was perhaps more reluctant to renounce such ideals than someone for whom renunciation in this respect appeared to be the only way open to proceed with the immediate task of co-ordinating the multifarious evidence regarding atomic phenomena, which accumulated from day to day in the exploration of this new field of knowledge.

In the following years, during which the atomic problems attracted the attention of rapidly increasing circles of physicists, the apparent contradictions inherent in quantum theory were felt ever more acutely. Illustrative of this situation is the discussion raised by the discovery of the Stern-Gerlach effect in 1922. On the one hand, this effect gave striking support to the idea of stationary states and in particular to the quantum theory of the Zeeman effect developed by Sommerfeld; on the other hand, as exposed so clearly by Einstein and Ehrenfest,[4] it presented with unsurmountable difficulties any attempt at forming a picture of the behaviour of atoms in a magnetic field. Similar paradoxes were raised by the discovery by Compton (1924) of the change in wave-length accompanying the scattering of X-rays by electrons. This phenomenon afforded, as is well known, a most direct proof of the adequacy of Einstein's view regarding the transfer of energy and momentum in radiative processes; at the same time, it was equally clear that no simple picture of a corpuscular collision could offer an exhaustive description of the phenomenon. Under the impact of such difficulties, doubts

[4] A. Einstein and P. Ehrenfest, *Zs. f. Phys.*, *11*, 31, (1922).

were for a time entertained even regarding the conservation of energy and momentum in the individual radiation processes;[5] a view, however, which very soon had to be abandoned in face of more refined experiments bringing out the correlation between the deflection of the photon and the corresponding electron recoil.

The way to the clarification of the situation was, indeed, first to be paved by the development of a more comprehensive quantum theory. A first step towards this goal was the recognition by de Broglie in 1925 that the wave-corpuscle duality was not confined to the properties of radiation, but was equally unavoidable in accounting for the behaviour of material particles. This idea, which was soon convincingly confirmed by experiments on electron interference phenomena, was at once greeted by Einstein, who had already envisaged the deep-going analogy between the properties of thermal radiation and of gases in the so-called degenerate state.[6] The new line was pursued with the greatest success by Schrödinger (1926) who, in particular, showed how the stationary states of atomic systems could be represented by the proper solutions of a wave-equation to the establishment of which he was led by the formal analogy, originally traced by Hamilton, between mechanical and optical problems. Still, the paradoxical aspects of quantum theory were in no way ameliorated, but even emphasized, by the apparent contradiction between the exigencies of the general superposition principle of the wave description and the feature of individuality of the elementary atomic processes.

At the same time, Heisenberg (1925) had laid the foundation of a rational quantum mechanics, which was rapidly developed through important contributions by Born and Jordan as well as by Dirac. In this theory, a formalism is introduced, in which the kinematical and dynamical variables of classical mechanics are replaced by symbols subjected to a non-commutative algebra. Notwithstanding the renunciation of orbital pictures, Hamilton's canonical equations of mechanics are kept unaltered and

[5] N. Bohr, H. A. Kramers and J. C. Slater, *Phil. Mag.*, 47, 785, (1924).
[6] A. Einstein, *Berl. Ber.*, (1924), 261, and (1925), 3 and 18.

Planck's constant enters only in the rules of commutation

$$qp - pq = \sqrt{-1}\,\frac{h}{2\pi} \qquad (2)$$

holding for any set of conjugate variables q and p. Through a representation of the symbols by matrices with elements referring to transitions between stationary states, a quantitative formulation of the correspondence principle became for the first time possible. It may here be recalled that an important preliminary step towards this goal was reached through the establishment, especially by contributions of Kramers, of a quantum theory of dispersion making basic use of Einstein's general rules for the probability of the occurrence of absorption and emission processes.

This formalism of quantum mechanics was soon proved by Schrödinger to give results identical with those obtainable by the mathematically often more convenient methods of wave theory, and in the following years general methods were gradually established for an essentially statistical description of atomic processes combining the features of individuality and the requirements of the superposition principle, equally characteristic of quantum theory. Among the many advances in this period, it may especially be mentioned that the formalism proved capable of incorporating the exclusion principle which governs the states of systems with several electrons, and which already before the advent of quantum mechanics had been derived by Pauli from an analysis of atomic spectra. The quantitative comprehension of a vast amount of empirical evidence could leave no doubt as to the fertility and adequacy of the quantum-mechanical formalism, but its abstract character gave rise to a widespread feeling of uneasiness. An elucidation of the situation should, indeed, demand a thorough examination of the very observational problem in atomic physics.

This phase of the development was, as is well known, initiated in 1927 by Heisenberg,[7] who pointed out that the knowledge obtainable of the state of an atomic system will always involve a peculiar "indeterminacy." Thus, any measurement of the position of an electron by means of some device,

[7] W. Heisenberg, *Zs. f. Phys.*, 43, 172, (1927).

like a microscope, making use of high frequency radiation, will, according to the fundamental relations (1), be connected with a momentum exchange between the electron and the measuring agency, which is the greater the more accurate a position measurement is attempted. In comparing such considerations with the exigencies of the quantum-mechanical formalism, Heisenberg called attention to the fact that the commutation rule (2) imposes a reciprocal limitation on the fixation of two conjugate variables, q and p, expressed by the relation

$$\Delta q \cdot \Delta p \approx h, \qquad (3)$$

where Δq and Δp are suitably defined latitudes in the determination of these variables. In pointing to the intimate connection between the statistical description in quantum mechanics and the actual possibilities of measurement, this so-called indeterminacy relation is, as Heisenberg showed, most important for the elucidation of the paradoxes involved in the attempts of analyzing quantum effects with reference to customary physical pictures.

The new progress in atomic physics was commented upon from various sides at the International Physical Congress held in September 1927, at Como in commemoration of Volta. In a lecture on that occasion,[8] I advocated a point of view conveniently termed "complementarity," suited to embrace the characteristic features of individuality of quantum phenomena, and at the same time to clarify the peculiar aspects of the observational problem in this field of experience. For this purpose, it is decisive to recognize that, *however far the phenomena transcend the scope of classical physical explanation, the account of all evidence must be expressed in classical terms.* The argument is simply that by the word "experiment" we refer to a situation where we can tell others what we have done and what we have learned and that, therefore, the account of the experimental arrangement and of the results of the observations must be expressed in unambiguous language with suitable application of the terminology of classical physics.

This crucial point, which was to become a main theme of the

[8] Atti del Congresso Internazionale dei Fisici, Como, Settembre 1927 (reprinted in *Nature*, *121*, 78 and 580, 1928).

discussions reported in the following, implies the *impossibility of any sharp separation between the behaviour of atomic objects and the interaction with the measuring instruments which serve to define the conditions under which the phenomena appear.* In fact, the individuality of the typical quantum effects finds its proper expression in the circumstance that any attempt of subdividing the phenomena will demand a change in the experimental arrangement introducing new possibilities of interaction between objects and measuring instruments which in principle cannot be controlled. Consequently, evidence obtained under different experimental conditions cannot be comprehended within a single picture, but must be regarded as *complementary* in the sense that only the totality of the phenomena exhausts the possible information about the objects.

Under these circumstances an essential element of ambiguity is involved in ascribing conventional physical attributes to atomic objects, as is at once evident in the dilemma regarding the corpuscular and wave properties of electrons and photons, where we have to do with contrasting pictures, each referring to an essential aspect of empirical evidence. An illustrative example, of how the apparent paradoxes are removed by an examination of the experimental conditions under which the complementary phenomena appear, is also given by the Compton effect, the consistent description of which at first had presented us with such acute difficulties. Thus, any arrangement suited to study the exchange of energy and momentum between the electron and the photon must involve a latitude in the space-time description of the interaction sufficient for the definition of wave-number and frequency which enter into the relation (1). Conversely, any attempt of locating the collision between the photon and the electron more accurately would, on account of the unavoidable interaction with the fixed scales and clocks defining the space-time reference frame, exclude all closer account as regards the balance of momentum and energy.

As stressed in the lecture, an adequate tool for a complementary way of description is offered precisely by the quantum-mechanical formalism which represents a purely symbolic scheme permitting only predictions, on lines of the correspondence principle, as to results obtainable under conditions specified

by means of classical concepts. It must here be remembered that even in the indeterminacy relation (3) we are dealing with an implication of the formalism which defies unambiguous expression in words suited to describe classical physical pictures. Thus, a sentence like "we cannot know both the momentum and the position of an atomic object" raises at once questions as to the physical reality of two such attributes of the object, which can be answered only by referring to the conditions for the unambiguous use of space-time concepts, on the one hand, and dynamical conservation laws, on the other hand. While the combination of these concepts into a single picture of a causal chain of events is the essence of classical mechanics, room for regularities beyond the grasp of such a description is just afforded by the circumstance that the study of the complementary phenomena demands mutually exclusive experimental arrangements.

The necessity, in atomic physics, of a renewed examination of the foundation for the unambiguous use of elementary physical ideas recalls in some way the situation that led Einstein to his original revision on the basis of all application of space-time concepts which, by its emphasis on the primordial importance of the observational problem, has lent such unity to our world picture. Notwithstanding all novelty of approach, causal description is upheld in relativity theory within any given frame of reference, but in quantum theory the uncontrollable interaction between the objects and the measuring instruments forces us to a renunciation even in such respect. This recognition, however, in no way points to any limitation of the scope of the quantum-mechanical description, and the trend of the whole argumentation presented in the Como lecture was to show that the viewpoint of complementarity may be regarded as a rational generalization of the very ideal of causality.

At the general discussion in Como, we all missed the presence of Einstein, but soon after, in October 1927, I had the opportunity to meet him in Brussels at the Fifth Physical Conference of the Solvay Institute, which was devoted to the theme "Electrons and Photons." At the Solvay meetings, Einstein had from their beginning been a most prominent figure, and several

of us came to the conference with great anticipations to learn his reaction to the latest stage of the development which, to our view, went far in clarifying the problems which he had himself from the outset elicited so ingeniously. During the discussions, where the whole subject was reviewed by contributions from many sides and where also the arguments mentioned in the preceding pages were again presented, Einstein expressed, however, a deep concern over the extent to which causal account in space and time was abandoned in quantum mechanics.

To illustrate his attitude, Einstein referred at one of the sessions[9] to the simple example, illustrated by Fig. 1, of a particle (electron or photon) penetrating through a hole or a narrow slit in a diaphragm placed at some distance before a photographic plate. On account of the diffraction of the wave con-

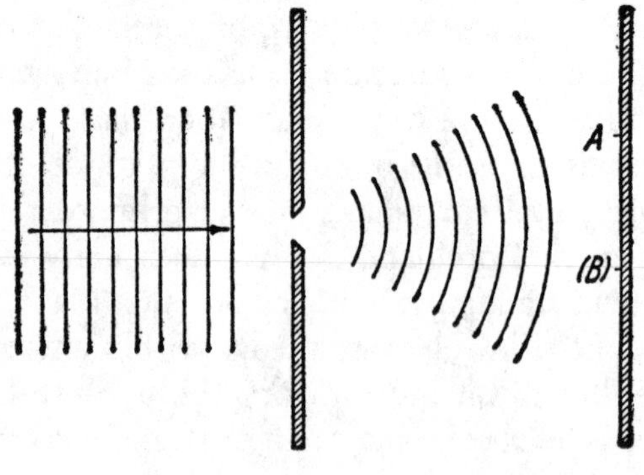

FIG. 1

nected with the motion of the particle and indicated in the figure by the thin lines, it is under such conditions not possible to predict with certainty at what point the electron will arrive at the photographic plate, but only to calculate the probability that, in an experiment, the electron will be found within any given region of the plate. The apparent difficulty, in this description, which Einstein felt so acutely, is the fact that, if in the experiment the electron is recorded at one point A of the plate,

[9] Institut International de Physique Solvay, *Rapport et discussions* du 5[e] Conseil, Paris 1928, 253ff.

then it is out of the question of ever observing an effect of this electron at another point (B), although the laws of ordinary wave propagation offer no room for a correlation between two such events.

Einstein's attitude gave rise to ardent discussions within a small circle, in which Ehrenfest, who through the years had been a close friend of us both, took part in a most active and helpful way. Surely, we all recognized that, in the above example, the situation presents no analogue to the application of statistics in dealing with complicated mechanical systems, but rather recalled the background for Einstein's own early conclusions about the unidirection of individual radiation effects which contrasts so strongly with a simple wave picture (cf. p. 205). The discussions, however, centered on the question of whether the quantum-mechanical description exhausted the possibilities of accounting for observable phenomena or, as Einstein maintained, the analysis could be carried further and, especially, of whether a fuller description of the phenomena could be obtained by bringing into consideration the detailed balance of energy and momentum in individual processes.

To explain the trend of Einstein's arguments, it may be illustrative here to consider some simple features of the momentum and energy balance in connection with the location of a particle in space and time. For this purpose, we shall examine the simple case of a particle penetrating through a hole in a diaphragm without or with a shutter to open and close the hole, as indicated in Figs. 2a and 2b, respectively. The equidistant parallel lines to the left in the figures indicate the train of plane waves corresponding to the state of motion of a particle which, before reaching the diaphragm, has a momentum P related to the wave-number σ by the second of equations (1). In accordance with the diffraction of the waves when passing through the hole, the state of motion of the particle to the right of the diaphragm is represented by a spherical wave train with a suitably defined angular aperture ϑ and, in case of Fig. 2b, also with a limited radial extension. Consequently, the description of this state involves a certain latitude Δp in the momentum component of the particle parallel to the diaphragm and, in the case of a

diaphragm with a shutter, an additional latitude ΔE of the kinetic energy.

Since a measure for the latitude Δq in location of the particle in the plane of the diaphragm is given by the radius a of the hole, and since $\vartheta \approx (1/\sigma a)$, we get, using (1), just $\Delta p \approx \vartheta P \approx (h/\Delta q)$, in accordance with the indeterminacy relation (3). This result could, of course, also be obtained directly by noticing that, due to the limited extension of the wave-field at the place of the slit, the component of the wave-number parallel to the plane of the diaphragm will involve a latitude $\Delta\sigma \approx (1/a) \approx (1/\Delta q)$. Similarly, the spread of the frequencies

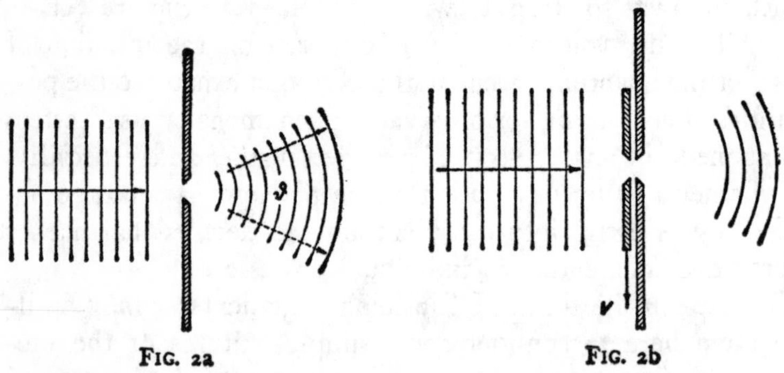

FIG. 2a FIG. 2b

of the harmonic components in the limited wave-train in Fig. 2b is evidently $\Delta\nu \approx (1/\Delta t)$, where Δt is the time interval during which the shutter leaves the hole open and, thus, represents the latitude in time of the passage of the particle through the diaphragm. From (1), we therefore get

$$\Delta E \cdot \Delta t \approx h, \qquad (4)$$

again in accordance with the relation (3) for the two conjugated variables E and t.

From the point of view of the laws of conservation, the origin of such latitudes entering into the description of the state of the particle after passing through the hole may be traced to the possibilities of momentum and energy exchange with the diaphragm

or the shutter. In the reference system considered in Figs. 2a and 2b, the velocity of the diaphragm may be disregarded and only a change of momentum Δp between the particle and the diaphragm needs to be taken into consideration. The shutter, however, which leaves the hole opened during the time Δt, moves with a considerable velocity $v \approx (a/\Delta t)$, and a momentum transfer Δp involves therefore an energy exchange with the particle, amounting to $v\Delta p \approx (1/\Delta t)\ \Delta q\ \Delta p \approx (h/\Delta t)$, being just of the same order of magnitude as the latitude ΔE given by (4) and, thus, allowing for momentum and energy balance.

The problem raised by Einstein was now to what extent a control of the momentum and energy transfer, involved in a location of the particle in space and time, can be used for a further specification of the state of the particle after passing through the hole. Here, it must be taken into consideration that the position and the motion of the diaphragm and the shutter have so far been assumed to be accurately co-ordinated with the space-time reference frame. This assumption implies, in the description of the state of these bodies, an essential latitude as to their momentum and energy which need not, of course, noticeably affect the velocities, if the diaphragm and the shutter are sufficiently heavy. However, as soon as we want to know the momentum and energy of these parts of the measuring arrangement with an accuracy sufficient to control the momentum and energy exchange with the particle under investigation, we shall, in accordance with the general indeterminacy relations, lose the possibility of their accurate location in space and time. We have, therefore, to examine how far this circumstance will affect the intended use of the whole arrangement and, as we shall see, this crucial point clearly brings out the complementary character of the phenomena.

Returning for a moment to the case of the simple arrangement indicated in Fig. 1, it has so far not been specified to what use it is intended. In fact, it is only on the assumption that the diaphragm and the plate have well-defined positions in space that it is impossible, within the frame of the quantum-mechanical formalism, to make more detailed predictions as to the point

of the photographic plate where the particle will be recorded. If, however, we admit a sufficiently large latitude in the knowledge of the position of the diaphragm it should, in principle, be possible to control the momentum transfer to the diaphragm and, thus, to make more detailed predictions as to the direction of the electron path from the hole to the recording point. As regards the quantum-mechanical description, we have to deal here with a two-body system consisting of the diaphragm as well as of the particle, and it is just with an explicit application of conservation laws to such a system that we are concerned in the Compton effect where, for instance, the observation of the recoil of the electron by means of a cloud chamber allows us to predict in what direction the scattered photon will eventually be observed.

The importance of considerations of this kind was, in the course of the discussions, most interestingly illuminated by the examination of an arrangement where between the diaphragm with the slit and the photographic plate is inserted another

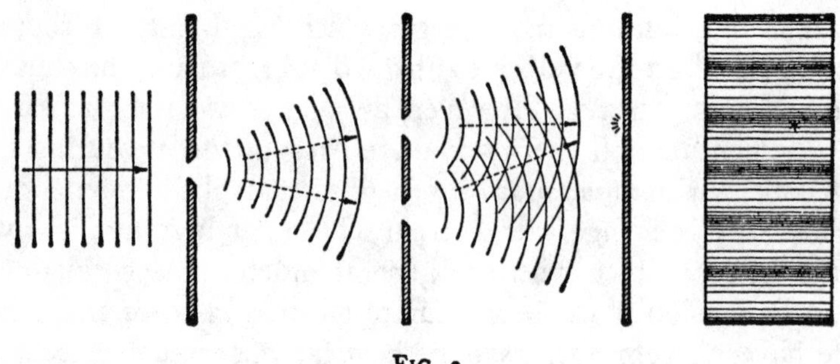

FIG. 3

diaphragm with two parallel slits, as is shown in Fig. 3. If a parallel beam of electrons (or photons) falls from the left on the first diaphragm, we shall, under usual conditions, observe on the plate an interference pattern indicated by the shading of the photographic plate shown in front view to the right of the figure. With intense beams, this pattern is built up by the accumulation of a large number of individual processes, each giving rise to a small spot on the photographic plate, and the distribution of these spots follows a simple law derivable from

the wave analysis. The same distribution should also be found in the statistical account of many experiments performed with beams so faint that in a single exposure only one electron (or photon) will arrive at the photographic plate at some spot shown in the figure as a small star. Since, now, as indicated by the broken arrows, the momentum transferred to the first diaphragm ought to be different if the electron was assumed to pass through the upper or the lower slit in the second diaphragm, Einstein suggested that a control of the momentum transfer would permit a closer analysis of the phenomenon and, in particular, to decide through which of the two slits the electron had passed before arriving at the plate.

A closer examination showed, however, that the suggested control of the momentum transfer would involve a latitude in the knowledge of the position of the diaphragm which would exclude the appearance of the interference phenomena in question. In fact, if ω is the small angle between the conjectured paths of a particle passing through the upper or the lower slit, the difference of momentum transfer in these two cases will, according to (1), be equal to $h\sigma\omega$ and any control of the momentum of the diaphragm with an accuracy sufficient to measure this difference will, due to the indeterminacy relation, involve a minimum latitude of the position of the diaphragm, comparable with $1/\sigma\omega$. If, as in the figure, the diaphragm with the two slits is placed in the middle between the first diaphragm and the photographic plate, it will be seen that the number of fringes per unit length will be just equal to $\sigma\omega$ and, since an uncertainty in the position of the first diaphragm of the amount of $1/\sigma\omega$ will cause an equal uncertainty in the positions of the fringes, it follows that no interference effect can appear. The same result is easily shown to hold for any other placing of the second diaphragm between the first diaphragm and the plate, and would also be obtained if, instead of the first diaphragm, another of these three bodies were used for the control, for the purpose suggested, of the momentum transfer.

This point is of great logical consequence, since it is only the circumstance that we are presented with a choice of *either* tracing the path of a particle *or* observing interference effects, which

allows us to escape from the paradoxical necessity of concluding that the behaviour of an electron or a photon should depend on the presence of a slit in the diaphragm through which it could be proved not to pass. We have here to do with a typical example of how the complementary phenomena appear under mutually exclusive experimental arrangements (cf. p. 210) and are just faced with the impossibility, in the analysis of quantum effects, of drawing any sharp separation between an independent behaviour of atomic objects and their interaction with the measuring instruments which serve to define the conditions under which the phenomena occur.

Our talks about the attitude to be taken in face of a novel situation as regards analysis and synthesis of experience touched naturally on many aspects of philosophical thinking, but, in spite of all divergencies of approach and opinion, a most humorous spirit animated the discussions. On his side, Einstein mockingly asked us whether we could really believe that the providential authorities took recourse to dice-playing (". . . *ob der liebe Gott würfelt*"), to which I replied by pointing at the great caution, already called for by ancient thinkers, in ascribing attributes to Providence in every-day language. I remember also how at the peak of the discussion Ehrenfest, in his affectionate manner of teasing his friends, jokingly hinted at the apparent similarity between Einstein's attitude and that of the opponents of relativity theory; but instantly Ehrenfest added that he would not be able to find relief in his own mind before concord with Einstein was reached.

Einstein's concern and criticism provided a most valuable incentive for us all to reexamine the various aspects of the situation as regards the description of atomic phenomena. To me it was a welcome stimulus to clarify still further the rôle played by the measuring instruments and, in order to bring into strong relief the mutually exclusive character of the experimental conditions under which the complementary phenomena appear, I tried in those days to sketch various apparatus in a pseudo-realistic style of which the following figures are examples. Thus, for the study of an interference phenomenon of the type

indicated in Fig. 3, it suggests itself to use an experimental arrangement like that shown in Fig. 4, where the solid parts of the apparatus, serving as diaphragms and plate-holder, are

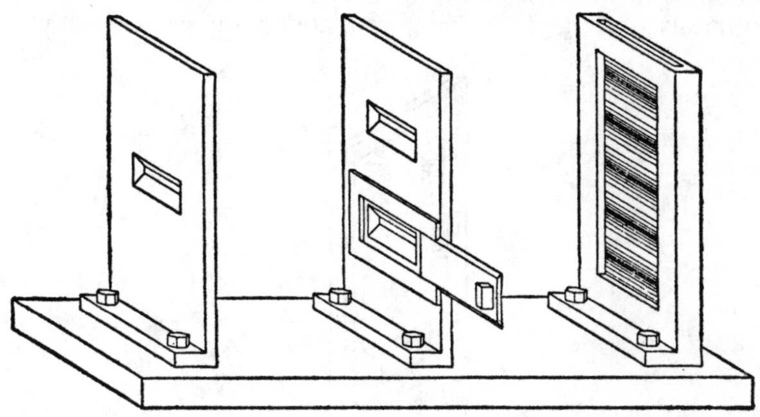

Fig. 4

firmly bolted to a common support. In such an arrangement, where the knowledge of the relative positions of the diaphragms and the photographic plate is secured by a rigid connection, it is obviously impossible to control the momentum exchanged between the particle and the separate parts of the apparatus. The only way in which, in such an arrangement, we could insure that the particle passed through one of the slits in the second diaphragm is to cover the other slit by a lid, as indicated in the figure; but if the slit is covered, there is of course no question of any interference phenomenon, and on the plate we shall simply observe a continuous distribution as in the case of the single fixed diaphragm in Fig. 1.

In the study of phenomena in the account of which we are dealing with detailed momentum balance, certain parts of the whole device must naturally be given the freedom to move independently of others. Such an apparatus is sketched in Fig. 5, where a diaphragm with a slit is suspended by weak springs from a solid yoke bolted to the support on which also other immobile parts of the arrangement are to be fastened. The scale on the diaphragm together with the pointer on the bearings of

the yoke refer to such study of the motion of the diaphragm, as may be required for an estimate of the momentum transferred to it, permitting one to draw conclusions as to the deflection suffered by the particle in passing through the slit. Since, however, any reading of the scale, in whatever way performed, will

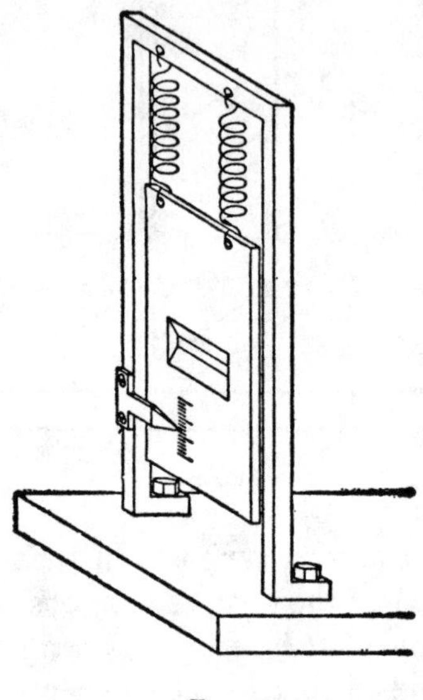

FIG. 5

involve an uncontrollable change in the momentum of the diaphragm, there will always be, in conformity with the indeterminacy principle, a reciprocal relationship between our knowledge of the position of the slit and the accuracy of the momentum control.

In the same semi-serious style, Fig. 6 represents a part of an arrangement suited for the study of phenomena which, in contrast to those just discussed, involve time co-ordination explicitly. It consists of a shutter rigidly connected with a robust clock resting on the support which carries a diaphragm and on which further parts of similar character, regulated by the same clock-work or by other clocks standardized relatively to it, are also to be fixed. The special aim of the figure is to underline that a clock is a piece of machinery, the working of which can completely be accounted for by ordinary mechanics and will be

affected neither by reading of the position of its hands nor by the interaction between its accessories and an atomic particle. In securing the opening of the hole at a definite moment, an apparatus of this type might, for instance, be used for an accurate measurement of the time an electron or a photon takes to come from the diaphragm to some other place, but evidently, it would leave no possibility of controlling the energy transfer to

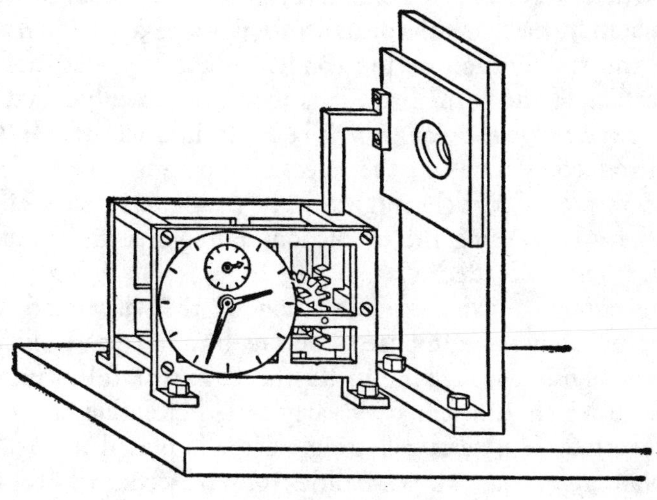

FIG. 6

the shutter with the aim of drawing conclusions as to the energy of the particle which has passed through the diaphragm. If we are interested in such conclusions we must, of course, use an arrangement where the shutter devices can no longer serve as accurate clocks, but where the knowledge of the moment when the hole in the diaphragm is open involves a latitude connected with the accuracy of the energy measurement by the general relation (4).

The contemplation of such more or less practical arrangements and their more or less fictitious use proved most instructive in directing attention to essential features of the problems. The main point here is the distinction between the *objects* under investigation and the *measuring instruments* which serve to define, in classical terms, the conditions under which the

phenomena appear. Incidentally, we may remark that, for the illustration of the preceding considerations, it is not relevant that experiments involving an accurate control of the momentum or energy transfer from atomic particles to heavy bodies like diaphragms and shutters would be very difficult to perform, if practicable at all. It is only decisive that, in contrast to the proper measuring instruments, these bodies together with the particles would in such a case constitute the system to which the quantum-mechanical formalism has to be applied. As regards the specification of the conditions for any well-defined application of the formalism, it is moreover essential that the *whole experimental arrangement* be taken into account. In fact, the introduction of any further piece of apparatus, like a mirror, in the way of a particle might imply new interference effects essentially influencing the predictions as regards the results to be eventually recorded.

The extent to which renunciation of the visualization of atomic phenomena is imposed upon us by the impossibility of their subdivision is strikingly illustrated by the following example to which Einstein very early called attention and often has reverted. If a semi-reflecting mirror is placed in the way of a photon, leaving two possibilities for its direction of propagation, the photon may either be recorded on one, and only one, of two photographic plates situated at great distances in the two directions in question, or else we may, by replacing the plates by mirrors, observe effects exhibiting an interference between the two reflected wave-trains. In any attempt of a pictorial representation of the behaviour of the photon we would, thus, meet with the difficulty: to be obliged to say, on the one hand, that the photon always chooses *one* of the two ways and, on the other hand, that it behaves as if it had passed *both* ways.

It is just arguments of this kind which recall the impossibility of subdividing quantum phenomena and reveal the ambiguity in ascribing customary physical attributes to atomic objects. In particular, it must be realized that—besides in the account of the placing and timing of the instruments forming the experimental arrangement—all unambiguous use of space-time concepts in the description of atomic phenomena is confined to the

recording of observations which refer to marks on a photographic plate or to similar practically irreversible amplification effects like the building of a water drop around an ion in a cloud-chamber. Although, of course, the existence of the quantum of action is ultimately responsible for the properties of the materials of which the measuring instruments are built and on which the functioning of the recording devices depends, this circumstance is not relevant for the problems of the adequacy and completeness of the quantum-mechanical description in its aspects here discussed.

These problems were instructively commented upon from different sides at the Solvay meeting,[10] in the same session where Einstein raised his general objections. On that occasion an interesting discussion arose also about how to speak of the appearance of phenomena for which only predictions of statistical character can be made. The question was whether, as to the occurrence of individual effects, we should adopt a terminology proposed by Dirac, that we were concerned with a choice on the part of "nature" or, as suggested by Heisenberg, we should say that we have to do with a choice on the part of the "observer" constructing the measuring instruments and reading their recording. Any such terminology would, however, appear dubious since, on the one hand, it is hardly reasonable to endow nature with volition in the ordinary sense, while, on the other hand, it is certainly not possible for the observer to influence the events which may appear under the conditions he has arranged. To my mind, there is no other alternative than to admit that, in this field of experience, we are dealing with individual phenomena and that our possibilities of handling the measuring instruments allow us only to make a choice between the different complementary types of phenomena we want to study.

The epistemological problems touched upon here were more explicitly dealt with in my contribution to the issue of *Naturwissenschaften* in celebration of Planck's 70th birthday in 1929. In this article, a comparison was also made between the lesson derived from the discovery of the universal quantum of action

[10] *Ibid.*, 248ff.

and the development which has followed the discovery of the finite velocity of light and which, through Einstein's pioneer work, has so greatly clarified basic principles of natural philosophy. In relativity theory, the emphasis on the dependence of all phenomena on the reference frame opened quite new ways of tracing general physical laws of unparalleled scope. In quantum theory, it was argued, the logical comprehension of hitherto unsuspected fundamental regularities governing atomic phenomena has demanded the recognition that no sharp separation can be made between an independent behaviour of the objects and their interaction with the measuring instruments which define the reference frame.

In this respect, quantum theory presents us with a novel situation in physical science, but attention was called to the very close analogy with the situation as regards analysis and synthesis of experience, which we meet in many other fields of human knowledge and interest. As is well known, many of the difficulties in psychology originate in the different placing of the separation lines between object and subject in the analysis of various aspects of psychical experience. Actually, words like "thoughts" and "sentiments," equally indispensable to illustrate the variety and scope of conscious life, are used in a similar complementary way as are space-time co-ordination and dynamical conservation laws in atomic physics. A precise formulation of such analogies involves, of course, intricacies of terminology, and the writer's position is perhaps best indicated in a passage in the article, hinting at the mutually exclusive relationship which will always exist between the practical use of any word and attempts at its strict definition. The principal aim, however, of these considerations, which were not least inspired by the hope of influencing Einstein's attitude, was to point to perspectives of bringing general epistemological problems into relief by means of a lesson derived from the study of new, but fundamentally simple physical experience.

At the next meeting with Einstein at the Solvay Conference in 1930, our discussions took quite a dramatic turn. As an objection to the view that a control of the interchange of momen-

tum and energy between the objects and the measuring instruments was excluded if these instruments should serve their purpose of defining the space-time frame of the phenomena, Einstein brought forward the argument that such control should be possible when the exigencies of relativity theory were taken into consideration. In particular, the general relationship between energy and mass, expressed in Einstein's famous formula

$$E = mc^2 \qquad (5)$$

should allow, by means of simple weighing, to measure the total energy of any system and, thus, in principle to control the energy transferred to it when it interacts with an atomic object.

As an arrangement suited for such purpose, Einstein proposed the device indicated in Fig. 7, consisting of a box with

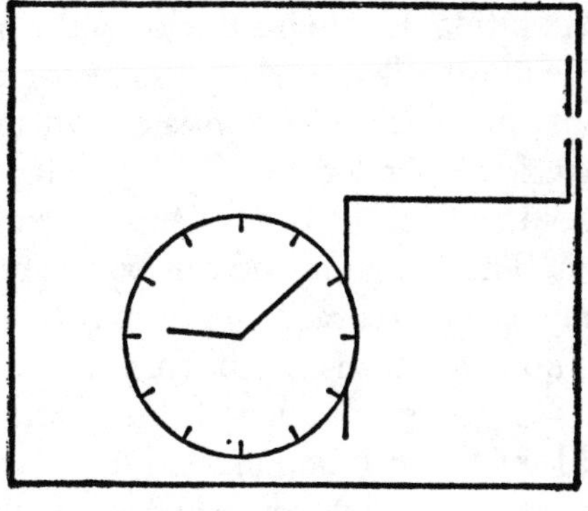

FIG. 7

a hole in its side, which could be opened or closed by a shutter moved by means of a clock-work within the box. If, in the beginning, the box contained a certain amount of radiation and the clock was set to open the shutter for a very short interval at a chosen time, it could be achieved that a single photon was released through the hole at a moment known with as great accuracy as desired. Moreover, it would apparently also be possible, by weighing the whole box before and after this event, to measure the energy of the photon with any accuracy wanted,

in definite contradiction to the reciprocal indeterminacy of time and energy quantities in quantum mechanics.

This argument amounted to a serious challenge and gave rise to a thorough examination of the whole problem. At the outcome of the discussion, to which Einstein himself contributed effectively, it became clear, however, that this argument could not be upheld. In fact, in the consideration of the problem, it was found necessary to look closer into the consequences of the identification of inertial and gravitational mass implied in the application of relation (5). Especially, it was essential to take into account the relationship between the rate of a clock and its position in a gravitational field—well known from the red-shift of the lines in the sun's spectrum—following from Einstein's principle of equivalence between gravity effects and the phenomena observed in accelerated reference frames.

Our discussion concentrated on the possible application of an apparatus incorporating Einstein's device and drawn in Fig. 8 in the same pseudo-realistic style as some of the preceding figures. The box, of which a section is shown in order to exhibit its interior, is suspended in a spring-balance and is furnished with a pointer to read its position on a scale fixed to the balance support. The weighing of the box may thus be performed with any given accuracy Δm by adjusting the balance to its zero position by means of suitable loads. The essential point is now that any determination of this position with a given accuracy Δq will involve a minimum latitude Δp in the control of the momentum of the box connected with Δq by the relation (3). This latitude must obviously again be smaller than the total impulse which, during the whole interval T of the balancing procedure, can be given by the gravitational field to a body with a mass Δm, or

$$\Delta p \approx \frac{h}{\Delta q} < T \cdot g \cdot \Delta m, \qquad (6)$$

where g is the gravity constant. The greater the accuracy of the reading q of the pointer, the longer must, consequently, be the balancing interval T, if a given accuracy Δm of the weighing of the box with its content shall be obtained.

Now, according to general relativity theory, a clock, when displaced in the direction of the gravitational force by an amount of Δq, will change its rate in such a way that its reading

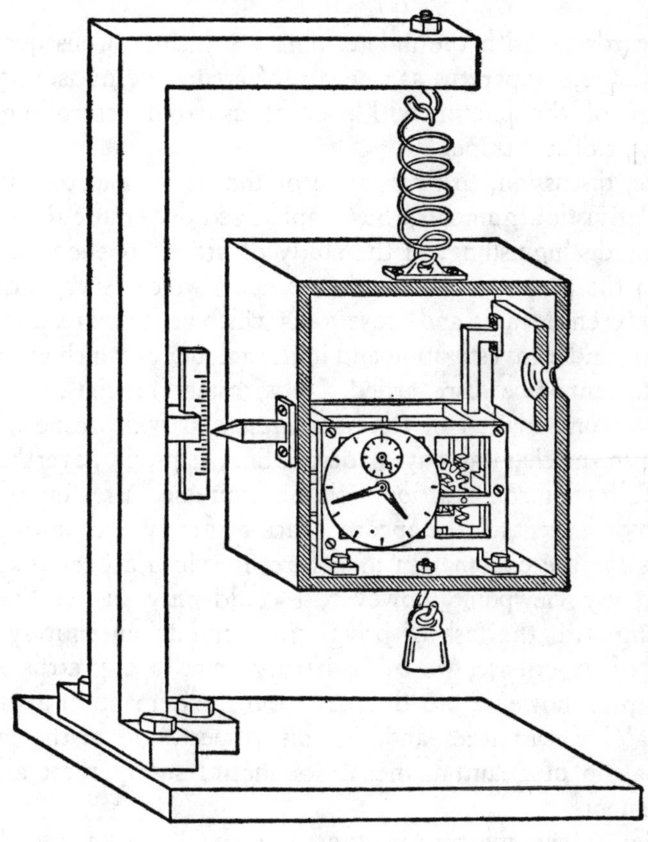

FIG. 8

in the course of a time interval T will differ by an amount ΔT given by the relation

$$\frac{\Delta T}{T} = \frac{1}{c^2} g\Delta q. \qquad (7)$$

By comparing (6) and (7) we see, therefore, that after the weighing procedure there will in our knowledge of the adjustment of the clock be a latitude

$$\Delta T > \frac{h}{c^2 \Delta m}.$$

Together with the formula (5), this relation again leads to

$$\Delta T \cdot \Delta E > h,$$

in accordance with the indeterminacy principle. Consequently, a use of the apparatus as a means of accurately measuring the energy of the photon will prevent us from controlling the moment of its escape.

The discussion, so illustrative of the power and consistency of relativistic arguments, thus emphasized once more the necessity of distinguishing, in the study of atomic phenomena, between the proper measuring instruments which serve to define the reference frame and those parts which are to be regarded as objects under investigation and in the account of which quantum effects cannot be disregarded. Notwithstanding the most suggestive confirmation of the soundness and wide scope of the quantum-mechanical way of description, Einstein nevertheless, in a following conversation with me, expressed a feeling of disquietude as regards the apparent lack of firmly laid down principles for the explanation of nature, in which all could agree. From my viewpoint, however, I could only answer that, in dealing with the task of bringing order into an entirely new field of experience, we could hardly trust in any accustomed principles, however broad, apart from the demand of avoiding logical inconsistencies and, in this respect, the mathematical formalism of quantum mechanics should surely meet all requirements.

The Solvay meeting in 1930 was the last occasion where, in common discussions with Einstein, we could benefit from the stimulating and mediating influence of Ehrenfest, but shortly before his deeply deplored death in 1933 he told me that Einstein was far from satisfied and with his usual acuteness had discerned new aspects of the situation which strengthened his critical attitude. In fact, by further examining the possibilities for the application of a balance arrangement, Einstein had perceived alternative procedures which, even if they did not allow the use he originally intended, might seem to enhance

the paradoxes beyond the possibilities of logical solution. Thus, Einstein had pointed out that, after a preliminary weighing of the box with the clock and the subsequent escape of the photon, one was still left with the choice of either repeating the weighing or opening the box and comparing the reading of the clock with the standard time scale. Consequently, we are at this stage still free to choose whether we want to draw conclusions either about the energy of the photon or about the moment when it left the box. Without in any way interfering with the photon between its escape and its later interaction with other suitable measuring instruments, we are, thus, able to make accurate predictions pertaining *either* to the moment of its arrival *or* to the amount of energy liberated by its absorption. Since, however, according to the quantum-mechanical formalism, the specification of the state of an isolated particle cannot involve both a well-defined connection with the time scale and an accurate fixation of the energy, it might thus appear as if this formalism did not offer the means of an adequate description.

Once more Einstein's searching spirit had elicited a peculiar aspect of the situation in quantum theory, which in a most striking manner illustrated how far we have here transcended customary explanation of natural phenomena. Still, I could not agree with the trend of his remarks as reported by Ehrenfest. In my opinion, there could be no other way to deem a logically consistent mathematical formalism as inadequate than by demonstrating the departure of its consequences from experience or by proving that its predictions did not exhaust the possibilities of observation, and Einstein's argumentation could be directed to neither of these ends. In fact, we must realize that in the problem in question we are not dealing with a *single* specified experimental arrangement, but are referring to *two* different, mutually exclusive arrangements. In the one, the balance together with another piece of apparatus like a spectrometer is used for the study of the energy transfer by a photon; in the other, a shutter regulated by a standardized clock together with another apparatus of similar kind, accurately timed relatively to the clock, is used for the study of the time of propagation of a photon over a given distance. In both these cases, as also as-

sumed by Einstein, the observable effects are expected to be in complete conformity with the predictions of the theory.

The problem again emphasizes the necessity of considering the *whole* experimental arrangement, the specification of which is imperative for any well-defined application of the quantum-mechanical formalism. Incidentally, it may be added that paradoxes of the kind contemplated by Einstein are encountered also in such simple arrangements as sketched in Fig. 5. In fact, after a preliminary measurement of the momentum of the diaphragm, we are in principle offered the choice, when an electron or photon has passed through the slit, either to repeat the momentum measurement or to control the position of the diaphragm and, thus, to make predictions pertaining to alternative subsequent observations. It may also be added that it obviously can make no difference as regards observable effects obtainable by a definite experimental arrangement, whether our plans of constructing or handling the instruments are fixed beforehand or whether we prefer to postpone the completion of our planning until a later moment when the particle is already on its way from one instrument to another.

In the quantum-mechanical description our freedom of constructing and handling the experimental arrangement finds its proper expression in the possibility of choosing the classically defined parameters entering in any proper application of the formalism. Indeed, in all such respects quantum mechanics exhibits a correspondence with the state of affairs familiar from classical physics, which is as close as possible when considering the individuality inherent in the quantum phenomena. Just in helping to bring out this point so clearly, Einstein's concern had therefore again been a most welcome incitement to explore the essential aspects of the situation.

The next Solvay meeting in 1933 was devoted to the problems of the structure and properties of atomic nuclei, in which field such great advances were made just in that period due to the experimental discoveries as well as to new fruitful applications of quantum mechanics. It need in this connection hardly be recalled that just the evidence obtained by the study of arti-

ficial nuclear transformations gave a most direct test of Einstein's fundamental law regarding the equivalence of mass and energy, which was to prove an evermore important guide for researches in nuclear physics. It may also be mentioned how Einstein's intuitive recognition of the intimate relationship between the law of radioactive transformations and the probability rules governing individual radiation effects (cf. p. 205) was confirmed by the quantum-mechanical explanation of spontaneous nuclear disintegrations. In fact, we are here dealing with a typical example of the statistical mode of description, and the complementary relationship between energy-momentum conservation and time-space co-ordination is most strikingly exhibited in the well-known paradox of particle penetration through potential barriers.

Einstein himself did not attend this meeting, which took place at a time darkened by the tragic developments in the political world which were to influence his fate so deeply and add so greatly to his burdens in the service of humanity. A few months earlier, on a visit to Princeton where Einstein was then guest of the newly founded Institute for Advanced Study to which he soon after became permanently attached, I had, however, opportunity to talk with him again about the epistemological aspects of atomic physics, but the difference between our ways of approach and expression still presented obstacles to mutual understanding. While, so far, relatively few persons had taken part in the discussions reported in this article, Einstein's critical attitude towards the views on quantum theory adhered to by many physicists was soon after brought to public attention through a paper[11] with the title "Can Quantum-Mechanical Description of Physical Reality Be Considered Complete?," published in 1935 by Einstein, Podolsky and Rosen.

The argumentation in this paper is based on a criterion which the authors express in the following sentence: "If, without in any way disturbing a system, we can predict with certainty (i.e., with probability equal to unity) the value of a physical quantity, then there exists an element of physical reality correspond-

[11] A. Einstein, B. Podolsky and N. Rosen, *Phys. Rev.*, 47, 777, (1935).

ing to this physical quantity." By an elegant exposition of the consequences of the quantum-mechanical formalism as regards the representation of a state of a system, consisting of two parts which have been in interaction for a limited time interval, it is next shown that different quantities, the fixation of which cannot be combined in the representation of one of the partial systems, can nevertheless be predicted by measurements pertaining to the other partial system. According to their criterion, the authors therefore conclude that quantum mechanics does not "provide a complete description of the physical reality," and they express their belief that it should be possible to develop a more adequate account of the phenomena.

Due to the lucidity and apparently incontestable character of the argument, the paper of Einstein, Podolsky and Rosen created a stir among physicists and has played a large rôle in general philosophical discussion. Certainly the issue is of a very subtle character and suited to emphasize how far, in quantum theory, we are beyond the reach of pictorial visualization. It will be seen, however, that we are here dealing with problems of just the same kind as those raised by Einstein in previous discussions, and, in an article which appeared a few months later,[12] I tried to show that from the point of view of complementarity the apparent inconsistencies were completely removed. The trend of the argumentation was in substance the same as that exposed in the foregoing pages, but the aim of recalling the way in which the situation was discussed at that time may be an apology for citing certain passages from my article.

Thus, after referring to the conclusions derived by Einstein, Podolsky and Rosen on the basis of their criterion, I wrote:

> Such an argumentation, however, would hardly seem suited to affect the soundness of quantum-mechanical description, which is based on a coherent mathematical formalism covering automatically any procedure of measurement like that indicated. The apparent contradiction in fact discloses only an essential inadequacy of the customary viewpoint of natural philosophy for a rational account of physical phenomena of the type with which we are concerned in quantum mechanics. Indeed the *finite interaction between object and measuring agencies* conditioned

[12] N. Bohr, *Phys. Rev.*, *48*, 696, (1935).

by the very existence of the quantum of action entails—because of the impossibility of controlling the reaction of the object on the measuring instruments, if these are to serve their purpose—the necessity of a final renunciation of the classical ideal of causality and a radical revision of our attitude towards the problem of physical reality. In fact, as we shall see, a criterion of reality like that proposed by the named authors contains—however cautious its formulation may appear—an essential ambiguity when it is applied to the actual problems with which we are here concerned.

As regards the special problem treated by Einstein, Podolsky and Rosen, it was next shown that the consequences of the formalism as regards the representation of the state of a system consisting of two interacting atomic objects correspond to the simple arguments mentioned in the preceding in connection with the discussion of the experimental arrangements suited for the study of complementary phenomena. In fact, although any pair q and p, of conjugate space and momentum variables obeys the rule of non-commutative multiplication expressed by (2), and can thus only be fixed with reciprocal latitudes given by (3), the difference $q_1 - q_2$ between two space-co-ordinates referring to the constituents of the system will commute with the sum $p_1 + p_2$ of the corresponding momentum components, as follows directly from the commutability of q_1 with p_2 and q_2 with p_1. Both $q_1 - q_2$ and $p_1 + p_2$ can, therefore, be accurately fixed in a state of the complex system and, consequently, we can predict the values of either q_1 or p_1 if either q_2 or p_2, respectively, are determined by direct measurements. If, for the two parts of the system, we take a particle and a diaphragm, like that sketched in Fig. 5, we see that the possibilities of specifying the state of the particle by measurements on the diaphragm just correspond to the situation described on p. 220 and further discussed on p. 230, where it was mentioned that, after the particle has passed through the diaphragm, we have in principle the choice of measuring either the position of the diaphragm or its momentum and, in each case, to make predictions as to subsequent observations pertaining to the particle. As repeatedly stressed, the principal point is here that such measurements demand mutually exclusive experimental arrangements.

The argumentation of the article was summarized in the following passage:

From our point of view we now see that the wording of the above-mentioned criterion of physical reality proposed by Einstein, Podolsky, and Rosen contains an ambiguity as regards the meaning of the expression 'without in any way disturbing a system.' Of course there is in a case like that just considered no question of a mechanical disturbance of the system under investigation during the last critical stage of the measuring procedure. But even at this stage there is essentially the question of *an influence on the very conditions which define the possible types of predictions regarding the future behaviour of the system.* Since these conditions constitute an inherent element of the description of any phenomenon to which the term "physical reality" can be properly attached, we see that the argumentation of the mentioned authors does not justify their conclusion that quantum-mechanical description is essentially incomplete. On the contrary, this description, as appears from the preceding discussion, may be characterized as a rational utilization of all possibilities of unambiguous interpretation of measurements, compatible with the finite and uncontrollable interaction between the objects and the measuring instruments in the field of quantum theory. In fact, it is only the mutual exclusion of any two experimental procedures, permitting the unambiguous definition of complementary physical quantities, which provides room for new physical laws, the coexistence of which might at first sight appear irreconcilable with the basic principles of science. It is just this entirely new situation as regards the description of physical phenomena that the notion of *complementarity* aims at characterizing.

Rereading these passages, I am deeply aware of the inefficiency of expression which must have made it very difficult to appreciate the trend of the argumentation aiming to bring out the essential ambiguity involved in a reference to physical attributes of objects when dealing with phenomena where no sharp distinction can be made between the behaviour of the objects themselves and their interaction with the measuring instruments. I hope, however, that the present account of the discussions with Einstein in the foregoing years, which contributed so greatly to make us familiar with the situation in quantum physics, may give a clearer impression of the necessity of a radical revision of basic principles for physical explanation in order to restore logical order in this field of experience.

Einstein's own views at that time are presented in an article "Physics and Reality," published in 1936 in the *Journal of the Franklin Institute.*[13]." Starting from a most illuminating exposition of the gradual development of the fundamental principles in the theories of classical physics and their relation to the problem of physical reality, Einstein here argues that the quantum-mechanical description is to be considered merely as a means of accounting for the average behaviour of a large number of atomic systems and his attitude to the belief that it should offer an exhaustive description of the individual phenomena is expressed in the following words: "To believe this is logically possible without contradiction; but it is so very contrary to my scientific instinct that I cannot forego the search for a more complete conception."

Even if such an attitude might seem well-balanced in itself, it nevertheless implies a rejection of the whole argumentation exposed in the preceding, aiming to show that, in quantum mechanics, we are not dealing with an arbitrary renunciation of a more detailed analysis of atomic phenomena, but with a recognition that such an analysis is *in principle* excluded. The peculiar individuality of the quantum effects presents us, as regards the comprehension of well-defined evidence, with a novel situation unforeseen in classical physics and irreconcilable with conventional ideas suited for our orientation and adjustment to ordinary experience. It is in this respect that quantum theory has called for a renewed revision of the foundation for the unambiguous use of elementary concepts, as a further step in the development which, since the advent of relativity theory, has been so characteristic of modern science.

In the following years, the more philosophical aspects of the situation in atomic physics aroused the interest of ever larger circles and were, in particular, discussed at the Second International Congress for the Unity of Science in Copenhagen in July 1936. In a lecture on this occasion,[14] I tried especially to

[13] A. Einstein, *Journ. Frankl. Inst.*, *221*, 349, (1936).

[14] N. Bohr, *Erkenntnis*, *6*, 293, (1937), and *Philosophy of Science*, *4*, 289, (1937).

stress the analogy in epistemological respects between the limitation imposed on the causal description in atomic physics and situations met with in other fields of knowledge. A principal purpose of such parallels was to call attention to the necessity in many domains of general human interest to face problems of a similar kind as those which had arisen in quantum theory and thereby to give a more familiar background for the apparently extravagant way of expression which physicists have developed to cope with their acute difficulties.

Besides the complementary features conspicuous in psychology and already touched upon (cf. p. 224), examples of such relationships can also be traced in biology, especially as regards the comparison between mechanistic and vitalistic viewpoints. Just with respect to the observational problem, this last question had previously been the subject of an address to the International Congress on Light Therapy held in Copenhagen in 1932,[15] where it was incidentally pointed out that even the psycho-physical parallelism as envisaged by Leibniz and Spinoza has obtained a wider scope through the development of atomic physics, which forces us to an attitude towards the problem of explanation recalling ancient wisdom, that when searching for harmony in life one must never forget that in the drama of existence we are ourselves both actors and spectators.

Utterances of this kind would naturally in many minds evoke the impression of an underlying mysticism foreign to the spirit of science; at the above mentioned Congress in 1936 I therefore tried to clear up such misunderstandings and to explain that the only question was an endeavour to clarify the conditions, in each field of knowledge, for the analysis and synthesis of experience.[14] Yet, I am afraid that I had in this respect only little success in convincing my listeners, for whom the dissent among the physicists themselves was naturally a cause of scepticism as to the necessity of going so far in renouncing customary demands as regards the explanation of natural phenomena. Not least through a new discussion with Einstein in Princeton in 1937, where we did not get beyond a humourous contest con-

[15] IIe Congrès international de la Lumière, Copenhague 1932 (reprinted in *Nature*, *131*, 421 and 457, 1933).

cerning which side Spinoza would have taken if he had lived to see the development of our days, I was strongly reminded of the importance of utmost caution in all questions of terminology and dialectics.

These aspects of the situation were especially discussed at a meeting in Warsaw in 1938, arranged by the International Institute of Intellectual Co-operation of the League of Nations.[16] The preceding years had seen great progress in quantum physics due to a number of fundamental discoveries regarding the constitution and properties of atomic nuclei as well as due to important developments of the mathematical formalism taking the requirements of relativity theory into account. In the last respect, Dirac's ingenious quantum theory of the electron offered a most striking illustration of the power and fertility of the general quantum-mechanical way of description. In the phenomena of creation and annihilation of electron pairs we have in fact to do with new fundamental features of atomicity, which are intimately connected with the non-classical aspects of quantum statistics expressed in the exclusion principle, and which have demanded a still more far-reaching renunciation of explanation in terms of a pictorial representation.

Meanwhile, the discussion of the epistemological problems in atomic physics attracted as much attention as ever and, in commenting on Einstein's views as regards the incompleteness of the quantum-mechanical mode of description, I entered more directly on questions of terminology. In this connection I warned especially against phrases, often found in the physical literature, such as "disturbing of phenomena by observation" or "creating physical attributes to atomic objects by measurements." Such phrases, which may serve to remind of the apparent paradoxes in quantum theory, are at the same time apt to cause confusion, since words like "phenomena" and "observations," just as "attributes" and "measurements," are used in a way hardly compatible with common language and practical definition.

As a more appropriate way of expression I advocated the ap-

[16] *New Theories in Physics* (Paris 1938), 11.

plication of the word *phenomenon* exclusively to refer to the observations obtained under specified circumstances, including an account of the whole experimental arrangement. In such terminology, the observational problem is free of any special intricacy since, in actual experiments, all observations are expressed by unambiguous statements referring, for instance, to the registration of the point at which an electron arrives at a photographic plate. Moreover, speaking in such a way is just suited to emphasize that the appropriate physical interpretation of the symbolic quantum-mechanical formalism amounts only to predictions, of determinate or statistical character, pertaining to individual phenomena appearing under conditions defined by classical physical concepts.

Notwithstanding all differences between the physical problems which have given rise to the development of relativity theory and quantum theory, respectively, a comparison of purely logical aspects of relativistic and complementary argumentation reveals striking similarities as regards the renunciation of the absolute significance of conventional physical attributes of objects. Also, the neglect of the atomic constitution of the measuring instruments themselves, in the account of actual experience, is equally characteristic of the applications of relativity and quantum theory. Thus, the smallness of the quantum of action compared with the actions involved in usual experience, including the arranging and handling of physical apparatus, is as essential in atomic physics as is the enormous number of atoms composing the world in the general theory of relativity which, as often pointed out, demands that dimensions of apparatus for measuring angles can be made small compared with the radius of curvature of space.

In the Warsaw lecture, I commented upon the use of not directly visualizable symbolism in relativity and quantum theory in the following way:

Even the formalisms, which in both theories within their scope offer adequate means of comprehending all conceivable experience, exhibit deep-going analogies. In fact, the astounding simplicity of the generalization of classical physical theories, which are obtained by the use of multidimensional geometry and non-commutative algebra, respectively, rests in both

cases essentially on the introduction of the conventional symbol $\sqrt{-1}$. The abstract character of the formalisms concerned is indeed, on closer examination, as typical of relativity theory as it is of quantum mechanics, and it is in this respect purely a matter of tradition if the former theory is considered as a completion of classical physics rather than as a first fundamental step in the thoroughgoing revision of our conceptual means of comparing observations, which the modern development of physics has forced upon us.

It is, of course, true that in atomic physics we are confronted with a number of unsolved fundamental problems, especially as regards the intimate relationship between the elementary unit of electric charge and the universal quantum of action; but these problems are no more connected with the epistemological points here discussed than is the adequacy of relativistic argumentation with the issue of thus far unsolved problems of cosmology. Both in relativity and in quantum theory we are concerned with new aspects of scientific analysis and synthesis and, in this connection, it is interesting to note that, even in the great epoch of critical philosophy in the former century, there was only question to what extent *a priori* arguments could be given for the adequacy of space-time co-ordination and causal connection of experience, but never question of rational generalizations or inherent limitations of such categories of human thinking.

Although in more recent years I have had several occasions of meeting Einstein, the continued discussions, from which I always have received new impulses, have so far not led to a common view about the epistemological problems in atomic physics, and our opposing views are perhaps most clearly stated in a recent issue of *Dialectica*,[17] bringing a general discussion of these problems. Realizing, however, the many obstacles for mutual understanding as regards a matter where approach and background must influence everyone's attitude, I have welcomed this opportunity of a broader exposition of the development by which, to my mind, a veritable crisis in physical science has been overcome. The lesson we have hereby received would seem to have brought us a decisive step further in the never-

[17] N. Bohr, *Dialectica*, *1*, 312 (1948).

ending struggle for harmony between content and form, and taught us once again that no content can be grasped without a formal frame and that any form, however useful it has hitherto proved, may be found to be too narrow to comprehend new experience.

Surely, in a situation like this, where it has been difficult to reach mutual understanding not only between philosophers and physicists but even between physicists of different schools, the difficulties have their root not seldom in the preference for a certain use of language suggesting itself from the different lines of approach. In the Institute in Copenhagen, where through those years a number of young physicists from various countries came together for discussions, we used, when in trouble, often to comfort ourselves with jokes, among them the old saying of the two kinds of truth. To the one kind belong statements so simple and clear that the opposite assertion obviously could not be defended. The other kind, the so-called "deep truths," are statements in which the opposite also contains deep truth. Now, the development in a new field will usually pass through stages in which chaos becomes gradually replaced by order; but it is not least in the intermediate stage where deep truth prevails that the work is really exciting and inspires the imagination to search for a firmer hold. For such endeavours of seeking the proper balance between seriousness and humour, Einstein's own personality stands as a great example and, when expressing my belief that through a singularly fruitful co-operation of a whole generation of physicists we are nearing the goal where logical order to a large extent allows us to avoid deep truth, I hope that it will be taken in his spirit and may serve as an apology for several utterances in the preceding pages.

The discussions with Einstein which have formed the theme of this article have extended over many years which have witnessed great progress in the field of atomic physics. Whether our actual meetings have been of short or long duration, they have always left a deep and lasting impression on my mind, and when writing this report I have, so-to-say, been arguing with Einstein all the time even when entering on topics ap-

parently far removed from the special problems under debate at our meetings. As regards the account of the conversations I am, of course, aware that I am relying only on my own memory, just as I am prepared for the possibility that many features of the development of quantum theory, in which Einstein has played so large a part, may appear to himself in a different light. I trust, however, that I have not failed in conveying a proper impression of how much it has meant to me to be able to benefit from the inspiration which we all derive from every contact with Einstein.

NIELS BOHR

UNIVERSITETETS INSTITUT
FOR TEORETISK FYSIK
COPENHAGEN, DENMARK

8

Henry Margenau

EINSTEIN'S CONCEPTION OF REALITY

8

EINSTEIN'S CONCEPTION OF REALITY

1. Introduction

An article which concerns itself with the philosophical views of a living scientist requires justification beyond the desire to honor his work; for such honor would be bestowed more properly by the pursuit and publication of significant research along lines marked out by the scientist himself. This consideration weighs heavily in relation to Einstein, a man who is particularly sensitive to writings about his person.

It is one thing to write a scientific exposition of the theory of relativity, but quite another to leave the realm of factual statement and to enter the wider domain of discourse in which words have a variety of meanings, where what is known is difficult to set apart from what is surmised and where, after all, Einstein's interest has never centered. This paper is not an attempt to *interpret* his views on reality, nor to embody them into a system for the reader's acceptance or rejection. If that were to be done, the originator of these views should be the author of their interpretation.

It is equally far from my intentions to present a criticism of ideas, physical or metaphysical, which inhere in the theory of relativity. The literature attempting this is already wide, too wide for the good of either physics or philosophy. A knowledge of the physical and mathematical structure of relativity theory will here be assumed, and its fundamental validity will never be drawn into question as far as present evidence goes. In fact this theory is now so well corroborated by experience and by assimilation into the whole of modern physics that its denial is almost unthinkable. The physicist is impressed not solely by its far flung empirical verifications, but above all by

the intrinsic beauty of its conception which predisposes the discriminating mind for acceptance even if there were no experimental evidence for the theory at all.

The purpose of the subsequent remarks is simply this: To distill from Einstein's work those elements of method, to draw from his miscellaneous writings those basic conceptions, which combine into a picture of what, to him, must be reality. That philosophers and physicists are interested in this picture, the background of the most creative effort of our time, goes without saying. That it be accurate can be insured, theoretically, by the opportunity available to its hero to point out its defects. The paper is written, therefore, in full expectation of being disavowed or corrected where it is in error. This valuable possibility of later correction has, I understand, inspired the publication of the present and of similar volumes.

Scientists, among them Einstein, have warned philosophers to give attention to their deeds rather than their words. Failure to heed this advice has produced a rather deplorable lack of understanding between philosophy and physics today. Every discoverer of a new physical principle makes an important contribution to philosophy, even though he may not discuss it in philosophic terms. The metaphysical wealth reposing largely untapped in modern physical theory is enormous and challenging to the investigator; it is available for everyone who will acquire the tools needed to explore it. The methodological content of relativity theory, both special and general, has not been exhausted and will here be made the primary source of information. Its author's own remarks on reality, illuminating indeed despite their relative paucity, will be used as corroborating evidence.

It is possible to construe a contradiction between the methodological implications of the theory of relativity and its founder's interpretative comments. Misconceptions have arisen as a result of this, and since they involve an erroneous identification of reality they should at once be exposed. One of the famous consequences of the special theory is the need for non-Newtonian time. According to Newton, time was a unique process of flow, independent of the circumstances of the observer. This empiri-

cal uniqueness was epitomized in Kant's system by a rationalization which attached transcendental necessity to the uniqueness of time, thus lifting it above empirical examination. Relativity shattered this isolation and again made time a matter for experimental inquiry. Indeed it went much farther than that, farther than Newton or anyone had ever gone; it wholly renounced rational preconceptions and made the meaning of time dependent upon one very specific physical process: the propagation of light. There was insistence on a definition of time which could be operationally circumscribed in great detail, a definition that stood the test of pragmatism. If the results of this innovation contradicted the alleged dictates of reason, common reasoning had to be modified: empirical facts forced inquiry into unaccustomed channels. It is hard to ignore the undercurrent of empiricism, and one might be tempted to impute the success of the relativity theory to a philosophic attitude which banishes rational, or mental, elements from the description of nature and replaces them by the solid facts of sensible experience. This is often done.

And yet, in his writings, Einstein frequently states that his position differs from Newton's inasmuch as he takes issue with the thought that time and space are concepts derived from experience. He claims that the distance between theoretical construction and verifiable conclusion in modern physics grows larger as theories take on simpler forms; indeed he regards fundamental principles as "free inventions of the human intellect."[1] Superficial examination senses here a contradiction which only closer analysis can remove. Einstein's position cannot be labelled by any one of the current names of philosophic attitudes; it contains features of rationalism and extreme empiricism, but not in logical isolation.

2. Ontological Beliefs

There is every indication that, to Einstein, reality means *physical* reality. While everywhere considerable respect is

[1] "On the Method of Theoretical Physics," by Albert Einstein (The Clarendon Press, Oxford, 1933; "The Herbert Spencer Lecture delivered at Oxford, 10 June 1933"); reprinted in *The World As I See It*, Covici Friede (1934), 33.

shown for those phases of experience which have not as yet been penetrated by scientific method, one feels, in reading his utterances, that all existence is essentially fathomable by means of the peculiar interplay of experience and analysis which characterizes physics. A certain pathos for the unknown, though often displayed, always intimates the ultimately knowable character of existence, knowable in scientific terms.

Little can be found which is at all relevant to the traditional questions of ontology: whether the real world contains traces of the human observer in a Kantian sense; whether it contains merely sensory qualities or the idealizations called laws of nature as well; whether logical concepts are to be regarded as part of it. In fact, one does not find a definition of reality. For my own part, I do not regard this as a lack, for it is increasingly evident that the best of modern physics avoids the term and operates entirely within the realm of epistemology, or methodology; leaving it for the spectator to construe the meaning of reality in any way he wishes. To some extent this seems to be true for the discoverer of relativity. Nevertheless there is a good deal of consistency in his usage of the word.

It is perfectly clear that Einstein, in common with practically all scientists, assumes the existence of an external world, an objective world, i.e., one that is largely independent of the human observer. To quote:

> The belief in an external world independent of the perceiving subject is the basis of all natural science. Since, however, sense perception only gives information of this external world or of 'physical reality' indirectly, we can only grasp the latter by speculative means. It follows from this that our notions of physical reality can never be final. We must always be ready to change these notions—that is to say, the axiomatic structure of physics —in order to do justice to perceived facts in the most logically perfect way.[2]

On the one hand one has here an identification of physical reality with the external world, on the other an insistence upon the difference between an essence of reality and what it appears

[2] "Clerk Maxwell's Influence on the Evolution of the Idea of Physical Reality," from Einstein, A., *The World As I See It*, 60.

to be. Indeed there is implied a three-fold distinction between an *external world*, the observer's *perception of that external world*, and our *notions* of it; for as we have seen before, the axiomatic structure of physics is not abstracted from sensory experience.

To some of the interesting questions which arise at this point answers seem to be lacking. Having been reared in the Kantian tradition Einstein conceivably espouses a *Ding an sich* which is intrinsically unknowable. More likely, however, he would hold any characterization of reality in terms other than those provided by science as irrelevant and regard the question as to the metaphysical attributes of reality as unimportant. Under those conditions, what is meant by the assertion that there *is* an external world independent of the perceiving subject becomes problematical. Like most scientists, Einstein leaves unanswered the basic metaphysical problem underlying all science, the meaning of externality.

There may be perceived a curious trace of rationalism in the passage last quoted. Sense perception, we are told, gives information about physical reality in a manner called indirect. This innocent word, of course, hides a multitude of epistemological problems upon which the scientist does not care to express himself. But the hint that, because of the indirect nature of sensuous knowledge, recourse is to be taken to speculation, is intensely interesting and reminds us again of that thoroughgoing conviction which separates Einstein, Planck and others who have had much to do with the creation of modern physics, from the more popular schools of current positivism and empiricism. However, to state this conviction very precisely is difficult, as the following quotation shows.

> Behind the tireless efforts of the investigator there lurks a stronger, more mysterious drive: it is existence and reality that one wishes to comprehend. But one shrinks from the use of such words, for one soon gets into difficulties when one has to explain what is really meant by 'reality' and by 'comprehend' in such a general statement.[3]

[3] Address at Columbia University from, *The World As I See It*, 137f.

3. Relation of Theory to Reality

While the exact manner in which theory represents physical reality is difficult to construe, it is quite clear from Einstein's work and writings that he was an opponent of the view according to which theory *copies* reality. On this point he takes sharp issue with Newton, and implicitly with the whole of British empiricism. The central recognition of the theory of relativity is that geometry, regarded by Newton as a set of descriptive propositions flowing from and summarizing physical experience, is a construct of the intellect. Only when this discovery is accepted can the mind feel free to tamper with the time-honored notions of space and time, to survey the range of possibilities available for defining them, and to select that formulation which agrees with observation. Conformation with experience must be achieved, not in the initial stages of theoretical analysis but in its final consequences. "The structure of the system is the work of reason; the empirical contents and their mutual relations must find their representation in the conclusions of the theory."[4]

Just how the contact with reality is to be made is obvious in the physical content of relativity theory, and is also a matter on which Einstein has expressed himself unambiguously. There is something ineffable about the real, something occasionally described as mysterious and awe-inspiring; the property alluded to is no doubt its ultimacy, its spontaneity, its failure to present itself as the perfect and articulate consequence of rational thought. On the other hand mathematics, and especially geometry, have exactly those attributes of internal order, the elements of predictability, which reality seems to lack. How do these incongruous counterparts of our experience get together? "As far as the laws of mathematics refer to reality, they are not certain; and as far as they are certain, they do not refer to reality."[5]

The point is that the two do not of themselves get together,

[4] "On the Method of Theoretical Physics" (1933); in *The World As I See It*, 33.

[5] "Geometry and Experience." An expanded form of an address to the Prussian Academy of Sciences, Berlin, Jan. 27, 1921, quoted from Einstein's *Sidelights of Relativity* (London, 1922).

but have to be brought together forcibly by means of a special postulate. Euclidean geometry is a hypothetical discipline based upon axioms which in themselves claim no relevance to reality. Other axioms generate different geometries. Reality, on the other hand, does not present the investigator with axioms. A physical theory, i.e., an intelligible picture of reality, results when one geometry is postulationally said to correspond to observation. Contact with reality has then been made. Mystic experience of the real is like a vast but formless reservoir of life-giving substance; mathematics alone is a gallery of robots. Select one of them and connect him with the real. If you have chosen the right one, you may witness the spectacle of man-made life; blood will course through the previously empty veins of the artifact and a functioning organism has been created. No one can tell in advance which robot will cause this success to be achieved; the scientist of genius makes the proper selection.

I should like to think that this crude pictorization will not do violence to Einstein's view. It emphasizes a point to which I have attached very great importance, namely that the central elements of any methodology of physics are these: the sensory facts of experience, the constructs generated to explain them, and the rules of correspondence which make possible the fruitful and valid intercommunication between the former two areas. All through "Geometry and Experience" one finds evidence for the need of such rules of correspondence.

In a number of places Einstein expresses his indebtedness to Mach, and it is easy to trace his concern over observability directly to this philosopher. Both reject theoretical concepts which by their nature do not lend themselves to verification. To get around the notion of unobservable absolute space, Mach tries to save the laws of mechanics by substituting for an acceleration with respect to absolute space an acceleration relative to the inertial system moving with the center of mass of all masses in the universe. This same attitude led Einstein to the rejection of the ether and, indeed, of Mach's proposal, for the latter annuls itself when thought through completely. To measure acceleration with reference to a universal inertial frame,

and even to define that frame, requires the concept of action at a distance and this, in turn, presupposes universal simultaneity which is operationally absurd. By this chain of logical reduction does the suggestion of Mach finally destroy itself. This example is nearly symbolic, for it happens that in many other instances the delicacy and the consistency of Einstein's physical reasoning controverts the original Machian stand, and the thoughtful observer sees throughout his work a progressive denial of the attitude that regards theories as inessential, labor saving adornments of reality which, though important for a time, are shed like dry leaves as the organism of science develops, to use Mach's phraseology.

4. The Concept of Objectivity

What makes the theory of relativity extraordinarily important for philosophy is its incisive answer to the problem of objectivity. It is agreed that the formalization which goes as the accepted view of reality must have the quality of being objective, or independent of the observer; it must have as few anthropomorphic traits as possible. One might mean thereby that reality must appear the same to all, appear, that is, in sensory perception. But this can certainly never be assured in view of the intrinsic subjectivity of all our sensory knowledge. Nor is there any use in wondering how reality could be constructed apart from sensory specification, for this would lead to an endless variety of reals. What the world would appear to be if our eyes were sensitive not to the range of optical frequencies but to X-rays, or even how a three-dimensional map of all electric and magnetic fields at any instant might be drawn, are philosophically not very significant questions. Relativity teaches that the meaning of objectivity can not be captured wholly in the external realm of science.

In Newton's physics space and time were objective because they manifested themselves unmistakably in everyone's experience. But this idea of objectivity was completely shattered when several different spaces and times suddenly clamored for acceptance. It then became necessary to distinguish between

the subjective time and space of every observer, and several kinds of formalized or public spaces and times. The latter had certain ideal properties such as being finite, or being isotropic, or constancy of metric, which the subjective counterparts did not possess. However, these ideal properties did not constitute them as objective.

Does objectivity, then, arise from agreement between experience and the predictions of theory? Is *any valid* theory objective? The answer to these questions is doubtless affirmative, but does not give a clue to the problem under consideration, for a theory, to be valid, must *also* be objective; correct prediction of events is not enough. It is thus seen that the criterion of objectivity lies somehow within the very structure of theory itself, that it must reside within some formal property of the ideal scheme which pretends to correspond to reality. And that is where the theory of relativity places it.

Objectivity becomes equivalent to *invariance* of physical laws, not physical phenomena or observations. A falling object may describe a parabola to an observer on a moving train, a straight line to an observer on the ground. These differences in appearance do not matter so long as the law of nature in its general form, i.e., in the form of a differential equation, is the same for both observers. Einstein's concept of objectivity takes every pretense to uniformity out of the sphere of perception and puts it in the basic form of theoretical statements. He rejected Newtonian mechanics because of its failure to satisfy this principle; he discarded the ether for that reason. Having produced the special theory of relativity, the conviction with regard to the ultimate significance of the axiom of invariance kept alive in Einstein, through the stunning series of successes encountered by the special theory, an acute realization of its limits. For the special theory had recognized invariance only with respect to inertial systems and had therefore not pushed objectivity far enough. From this defect the general theory took its origin.

The amazing results of Einstein's interpretation of objectivity have silenced almost completely all philosophical inquiry

into its logical status. On the face of it, it seems satisfactory to impose the demands of invariability upon the most basic tenets of theory, even though this creates variability in the sphere of immediate experience. From the mathematical point of view, however, this procedure fails to be impartial, for it favors differential equations over ordinary equations. The laws of physics, which are to remain invariant, are always differential equations. Their solutions, i.e., ordinary equations, contain constants which vary from one observer to the next. Now what distinguishes differential equations logically from ordinary ones is that they are less committal, and that requirements placed on them have less drastic effects than similar requirements on their solutions. One may put the meaning of objectivity, then, perhaps in this form: It amounts to invariance of that group of theoretical statements which are least specific.

The idea of invariance is the nucleus of the theory of relativity. To the layman, and sometimes to the philosopher, this theory represents quite the contrary, a set of laws which allow for variability from one observer to another. This one-sided conception is linguistically implied by the word relativity which does not characterize the theory as centrally as it should. The true state of affairs can be seen when attention is directed to the aforementioned postulate of objectivity, which requires that the basic laws (the differential equations of highest order used in the description of reality) shall be invariant with respect to certain transformations. From this the variability, or relativity, of detailed observation may be shown to follow as a logical consequence. To give a simple example: the basic laws of electrodynamics involve the speed of light, c. If these laws are to be invariant, c must be constant. But the constancy of c in different inertial systems requires that moving objects contract, that moving clocks be retarded, that there can be no universal simultaneity, and so forth. To achieve *objectivity* of basic description, the theory must confer *relativity* upon the domain of immediate observations. In philosophic discussions, too much emphasis has been placed upon the incidental consequence, doubtless because the spectacular tests of the theory involve this consequence.

5. Simplicity as a Criterion of Reality

Coupled with the hypothesis that our conception of reality must be objective one finds, throughout Einstein's work, the implicit belief that the best description of the world is the simplest. "Our experience . . . justifies us in believing that nature is the realisation of the simplest conceivable mathematical ideas."[6] The criterion of simplicity is frequently used by methodologists of science to distinguish acceptable from unacceptable theories. But it does not often attain complete clarity of statement.

Logically, it is extremely difficult to state the conditions under which a set of axioms may be regarded as simple or even as simpler than another, and this situation is likely to remain until theoretical physics has been penetrated completely by the methods of symbolic logic. Only when the number of independent fundamental axioms involved in a theory can be counted will simplicity become a quantitative concept.

Meanwhile, however, the scientist proceeds to use it intuitively, as a sort of topological measure upon which he relies when two competing theories, equally well verified, present themselves for acceptance. This happened, for example, in the days of Copernicus. The issue of simplicity was raised and it favored the heliocentric theory, although it would have been quite possible to patch up the Ptolemean system by adding deferents and epicycles *ad libitum.* It seems historically correct to say that Copernicus adopted his theory not because he held it to be true but because it was simpler. Similar instances have occurred in the later history of science.

Einstein's use of the principle of simplicity is not merely discriminating, it is constructive. In proposing new theories he employs it as a guide. This is made possible by limiting its meaning to some extent, by restricting it to the form of mathematical equations. For here it is not difficult to agree, for example, that a linear equation is simpler than one of higher order, that a constant is the simplest function, that a four-vector is a simpler construct than a tensor of the second rank, etc. Also,

[6] "On the Method of Theoretical Physics" (1933); in *The World As I See It,* 36.

in the mathematical field the hypothesis of simplicity combines beautifully with the postulate or invariance treated in the preceding section. To quote again, "In the limited nature of the mathematically existent simple fields and the simple equations possible between them, lies the theorist's hope of grasping the real in all its depth."[7]

We see this method at work, first of all, in the special theory with its choice of linear transformation equations;[8] in the explanation of the photoelectric effect where the simplest of all possible mathematical formulations worked so well; in the theory of radiation where mathematical simplicity and necessity led to the introduction of the coefficient of spontaneous emission for which the physical need was at the time not clear; in the formulation of Einstein's cosmological equation of the general theory of relativity; and finally in his discovery that the quantities used by Dirac in his successful theory of the electron were actually the simplest field quantities (spinors) suitable for that purpose.

It may well be that Einstein has carried his reliance on simplicity too far, for it has led him to criticize the recent advances in quantum theory on the basis of that criterion. But we shall defer discussion of this matter to a later section.

Although it is nowhere stated, the idea of simplicity seems to present itself to the man who used it so skillfully as one facet of a larger background of conviction, namely that our conception of reality while changing as time goes on, nevertheless converges toward some goal. The goal may never be reached, but it functions as a limit. And unless I am greatly in error, Einstein regards that goal as simple, and hence a simple theory as the best vehicle on which to approach it.

Considerations of mathematical simplicity play an important rôle in modern theories of cosmology. One of the chief arguments for supposing the universe to be bounded in space was the reminder that the boundary condition for a finite closed surface is very much simpler than the corresponding condition

[7] *Ibid.*, 38.

[8] This is not a good example, for there are reasons other than simplicity why linear equations must here be chosen; but we thought it worth mentioning.

at infinity, needed for a quasi-Euclidean universe. The story of the "cosmological constant" also throws an interesting side light on this issue. The simplest law of gravitation, which related the second order, divergence-free tensor $R_{\mu\nu} - \frac{1}{2} g_{\mu\nu} R$ directly to the matter-energy tensor $T_{\mu\nu}$, was regretfully found to be in error because it failed to account for the finite mean density of matter in the universe. Proceeding under the restraint of the simplicity conviction, Einstein introduced into his law the minimum complication by adding the term ΛG_{ik}, Λ being the cosmological constant. This amounted to a most unwelcome sacrifice. In reading the Appendix for the Second Edition of *The Meaning of Relativity* (1945) one senses the relief which the author of this augmented law of gravitation experienced at the work of Friedmann, who showed that the cosmological constant is, after all, not needed. Yet there looms a final dilemma, as yet unresolved. Friedmann's equations imply an age of the universe of a mere billion years, whereas all other evidence demands a greater span.

6. The Form of Physical Theories

Pre-quantum physics was marred by a peculiar dualism of conception, the irreconcilability of particles with fields, or, in more fundamental terms, the contrast between the discrete and the continuous. The particle notion received its confirmation at the hands of Newton and culminated in the brilliant speculations of Helmholtz. But the very idea of a particle becomes logically unsound unless it is stabilized by an absolute space or an ether to provide an invariable reference for its instantaneous position. The situation is well described by Einstein whom we quote at length.

—Before Clerk Maxwell people conceived of physical reality—in so far as it is supposed to represent events in nature—as material points, whose changes consist exclusively of motions, which are subject to *ordinary* [partial] differential equations. After Maxwell they conceived physical reality as represented by continuous fields, not mechanically explicable, which are subject to partial differential equations. This change in the conception of reality is the most profound and fruitful one that has come to physics since Newton; but it has at the same time to be admitted

that the programme has by no means been completely carried out yet. The successful systems of physics which have been evolved since rather represent compromises between these two schemes, which for that very reason bear a provisional, logically incomplete character, although they may have achieved great advances in certain particulars.

The first of these that calls for mention is Lorentz's theory of electrons, in which the field and the electrical corpuscles appear side by side as elements of equal value for the comprehension of reality. Next come the special and general theories of relativity, which, though based entirely on ideas connected with the field-theory, have so far been unable to avoid the independent introduction of material points and *ordinary* [total] differential equations.[9]

The author's preference is here very clearly stated. Reality is to be regarded as a continuous manifold. This view has inspired Einstein's recent researches, his quest for a unified field-theory on the model of general relativity which would include the laws of the electromagnetic as well as those of the gravitational fields. Simplicity would demand the absence of singularities in such a manifold, but if singularities appeared, and these could be correlated with electrical or material particles, that too would be a major achievement. But the successes of this research have thus far been limited, partly because it has been a lonely road and most physicists are preoccupied with the problems of quantum theory, which promise a better immediate yield.

Nevertheless, the need for unification, perhaps after the fashion of a continuum theory, is greater than would appear from philosophic considerations, or from predilections with regard to the representation of reality. For it must not be overlooked that one faces here also a problem of factual consistency. If the theory of relativity is correct, even only in its special form, the meaning of independent particles is an absurdity because their states cannot be specified in principle. There are further difficulties. Indications are that particles may not be re-

[9] From "Clark Maxwell's Influence on the Evolution of the Idea of Physical Reality," in Einstein's *The World As I See It*, pp. 65f. The only printed translation available uses the words "partial" and "total" differential equations in a manner confusing to me. I have taken the liberty, therefore, of replacing these words in accordance with presumed meanings (but I have been careful to *italicize* my own replacements and to print the original translations in brackets). *H.M.*

garded as points but as structures of finite size. Hence their states cannot be presumed to be given by a finite set of variables, and this condition threatens the validity of all causal description in an embarrassing way. It is clear, therefore, that physical description must either avail itself of the simplifying facilities offered by fields which satisfy partial differential equations and thereby insure sufficient regularity for causal analysis, or else it must entirely abandon the four-dimensional manifold and follow new lines such as those indicated by quantum mechanics. Einstein's view on these possibilities, which we shall now examine, throws further interesting light on his conception of reality.

7. Classical and Quantum-mechanical Description

As an introduction we first remind the reader of the essential differences between what is called *classical* and *quantum mechanical* description of reality. In Newtonian mechanics one conceives of matter as an aggregate of mass points, and the state of each mass point is specified by means of 6 numbers, three coordinates and three momenta. When the state is known at any instant, all future and all past states can be calculated from the laws of motion. Probabilities are introduced into this scheme only by ignorance of the states of all the particles, an ignorance occasioned only by difficulties of measurement, not of conception. According to the classical view, a particle *has* position and velocity in a simple possessive sense, just as a visible object has size, or color; and to say that quantities like position and velocity of a particle are *real* is an obvious statement which seems to require no further scrutiny.

The theory of relativity has greatly sharpened the outlines of this picture and has given it a degree of evidence and naturalness which is almost irresistible. For by showing that time may be regarded as a fourth co-ordinate, and by representing the changing universe as a system of world lines, it made the representation both more symmetrical and esthetically more appealing, and the sense in which particles *have* position, time, velocity has become even more obvious. But to this most perfect picture, as well as to its Newtonian predecessor, one may object on the

grounds that it takes no account of the finite size of particles and their internal structure, and that if it tried to do so it would become hopelessly non-causal.

Quantum mechanics changes all this by introducing a different concept of state. To be sure, it still uses particle language, but requires us no longer to commit ourselves to stating precisely where the particle is, or what is its velocity. It operates in fact with state functions, ψ (x,y,z), which have definite values for *all* positions of the physical system (e.g., particle). They are the best we have in the way of representing reality, but they do not in general permit a prediction of future and past positions, velocities etc. of the system. If we continue to use the word state in the classical sense of the term, these functions do not define a state at all.

Nevertheless they are immensely useful. For by simple and well-known mathematical procedures they allow the calculation of the *mean values* of all the measurements which can possibly be performed on the system. Or, if desired, the *probability* that a certain measurement shall yield a given value can be computed by similar rules. Many writers on quantum mechanics follow classical language to the extent of saying: Quantum mechanics allows the calculation of the probability that a certain *quantity*, such as momentum, shall be found to have a certain value upon measurement. To the physicist and his practical concerns this statement is acceptable as a working rule. To the philosopher, however, it carries a falsification which is most unfortunate because it looks so innocent. In fact, quantum mechanics never refers to *quantities* of systems; it gives no hint whatever that the system possesses quantities in the older sense. All it does is to say, in probability terms, what may be found when a measurement is made. All further implications arise from an injudicious use of classical language in a field foreign to such lingo. We shall see that Einstein's appreciation of quantum mechanics is troubled by this misfortune.

Knowledge of the state function represents the maximum knowledge attainable with regard to a physical system, and the quantum mechanical theory dealing with this optimum representation is called the theory of *pure cases* or *pure states*.

Almost all of useful modern atomic theory belongs to it; on the classical level it corresponds to ordinary dynamics. But classical physics includes also statistical mechanics, where states are known with a lesser measure of certainty. In quantum mechanics, too, there arises the possibility that knowledge exhausts itself in specifying merely the probabilities, w_i, that a system shall have given state functions ψ_i. As far as observation, or measurement is concerned, we are then dealing with a superposition of two kinds of probabilities; for even if we knew for certain that the system was in the state ψ_i, the results of measurements could still be calculated with probability only, and the uncertainty expressed by the w_i would further diffuse this knowledge. A state Φ, corresponding to this imperfect knowledge, and written $\Phi = \sum w_i \psi_i$, is called a mixture. The theory of mixtures has been developed by Von Neumann; its main fields of application are quantum-thermodynamics and the theory of measurement. Since Einstein is much interested in the latter it was necessary to mention it here. We shall briefly return to it.

To summarize these introductory considerations: Quantum mechanics does not define its states in terms of the classical variables of state. It uses functions which, however they may be related to reality, do not imply the *existence* of the old variables of state. These functions are connected with experience (observation, measurement) in a perfectly satisfactory way inasmuch as they allow prediction of probabilities of events, not of quantities or properties of systems. Less certain knowledge is represented in quantum mechanics by the idea of a mixture, which is subject to special treatment and must be distinguished from a pure case.

8. Quantum Theory and Reality

In contemplation of the changes induced by quantum theory in the description of physical states, Einstein, Rosen and Podolski published a paper with the significant title "Can Quantum-Mechanical Description of Physical Reality be Considered Complete?"[10] Aside from giving a negative answer to this ques-

[10] *Physical Review*, vol. 47, 777 (1935).

tion, the article contains a more or less systematic exposition of what the authors mean by reality, limited, to be sure, to the purposes at hand and confirming some of the points already made in this article. Here we read at length:

> Any serious consideration of a physical theory must take into account the distinction between the objective reality, which is independent of any theory, and the physical concepts with which the theory operates. These concepts are intended to correspond with the objective reality, and by means of these concepts we picture this reality to ourselves. . . .
>
> Whatever the meaning assigned to the term *complete,* the following requirement for a complete theory seems to be a necessary one: *every element of the physical reality must have a counterpart in the physical theory.* We shall call this the condition of completeness. The second question is thus easily answered, as soon as we are able to decide what are the elements of the physical reality.
>
> The elements of the physical reality cannot be determined by *a priori* philosophical considerations, but must be found by an appeal to results of experiments and measurements. A comprehensive definition of reality, is, however, unnecessary for our purpose. We shall be satisfied with the following criterion, which we regard as reasonable. *If, without in any way disturbing a system, we can predict with certainty (i.e., with probability equal to unity) the value of a physical quantity, then there exists an element of physical reality corresponding to this physical quantity.* It seems to us that this criterion, while far from exhausting all possible ways of recognizing a physical reality, at least provides us with one such way, whenever the conditions set down in it occur. Regarded not as a necessary, but merely as a sufficient, condition of reality, this criterion is in agreement with classical as well as quantum-mechanical ideas of reality.

Attention is called to the two italicised statements. The first sets up a correspondence between the elements of physical reality and physical theory. Unfortunately, one finds nowhere a concise exposition of the meaning of physical reality apart from physical theory; indeed it is my conviction that reality cannot be defined except by reference to successful physical theory. If this is true, Einstein's proposition becomes tautological, as I suspect it to be. On the other hand there is the possibility of a more favorable interpretation by construing physical reality, as used in that particular sentence, to mean sensory experience alone, or

perhaps the sum total of all possible experience, past, present and future. The disadvantage of this position is its divergence from the usual attitude with regard to reality. For the latter term customarily implies more permanence and uniformity than bare sense experience can convey.

As to the second italicised statement in the quotation above, we find it somewhat too specific for general use, and heavily weighted in favor of the classical definition of state. Reality is conferred upon physical quantities by their predictability. But what if physical quantities were ghostlike things to which no primary interest attaches, as indeed they are in quantum mechanics? What if physical theory seized upon the elements of experience directly, addressed itself at once to outcomes of observations without the interpolation of ideal quantities like position and momentum? To this question we shall return at the end of this article. For the present let it be said that, if the second italicised statement is accepted, the argument of Einstein, Podolski and Rosen does precisely what it sets out to do; it proves that quantum mechanical description of reality is not complete when the discussion is limited to pure cases, and this limitation is made in the paper, even if it is not explicitly stated. Nor is this an insignificant contribution, for the independent-quantity view of reality implicit in the quotation, here criticised as an incongruous relic from earlier days, was actually widely held by physicists and is still in vogue today.

We now examine briefly the logical content of the paper in question and present the detailed conclusions. This need not detain us long, for the steps are simple, clearly stated and the results are definite. Confusion which has subsequently arisen stems largely from the discussions which this paper has stimulated, discussions which did not always confine themselves to the issues clearly marked in that paper. The main content may be summarized in the following example.[11]

Let two physical systems be isolated from each other from the beginning of time to the present. Now, for a finite period, they interact, only to be isolated again forever after. According

[11] The following review is greatly condensed and will probably be somewhat incomprehensible to the reader who has not previously studied reference 10.

to the laws of quantum mechanics it is possible to represent the state function of the two isolated systems after interaction in two equivalent ways by means of biorthogonal expansions. One expansion correlates the probabilities for the outcomes of an observation of type A_1 on system 1 with those for observation of type A_2 on system 2, the other correlates the probabilities for outcomes of observation B_1 on system 1 with those for observation B_2 on system 2. In Einstein's language, A_1, A_2, B_1, B_2 are *quantities,* as they would be in classical physics. If now a measurement of type A_2 is made after isolation upon system 2, and the value measured is A_2, certain inferences can be drawn with regard to the state of system 1. The usual inference is this.

After the measurement, we know exactly what the state of system 2 must be. It is in fact such that further repetition of the measurement would yield the same value. In other words, the measurement has converted the original state function into an *Eigenstate*[12] for that kind of measurement. But associated with this eigenstate of system 2 there is also an eigenstate of system 1 corresponding to the value a_1, the existence of which may thus be concluded as a result of a measurement performed on system 2. This will in general correspond to some other "observable" than that measured on 1.

This inference leads to trouble. For suppose we had chosen to observe, after isolation, the outcome of another type of measurement, say of type B_2, on system 2, and let the measured value be b_2. This would then be correlated with certainty of measuring b_1 on system 1. If now b_1 were different from a_1 we should face the curious fact of a measurement on system 2 influencing the state of system 1, the systems being not at the time interacting. The situation is indeed worse than this, for it can be shown by definite examples that the results a_1 and b_1 not only may be different, they may even be *incompatible* (belong to non-commuting operators). They are of a kind which experience can never provide simultaneously. The following conclusion, within the framework of Einstein's query, is thus inescapable.

In accordance with his criterion, we must in one case regard

[12] For terminology, see any book on quantum mechanics.

a_1 as an element of reality, in the other case b_1. But both belong to the same reality, for system 1 has not been disturbed in the act of measurement. Hence, by slight further elaboration, Einstein, Podolski and Rosen finally remark: "We are thus forced to conclude that the quantum-mechanical description of physical reality given by wave functions (i.e., state functions) is not complete."

To judge the seriousness of this indictment, certain presuppositions of the argument must be examined. We note that the authors operate throughout with simple state functions and hence pure cases, and that they accept the axiom according to which a measurement converts a state into an eigenstate of the measured observable. In my opinion, as stated elsewhere,[13] this view cannot be maintained in spite of its reasonableness and its close alignment with classical physics. Empirically, the effect of a measurement upon the state of a system is extremely complicated, sometimes slight, sometimes—as in the case of absorption of photons—destructive to the identity of the physical system. It is difficult to make a simple theory about the dynamical fate of a system during measurement. Now quantum mechanics may be said to be that discipline which successfully overcomes this difficulty by recasting its entire method of physical description, by taking care of the uncertainties of empirical cognition in its very foundation. If we apply it correctly we must not ask: what happens to a system during measurement; but content ourselves with the information given to us in that measurement. Furthermore, a state function does not fix the outcome of a single observation; why should a single observation determine a state function? It thus appears that Einstein's analysis focuses attention upon an inadvertency frequently exhibited in the discussion of the foundations of quantum mechanics, and one which it was important to expose.

The fate of a system during measurement cannot be satisfactorily described by the formalism employed in the work under discussion. Its analysis requires the use of mixtures. It

[13] "Critical Points of Modern Physical Theory;" *Journal of Philosophy of Science*, vol. 4, 337 (1937).

has indeed been shown by various authors, first by Von Neumann, that the effect of a measurement is to convert a pure case into a mixture. When this is recognized, the logical difficulties disappear.

To round out the picture, let it be emphasized once more that a reformulation of the criterion of reality which regards classical quantities as parts of reality is greatly needed. Quantum theory denies the attachment of quantities to physical systems in a possessive manner. To say that an electron *has* momentum when it is not in an eigenstate of the momentum operator is meaningless, and in that state its momentum is not a significant component of reality. The possibility of "measuring its momentum" is of course always at hand; but properly speaking this is no more than an act of creating experience of a certain kind; this experience *is* a component of reality, as is the fact that, when the measurement is repeated, its result may be different from the first. Such positive experiences are honored by the quantum mechanical way of describing reality, yet the possibility of assigning persistent properties like position, momentum, is not. What Einstein has always correctly stressed is that classical continuity of properties is contradicted by quantum physics.

He has further objections to the new discipline. In reference 1 we read:

> Unfortunately, it [quantum mechanics] compels us to use a continuum the number of whose dimensions is not that ascribed to space by physics hitherto (4) but rises indefinitely with the number of particles constituting the system under consideration. I can not but confess that I attach only a transitory importance to this interpretation. I still believe in the possibility of a model of reality—that is to say, of a theory which represents things themselves and not merely the probability of their occurrence.

Here one might wonder what would become of models with preassigned properties if experience itself threw doubts upon their existence. Would not a model of an electron force us to a commitment as to whether it is a particle or a wave? This question, however, is unanswerable in the face of recent developments.

Einstein regards the Heisenberg uncertainty principle as true and important, but he prefers another kind of description.

> . . . to account for the atomic character of electricity, the field equations need only lead to the following conclusions: A portion of space (three-dimensional) at whose boundaries electrical density disappears everywhere, always contains a total electrical charge whose size is represented by a whole number. In a continuum-theory atomic characteristics would be satisfactorily expressed by integral laws without localization of the formation entity which constitutes the atomic structure.
>
> Not until the atomic structure has been successfully represented in such a manner would I consider the quantum-riddle solved.[14]

In conclusion, one is moved to this reflection. It is everywhere apparent that Einstein, with a keen intuitive sense for what is physically real, has come to recognize an impasse in the time-honored description of the universe. The independent particle concept must be abandoned because of the failure of space or ether to be absolute in the Newtonian sense. Furthermore, the assumption of a three-dimensional infinity of point particles, needed to account for structures of finite size, threatens the simplicity and indeed the feasibility of causal analysis. There are other indications of this kind.

One can at present see two paths leading out of the dilemma. One is to retain the epistemology of classical physics, to describe reality in terms of systems defined by stable properties having significance at all times. This is possible only by means of field theories, in which every point of a four-dimensional continuum becomes the permanent bearer of qualities, such as a metric, or an electromagnetic potential. To make the program practicable the field quantities must be subjected to partial differential equations which allow a large region of the continuum to be controlled by the properties of an infinitesimal portion of it, thus establishing a basis for causality. This is the path favored by Einstein.

The other road passes through less familiar terrain. To travel it, one must leave much of classical physics behind; one must redefine the notion of physical state and accept the more rhapsodic form of reality which it entails. This requires the

[14] "On the Method of Theoretical Physics" (1933); in *The World As I See It*, 40.

abandonment of the attempt to map experience upon a four-dimensional continuum, but leads into a branch of mathematics which has peculiar attractions of its own and is not unmanageable. Present successes in the exploration of the atom definitely recommend this road, which is quantum mechanics. But there are difficulties, already very vexing in the quantum theory of electromagnetic fields, which are beginning to dampen the enthusiasm of its travellers.

Perhaps the two roads will meet beyond our present horizon.

HENRY MARGENAU

SLOANE PHYSICS LABORATORY
YALE UNIVERSITY

9

Philipp Frank

EINSTEIN, MACH, AND LOGICAL POSITIVISM

9

EINSTEIN, MACH, AND LOGICAL POSITIVISM

ROUGHLY speaking, we may distinguish, according to Max Planck, two conflicting conceptions in the philosophy of science: the metaphysical and the positivistic conception. Each of these regards Einstein as its chief advocate and most distinguished witness. If there were a legal case to be decided, it would be possible to produce satisfactory evidence on behalf of either position by quoting Einstein. We do not, however, intend here to stretch the meaning of words like "positivism" and "metaphysics" as is done—a necessary evil—in legal disputes; we intend, rather, to describe Einstein's position in the philosophy of science and to use some arbitrary but precise meanings of "positivism" and "metaphysics" as points of reference for this description. As a matter of fact, Einstein has always felt the need for describing his position with respect to this frame of reference.

If we mean by "positivism" the philosophy of science which was advocated by Ernst Mach, we may describe it by quoting Einstein's essay of 1916, published as an obituary on Mach in the *Physikalische Zeitschrift*, as follows:

> Science is nothing else but the comparing and ordering of our observations according to methods and angles which we learn practically by trial and error. . . . As results of this ordering abstract concepts and the rules of their connection appear. . . . Concepts have meaning only if we can point to objects to which they refer and to the rules by which they are assigned to these objects. . . .
>
> He [Mach] conceived every science as the task of bringing order into the elementary single observations which he described as 'sensations.' This denotation was probably responsible for the fact that this sober and cautious thinker was called a philosophical idealist or solipsist by people who had not studied his work thoroughly.[1]

[1] *Physikalische Zeitschrift*, XVII (1916), 101ff.

We note here that Einstein obviously does not share a very common misinterpretation of Mach's philosophy. The "idealistic" (mis-)interpretation of Mach's philosophy, which Einstein rightly repudiates, has, as a matter of fact, become of historic importance by virtue of the fact that Lenin took it as the point of departure in this book on *Materialism and Empirio-Criticism,* in which he made a spirited attack on Mach's "idealism." As a result of this pronouncement by the highest Soviet political authority, Mach's philosophy of science has become a target of attack in every textbook and in every classroom in the Soviet Union where philosophy is being taught. Because of the close connection, which obviously exists between Einstein's theory of relativity and Mach's philosophy, Lenin feared that Einstein's theories might become a Trojan horse for the infiltration of idealistic currents of thought among Russian scientists and among educated classes in general. This suspicion accounts for the bittersweet reception which Einstein's theories frequently met in the first years of the Soviet regime in Russia.

In 1916 Einstein himself asserted:

> I can say with certainty that the study of Mach and Hume has been directly and indirectly a great help in my work. . . . Mach recognized the weak spots of classical mechanics and was not very far from requiring a general theory of relativity half a century ago [this was written in 1916]. . . . It is not improbable that Mach would have discovered the theory of relativity, if, at the time when his mind was still young and susceptible, the problem of the constancy of the speed of light had been discussed among physicists. . . . Mach's considerations about Newton's bucket experiment show how close to his way of thinking was the search for relativity in a general sense (relativity of acceleration).[3]

It is easy to see which lines of Mach's thought have been particularly helpful to Einstein. The definition of simultaneity in the special theory of relativity is based on Mach's requirement, that every statement in physics has to state relations between observable quantities. The same requirement appeared when Einstein started the theory of gravitation by asking what conditions are responsible for the flattening of a rotating liquid sphere.

[3] *Ibid.,* 103.

In this case Mach decided that the cause of flattening does not have to be the rotation in empty space, but the rotations with respect to some material and therefore observable bodies.

There is no doubt that in both cases Mach's requirement, the "positivistic" requirement, was of great heuristic value to Einstein. When Einstein actually developed his general theory, however, he found that it was an oversimplification to require that every statement of physics must be directly translatable into relations between observable quantities. Actually, in Einstein's general theory of relativity, the general statements of physics are relations between symbols (general co-ordinates, gravitational potentials, etc.) from which conclusions can be drawn, which latter are translatable into statements about observable quantities.

The original "positivistic requirement," as advocated by Mach and his immediate followers, had to be replaced by a more general requirement, which allows for any symbols or words in the formulation of the principles, provided that statements about observable quantities can logically be derived from them. In the original "positivistic conception of science," as advocated by Mach, the concepts of which the principles consisted were very near to direct observation and, therefore, very near to possible physical experiments. The road from these experiments to the principles was short and easy to understand.

In his Herbert Spencer Lecture, delivered in London in 1933, Einstein says:

> The natural philosophers of those days [18th and 19th centuries] were . . . most of them possessed with the idea that the fundamental concepts and postulates of physics were not in the logical sense free inventions of the human mind but could be deduced from experience by 'abstraction'—that is to say by logical means. A clear recognition of the erroneousness of this notion really only came with the general theory of relativity, . . . the fictitious character of the fundamental principles is perfectly evident from the fact that we can point to two essentially different principles, both of which correspond with experience to a large extent. . . .

These bases are Newton's and Einstein's principles of gravitation. "This proves," Einstein continues, "that every attempt at a

logical deduction of the basic concepts and postulates of mechanics from elementary experiences is doomed to failure."[3]

This logical derivation of laws from experience by "abstraction" was certainly not regarded as possible by Mach. But it was a typical belief of nineteenth century physicists as represented, for instance, in J. Tyndall's famous *Fragments of Science*. It is, however, probable that Mach did not believe that there was a wide gap between the concepts which were used in the description of our physical experiments and the concepts used in the formulation of general laws. Einstein, however, emphasized

> . . . the distance in thought between the fundamental concepts and laws on one side and, on the other, the conclusions which have to be brought into relation with our experience grows larger and larger, the simpler the logical structure becomes—that is to say, the smaller the number of logically independent conceptual elements which are found necessary to support the structure.[4]

Einstein's conception of modern science departs from Mach's "positivistic requirement" in the following point: According to Mach and his immediate followers, the fundamental laws of physics should be formulated so that they would contain only concepts which could be defined by direct observations or at least by a short chain of thoughts connected with direct observations. Einstein, however, recognized that this requirement is an oversimplification. In twentieth-century physics the general principles have been formulated by using words or symbols which are connected with observational concepts by long chains of mathematical and logical argument. Einstein, of course, holds in addition that there must be some consequences of these general principles which can be formulated in terms of observational concepts and which can, therefore, be checked by direct observation. This requirement is "positivistic" in the sense that the "truth" of general principles is ultimately based on a check by direct physical experiment and observation. Einstein does not believe—as Mach's contemporaries did—that the basic principles can be checked directly or by means of a short chain of

[3] "On the Methods of Theoretical Physics," in *The World As I See It*, 35f.
[4] *Ibid.*, 34.

conclusions. It had now become clear that the road between principles and observation was a long and arduous one. In the same Herbert Spencer Lecture already quoted, Einstein says that "it is the grand object of all theory to make these irreducible elements as simple and as few in number as possible, without having to renounce the adequate representation of any empirical content whatever."[5]

Einstein requires, accordingly, that two criteria have to be met by a set of basic principles: logical consistency and simplicity, on the one hand, and agreement with the observed facts, on the other—briefly speaking, a logical and an empirical criterion. It is irrelevant by means of what concepts or symbols the principles are formulated. They become, from the purely logical viewpoint, free creations of the human mind. But they also have to meet the empirical criterion; they have to obey the restriction of the free imagination which is necessary to represent the data of experience.

The growing understanding of the general theory of relativity and similar theories accounted for a new development within the views held by Mach's "positivistic" followers. A modification and generalization of Mach's "positivistic requirement" occurred among the scientists who worked in the logic of science after 1920. They tried to adjust their formulations to the methods which had been used successfully in general relativity. Under the name of "logical empiricism" a new school of thought appeared, which can be regarded as an attempt to develop Mach's philosophy of science according to the new developments in theoretical physics. The basic principles of physics were no longer to contain only concepts like "red," "warm," "one spot touching a second spot," etc., which were called "elementary terms" or "observational terms." Instead, the principles themselves were regarded as products of the free human imagination and could contain any "abstract terms" or symbols. But these principles cannot be proved or validated by an appeal to the imagination, to intuition, or even to logical simplicity or beauty. The principles are regarded as "true" only if by logical conclusions statements about observations can be

[5] *Ibid.*, 33f.

derived which can be confirmed by actual experience.

As an example of this line of thought, I quote from Rudolf Carnap's *Foundations of Logic and Mathematics*, which was published in the *Encyclopedia of Unified Science* in 1939:

> Would it be possible to formulate all laws of physics in elementary terms, admitting more abstract terms only as abbreviations? If so, we would have that ideal of a science in sensationalistic form which Goethe in his polemic against Newton, as well as some positivists, seems to have had in mind. But it turns out—this is an empirical fact, not a logical necessity—that it is not possible to arrive in this way at a powerful and efficacious system of laws. To be sure, historically, science started with laws formulated in terms of a low level of abstractness. But for any law of this kind, one nearly always later found some exceptions and thus had to confine it to a narrower realm of validity. Hence we understand that they [the physicists] are inclined to choose the *second method*. This method begins at the top of the system, . . . It consists in taking a few abstract terms as primitive science and a few fundamental laws of great generality as axioms. . . . If, . . . abstract terms are taken as primitive—according to the second method, the one used in scientific physics—then the semantical rules [which connect the abstract terms with observational terms] have no direct relations to the primitive [abstract] terms of the system but refer to terms introduced by long chains of definitions. The calculus is first constructed floating in the air, so to speak; the construction begins at the top and then adds lower and lower levels. Finally, by the semantical rules, the lowest level is anchored at the solid ground of the observable facts. The laws . . . are not directly interpreted, but only the singular sentences.[6]

This conception of logical empiricism seems to be fairly in accordance with the way Einstein anchored his theory of gravitation in the solid grounds of observable facts by deriving phenomena like the redshift of spectral lines, etc. Whether this generalized conception of the relation between theory and facts is a "positivistic conception" is certainly a question of terminology. Some authors in the United States have given to this conception the name "logical positivism," whereas Charles W. Morris recommends the name "logical empiricism," which I have used in this paper. It is simply a matter of a practical

[6] R. Carnap, *Foundations of Logic and Mathematics*, 64f.

scheme in one's history of thought, whether one includes this conception in his chapter on "positivism" or whether one starts a new chapter.

One thing is certain: the classical authors of "positivism," Ernst Mach and even Auguste Comte, understood very well that to say that the laws of science can be expressed in terms of observational concepts is an oversimplification. They hinted quite pointedly at the necessity of a more general conception; but they did not elaborate this hint at length, because at that time theories of the type of Einstein's theory of gravitation did not exist. But, from the strictly logical viewpoint, it is certain that even Newton's mechanics can not be formulated correctly unless we make use of the Einsteinian type of theory, which Carnap calls "starting from the top" or, in other words, unless we start from relations between symbols and draw conclusions which later can then be interpreted in terms of observable facts.

In 1894 Ernst Mach gave a lecture on the topic, "The Principle of Comparison in Physics" (published in his *Popular Scientific Lectures*), in which he distinguishes between "direct description" and "indirect description." The latter type does not describe facts in observational terms but by comparison with a mathematical scheme. Mach uses the example of the wave theory of light, which describes the optical phenomena by starting from a purely symbolic system of axioms which allows a much more practical description of the observed optical phenomena than a "direct" description in terms of optical sensations.

Auguste Comte, the founder of "positivism," was far from assuming that a physical theory should be expressed in observational terms only. He stresses the point, in fact, that no observation is possible without a theory or, at least, no description of observations is possible without previous acceptance of a conceptual scheme. In 1829 Comte wrote in his *Positive Philosophy:*

> If, on the one hand, every positive theory has to be based on observations, it is, on the other hand, also true that our mind needs a theory in order to make observations. If in contemplating the phenomena we did not link them immediately with some principles, it would not only

be impossible to combine the isolated observation and draw any useful conclusions, we would not even be able to remember them, and, for the most part, the facts would not be noticed by our eyes.[7]

Comte was so profoundly convinced of the necessity of having to start from a theory that he regarded man at the beginning of scientific research as being entangled in a vicious circle. He continues:

> Hence, squeezed between the necessity of observing in order to form real theories, and the no less urgent necessity of producing some theories in order to make coherent observations, the human mind had not been able to break this circle if not a natural way out had been opened by the spontaneous growth of theological conceptions.[8]

From these quotations it seems to become clear that even the "classical positivism" of Comte or Mach did not hold the opinion that the laws of nature could be simply "derived" from experience. These men knew very well that there must be a theoretical starting-point, a system of principles constructed by the human imagination in order to compare its consequences with observations. This feeling was so strong that Comte accepted even the theological principles as a starting-point to "get science going."

The principal feature which modern logical empiricism has in common with classical positivism is the requirement that, whatever the basic symbols and the laws of their connection may look like, there must be logical conclusions from these principles which can be confronted with direct experience. A set of principles from which no consequences of this type could be derived were called "meaningless" or "metaphysical" by the logical empiricists, thus giving to the time-honored word "metaphysics" a slightly derogatory meaning.

In order to understand Einstein's attitude towards this conception, we may quote his remarks in the volume on *The Philosophy of Bertrand Russell* in the present series:

> In order that thinking might not degenerate into "metaphysics," or into empty talk, it is only necessary that enough propositions of the con-

[7] Comte, A., *Cours de philosophie positive,* Premiére leçon.

[8] *Ibid.*

ceptual system be firmly enough connected with sensory experience and that the conceptual system, in view of its task of ordering and surveying sense-experience, should show as much unity and parsimony as possible. Beyond that, however, the "system" is (as regards logic) a free play with symbols according to (logical) arbitrarily given rules of the game. . . . The concepts which arise in our thought and in our linguistic expressions are all—when viewed logically—the free creations of thought which can not inductively be gained from sense-experiences.[9]

Einstein speaks here almost completely in the line of the logical empiricists; which is not surprising, inasmuch as logical empiricism is, to a considerable extent, a formulation of the very way in which Einstein envisaged the logical structure of his later theories, e.g., the theory of gravitation. Occasionally even Einstein himself uses the term "metaphysics" in exactly the same sense in which it has been used by the logical empiricists. He speaks of "metaphysics or empty talk," meaning by it any set of principles from which no conclusion—i.e., no statement about possible sense-experience—can be derived. Einstein shares the opinion of logical empiricism that the principles of science, e.g., the theories of physics, contain tools which are invented by human ingenuity in order to enable us to survey our sense-experiences in as simple a way as possible. He says, e.g., about the integer numbers: ". . . the series of integers is obviously an invention of the human mind, a self-created tool which simplifies the ordering of certain sensory experiences."[10]

In this context it is instructive to learn how Einstein himself describes the psychology of his creative work. The great French mathematician, Jacques Hadamard, in 1945 published a work on *The Psychology of Invention in the Mathematical Field*, in which he put some questions to prominent scientists concerning their respective way of procedure in mathematical science. Among these was Einstein, who described his work in a letter to Hadamard. Einstein, in this letter, stresses particularly the

[9] Albert Einstein, in "Remarks on Bertrand Russell's Theory of Knowledge" in Paul A. Schilpp's *The Philosophy of Bertrand Russell* (1944), 289 and, the last part of the quotation: 287.

[10] Einstein, A., in *ibid.*, 287.

way in which he finds the symbolic structure which is at the top of every theory:

> The words or the language, as they are written or spoken, do not seem to play any role in my mechanism of thought. The psychical entities which seem to serve as elements in thought are certain signs and more or less clear images which can be "voluntarily" reproduced and combined.
>
> There is, of course, a certain connection between those elements and relevant logical concepts. It is also clear that the desire to arrive finally at logically connected concepts is the emotional basis of this rather vague play with the above mentioned elements. But taken from the psychological viewpoint, this combinatory play seems to be the essential feature in productive thought.[11]

According to the conception of logical empiricism the relations between symbols which form the "top" of any scientific theory cannot be produced by any logical method. Their origin can only be explained psychologically. This production is the real nucleus of what one may call "creative thinking." This conception is fairly well confirmed by Einstein's statements. According to his own experience, the "combinatory play with symbols is the essential feature of productive thought."

These relations between symbols are, according to logical empiricism, the first part of any scientific theory. But there is a second part, which connects these symbols with the words of our everyday language: the "semantical rules" or, as P. W. Bridgman puts it, the "operational definitions."

Einstein continues the description of the procedure involved in developing new theories: "Conventional words or other signs have to be sought for laboriously only in a secondary stage, when the mentioned associative play is sufficiently established and can be reproduced at will. . . ." Then starts what Einstein calls "the connection with logical construction in words or other signs which can be communicated to others."[12] This means exactly that "semantical rules" have to be added to the symbolic expressions.

[11] Einstein, A., in Jacques Hadamard's *An Essay on the Psychology of Invention in the Mathematical Field* (Princeton, 1945), Appendix II, 142.

[12] *Ibid.*, 143, 142.

Although Einstein seems to be in considerable agreement with the logical empiricists on a great many points, he speaks occasionally of the "fateful 'fear of metaphysics' . . . which has come to be a malady of contemporary empiricistic philosophizing."[13] It is obvious that in this statement, by which "metaphysics" is being encouraged, he does *not* mean the same type of "metaphysics" which he discouraged in the statement, quoted above, where he uses the phrase, "metaphysics and empty talk." If we read this statement in *The Philosophy of Bertrand Russell* carefully, we see clearly that he disagreed with the belief "that all those concepts and propositions which cannot be deduced from the sensory raw material are, on account of their 'metaphysical' character, to be removed from thinking."[14] Einstein calls here "metaphysical" every concept that cannot be deduced from sensory raw material. But this kind of "metaphysical" concepts have certainly not been rejected by the logical empiricists. The admission of these concepts is exactly the point which distinguishes twentieth century logical empiricism from nineteenth century "positivism" of men like Mach. One could, therefore, give good reasons for not regarding logical empiricism as a kind of "positivism." It has often been called "logical positivism" because it rejected principles, from which, according to their structure, no observable facts could be deduced. But in this rejection there was again agreement with Einstein who called such systems "metaphysics and empty talk" exactly as they have been called by the logical empiricists and, for that matter, already by Hume, Mach, and Comte.

There is even the question, whether Mach, if pinned down, would not have agreed that the general conceptions of science are not "derived" from sensory experience, but constructed by the human imagination to derive observable facts logically from these concepts. This becomes probable if we consider Einstein's personal talk with Mach which occurred in 1913. From this conversation[15] it seems plausible that Mach could be pinned

[13] Einstein, in *The Philosophy of Bertrand Russell* (Schilpp, ed.), 289.

[14] *Ibid.*, 287-9.

[15] Frank, Philipp, *Einstein, His Life and Times* (New York, 1947), 104f.

down to admit the usefulness of these constructed concepts in science, although his emphasis and predilection belonged to the direct deduction from sensory material.

Concerning this question the difference between Einstein's approach and that of logical empiricism is only a verbal one. Whereas Einstein would, apparently, not use the term "positivism" for his twentieth century group, they in turn would not use the term "metaphysical" for concepts which are constructed by the human imagination in the process of deriving our sense-perceptions.

The extent of this agreement can best be judged, perhaps, by some of Einstein's statements from his Princeton Lecture of 1921, which do not deal with philosophy but with a presentation of the theory of relativity to physicists. In this lecture occur the following remarks:

> The object of all science, whether natural science or psychology, is to coördinate our experiences and to bring them into a logical system. . . . The only justification for our concepts is that they serve to represent the complex of our experiences; beyond this they have no legitimacy. I am convinced that the philosophers have had a harmful effect upon the progress of scientific thinking in removing certain fundamental concepts from the domain of empiricism, where they are under control, to the intangible heights of the *a priori*. For even if it should appear that the universe of ideas cannot be deduced from experience by logical means, but is, in a sense, a creation of the human mind, without which no science is possible, nevertheless the universe of ideas is just as little independent of the nature of our experiences as clothes are of the form of the human body. This is particularly true of our conceptions of time and space, which physicists have been obliged by the facts to bring down from the Olympus of the *a priori* in order to adjust them and put them in a serviceable condition.[16]

Briefly, I do not see in the question of the origin of the fundamental concepts of science any essential divergence between Einstein and twentieth century logical empiricism. But from the belief that the basic conceptions of science are creations of the human imagination—a belief which is common to both Einstein and the logical empiricists—one could easily draw the conclusion

[16] Einstein, A., *The Meaning of Relativity* (Princeton, 1923), 2f.

that we shall never reach the definitive basic principles of science. One could even be inclined to believe that such a "correct basis" does not at all exist. Conclusions of this kind have been widely drawn by Henri Poincaré, the godfather of logical empiricism, and by a great many of his followers. Einstein, however, in his Herbert Spencer Lecture of 1933, says:

> If it is true that this axiomatic basis of theoretical physics cannot be extracted from experience but must be freely invented, can we ever hope to find the right way? Nay more, has this right way any existence outside our illusions? . . . I answer without hesitation that there is, in my opinion, a right way, and that we are capable of finding it. . . . I am convinced that we can discover by means of purely mathematical constructions the concepts and the laws connecting them with each other, which furnish the key to the understanding of natural phenomena.[17]

By extolling the great heuristic value of mathematics Einstein does not want to suggest that a statement of physics could be proved to be true by this purely logical argument. For he continues: "Experience remains, of course, the sole criterion of the physical utility of a mathematical construction. But the creative principle resides in mathematics."[18] This means that the criterion of truth in physics is experience, but that the method by which the principles are found, or, in other words, produced, is mathematics. Einstein is so convinced of the creative power of mathematics that he says: "In a certain sense . . . I hold it to be true that pure thought can grasp reality, as the ancients dreamed."[19]

This statement could be interpreted as meaning that Einstein agrees with the Platonic belief that a statement of physics could be proved by mathematics. According to Einstein, however, this is true only "in a certain sense." This "certain sense" means "in the sense of heuristic method," but not "in the sense of a criterion of truth."

Nobody would deny the fact that this heuristic method, looking for mathematical simplicity and beauty, has led to successful theories, which have turned out to be "true" in the empiri-

[17] Einstein, A., in *The World As I See It*, 36.
[18] *Ibid.*, 36f.
[19] *Ibid.*, 37.

cal sense. Everybody, notwithstanding his special philosophic creed, who has had any glimpse of theoretical physics, will agree that this fact is a property of our world. It is itself an empirical fact. It is even—as some people like to express themselves—a "hard fact." The emotional reaction to this "hard fact" can, of course, be of various kinds. Einstein calls this fact the basis of cosmic religion. It is a "mystical experience." As "hard facts" cannot be "explained" but only derived from principles which are themselves "inexplicable hard facts," we can say that the most mystical experience is the experience of hard facts. In his paper "On Physical Reality" (1936) Einstein said: "The most incomprehensible thing about the world is that it is comprehensible."[20]

There are, however, scientists whose personal reaction to this fact is different. As an example we may quote P. W. Bridgman. In his *Logic of Modern Physics* (1927), Bridgman writes:

> With regard to the general question of simple laws, there are at least two attitudes; one is that there are probably simple general laws still undiscovered, the other is that nature has a predilection for simple laws. I do not see how there can be any quarrel with the first of these attitudes. Let us examine the second. We have in the first place to notice that "simple" means simple to us, when stated in terms of our concepts. This is in itself sufficient to raise a presumption against this general attitude. It is evident that our thinking must follow those lines imposed by the nature of our thinking mechanism: does it seem likely that all nature accepts these same limitations? If this were the case, our conceptions ought to stand in certain simple and definite relations to nature. Now if our discussion has brought out any one thing, it is that our concepts are not well defined things, but they are hazy and do not fit nature exactly, and many of them fit even approximately only within restricted range. . . . Considering, then, the nature of our conceptual material, it seems to me that the overwhelming presumption is against the laws of nature having any predisposition to simplicity as formulated in terms of our concepts (which is of course all that simplicity means), and the wonder is that there are apparently so many simple laws. There is this observation to be made about all the simple laws of nature that have hitherto been formulated; they apply only over a certain range.

[20] Einstein, A., "On Physical Reality," in *Franklin Institute, Journal*, vol. 221 (1936), 349ff.

. . . It does not seem so very surprising that over a limited domain, in which the most important phenomena are a restricted type, the conduct of nature should follow comparatively simple rules.[21]

Although this interpretation of the simplicity of nature sounds very different from Einstein's, the difference lies not in the assertion of facts or of logical relations but in the emphasis. Einstein stresses the marvelous simplicity and beauty of such symbolic structures as Maxwell's equations of the electromagnetic field or the field equations of the general theory of relativity. This beauty produces, according to Einstein, the feeling of admiration and even of "awe;" whereas Bridgman, in the passage quoted, is simply "wondering" about the existence of so many simple laws. These attitudes do not imply different assertions about the physical world or about the logical system by which this world is scientifically described. The difference is totally within the domain of personal reaction. In his address to the Conference on Science, Philosophy and Religion (1940), Einstein states clearly that the belief in the existence of this regularity in nature belongs to religion.

To this [sphere of religion] there also belongs the faith in the possibility that the regulations valid for the world of existence are rational, that is comprehensible to reason. I cannot conceive of a genuine scientist without that profound faith. The situation may be expressed by an image: science without religion is lame, religion without science is blind.[22]

Although this personal reaction, which, with Einstein, we may call "cosmic religion," is not implied logically by the facts and principles of physics, it may well be that the kind of reaction which is produced in the mind of the physicists is of relevance for his creative power in science. This is obviously Einstein's opinion. He stresses that this "knowledge, this feeling, is at the center of true religiousness. In this sense, and in this sense only, I belong to the ranks of devoutly religious men."

We see from these words that for Einstein this belief in the

[21] Bridgman, P. W., *The Logic of Modern Physics*, (New York, 1927); 2nd ed., (1946), 201, 203.

[22] *Science, Philosophy and Religion*, A Symposium (New York, Harper, 1941), 211.

"possibility of mathematical physics," if we put it perfunctorily, is almost identical with religion. But, on the other hand, Einstein has never agreed with some contemporary philosophical interpretations of physics, according to which relativity and quantum theory are interpreted as having been a decisive step in the reconciliation between science and religion. He has never agreed with men like Jeans or Eddington, who regarded the Heisenberg principle of indeterminacy in quantum theory as an argument for the freedom of the will and for the moral responsibility of man in contrast to the "iron causality of classical physics." Einstein's cosmic religion has been the belief in the possibility of a symbolic system of great beauty and conceptual simplicity from which the observed facts can be logically derived. Whatever his system may look like and whatever symbols may be used does not matter. Newtonian physics bolsters up cosmic religion in this sense just as well as twentieth century physics does.

Eventually the truly interested student of science should follow Einstein's advice, when he says: "If you want to find out anything from the theoretical physicists about the methods they use, . . . don't listen to their words, fix your attention on their deeds."

Philipp Frank

Research Laboratory of Physics
Harvard University

10

Hans Reichenbach

THE PHILOSOPHICAL SIGNIFICANCE OF THE THEORY OF RELATIVITY

10

THE PHILOSOPHICAL SIGNIFICANCE OF THE THEORY OF RELATIVITY

I

THE philosophical significance of the theory of relativity has been the subject of contradictory opinions. Whereas many writers have emphasized the philosophical implications of the theory and have even tried to interpret it as a sort of philosophical system, others have denied the existence of such implications and have voiced the opinion that Einstein's theory is merely a physical matter, of interest only to the mathematical physicist. These critics believe that philosophical views are constructed by other means than the methods of the scientist and are independent of the results of physics.

Now it is true that what has been called the philosophy of relativity represents, to a great extent, the fruit of misunderstandings of the theory rather than of its physical content. Philosophers who regard it as an ultimate wisdom that everything is relative are mistaken when they believe that Einstein's theory supplies evidence for such a sweeping generalization; and their error is even deeper when they transfer such a relativity to the field of ethics, when they claim that Einstein's theory implies a relativism of men's duties and rights. The theory of relativity is restricted to the cognitive field. That moral conceptions vary with the social class and the structure of civilization is a fact which is not derivable from Einstein's theory; the parallelism between the relativity of ethics and that of space and time is nothing more than a superficial analogy, which blurs the essential logical differences between the fields of volition and cognition. It appears understandable that those who were trained in the precision of mathematico-physical

methods wish to divorce physics from such blossoms of philosophizing.

Yet it would be another mistake to believe that Einstein's theory is not a philosophical theory. This discovery of a physicist has radical consequences for the theory of knowledge. It compels us to revise certain traditional conceptions that have played an important part in the history of philosophy, and it offers solutions for certain questions which are as old as the history of philosophy and which could not be answered earlier. Plato's attempt to solve the problems of geometry by a theory of ideas, Kant's attempt to account for the nature of space and time by a "*reine Anschauung*" and by a transcendental philosophy, these represent answers to the very questions to which Einstein's theory has given a different answer at a later time. If Plato's and Kant's doctrines are philosophical theories, then Einstein's theory of relativity is a philosophical and not a merely physical matter. And the questions referred to are not of a secondary nature but of primary import for philosophy; that much is evident from the central position they occupy in the systems of Plato and Kant. These systems are untenable if Einstein's answer is put in the place of the answers given to the same questions by their authors; their foundations are shaken when space and time are not the revelations of an insight into a world of ideas, or of a vision grown from pure reason, which a philosophical apriorism claimed to have established. The analysis of knowledge has always been the basic issue of philosophy; and if knowledge in so fundamental a domain as that of space and time is subject to revision, the implications of such criticism will involve the whole of philosophy.

To advocate the philosophical significance of Einstein's theory, however, does not mean to make Einstein a philosopher; or, at least, it does not mean that Einstein is a philosopher of primary intent. Einstein's primary objectives were all in the realm of physics. But he saw that certain physical problems could not be solved unless the solutions were preceded by a logical analysis of the fundamentals of space and time, and he saw that this analysis, in turn, presupposed a philosophic readjustment of certain familiar conceptions of knowledge. The

physicist who wanted to understand the Michelson experiment had to commit himself to a philosophy for which the meaning of a statement is reducible to its verifiability, that is, he had to adopt the verifiability theory of meaning if he wanted to escape a maze of ambiguous questions and gratuitous complications. It is this positivist, or let me rather say, empiricist commitment which determines the philosophical position of Einstein. It was not necessary for him to elaborate on it to any great extent; he merely had to join a trend of development characterized, within the generation of physicists before him, by such names as Kirchhoff, Hertz, Mach, and to carry through to its ultimate consequences a philosophical evolution documented at earlier stages in such principles as Occam's razor and Leibnitz' identity of indiscernibles.

Einstein has referred to this conception of meaning in various remarks, though he has never felt it necessary to enter into a discussion of its grounds or into an analysis of its philosophical position. The exposition and substantiation of a philosophical theory is nowhere to be found in his writings. In fact, Einstein's philosophy is not so much a philosophical system as a philosophical attitude; apart from occasional remarks, he left it to others to say what philosophy his equations entail and thus remained a philosopher by implication, so to speak. That is both his strength and his weakness; his strength, because it made his physics so conclusive; his weakness, because it left his theory open to misunderstandings and erroneous interpretations.

It seems to be a general law that the making of a new physics precedes a new philosophy of physics. Philosophic analysis is more easily achieved when it is applied to concrete purposes, when it is done within the pursuit of research aimed at an interpretation of observational data. The philosophic results of the procedure are often recognized at a later stage; they are the fruit of reflection about the methods employed in the solution of the concrete problem. But those who make the new physics usually do not have the leisure, or do not regard it as their objective, to expound and elaborate the philosophy implicit in their constructions. Occasionally, in popular presentations, a physicist attempts to explain the logical background of his

theories; thus many a physicist has been misled into believing that philosophy of physics is the same as a popularization of physics. Einstein himself does not belong to this group of writers who do not realize that what they achieve is as much a popularization of philosophy as it is one of physics, and that the philosophy of physics is as technical and intricate as is physics itself. Nevertheless, Einstein is not a philosopher in the technical sense either. It appears to be practically impossible that the man who is looking for new physical laws should also concentrate on the analysis of his method; he will perform this second task only when such analysis is indispensable for the finding of physical results. The division of labor between the physicist and the philosopher seems to be an inescapable consequence of the organization of the human mind.

It is not only a limitation of human capacities which calls for a division of labor between the physicist and the philosopher. The discovery of general relations that lend themselves to empirical verification requires a mentality different from that of the philosopher, whose methods are analytic and critical rather than predictive. The physicist who is looking for new discoveries must not be too critical; in the initial stages he is dependent on guessing, and he will find his way only if he is carried along by a certain faith which serves as a directive for his guesses. When I, on a certain occasion, asked Professor Einstein how he found his theory of relativity, he answered that he found it because he was so strongly convinced of the harmony of the universe. No doubt his theory supplies a most successful demonstration of the usefulness of such a conviction. But a creed is not a philosophy; it carries this name only in the popular interpretation of the term. The philosopher of science is not much interested in the thought processes which lead to scientific discoveries; he looks for a logical analysis of the completed theory, including the relationships establishing its validity. That is, he is not interested in the context of discovery, but in the context of justification. But the critical attitude may make a man incapable of discovery; and, as long as he is successful, the creative physicist may very well prefer his creed to the logic of the analytic philosopher.

The philosopher has no objections to a physicist's beliefs, so long as they are not advanced in the form of a philosophy. He knows that a personal faith is justified as an instrument of finding a physical theory, that it is but a primitive form of guessing, which is eventually replaced by the elaborate theory, and that it is ultimately subject to the same empirical tests as the theory. The philosophy of physics, on the other hand, is not a product of creed but of analysis. It incorporates the physicist's beliefs into the psychology of discovery; it endeavors to clarify the meanings of physical theories, independently of the interpretation by their authors, and is concerned with logical relationships alone.

Seen from this viewpoint it appears amazing to what extent the logical analysis of relativity coincides with the original interpretation by its author, as far as it can be constructed from the scanty remarks in Einstein's publications. In contradistinction to some developments in quantum theory, the logical schema of the theory of relativity corresponds surprisingly with the program which controlled its discovery. His philosophic clarity distinguishes Einstein from many a physicist whose work became the source of a philosophy different from the interpretation given by the author. In the following pages I shall attempt to outline the philosophical results of Einstein's theory, hoping to find a friendly comment by the man who was the first to see all these relations, even though he did not always formulate them explicitly. And the gratitude of the philosopher goes to this great physicist whose work includes more implicit philosophy than is contained in many a philosophical system.

II

The logical basis of the theory of relativity is the discovery that many statements, which were regarded as capable of demonstrable truth or falsity, are mere definitions.

This formulation sounds like the statement of an insignificant technical discovery and does not reveal the far-reaching implications which make up the philosophical significance of the theory. Nonetheless it is a complete formulation of the *logical* part of the theory.

Consider, for instance, the problem of geometry. That the unit of measurement is a matter of definition is a familiar fact; everybody knows that it does not make any difference whether we measure distances in feet or meters or light-years. However, that the comparison of distances is also a matter of definition is known only to the expert of relativity. This result can also be formulated as the definitional character of congruence. That a certain distance is congruent to another distance situated at a different place can never be proved to be true; it can only be maintained in the sense of a definition. More precisely speaking, it can be maintained as true only after a definition of congruence is given; it therefore depends on an original comparison of distances which is a matter of definition. A comparison of distances by means of the transport of solid bodies is but one definition of congruence. Another definition would result if we regarded a rod, once it had been transported to another location, as twice as long, thrice transported as three times as long, and so on. A further illustration refers to time: that the simultaneity of events occurring at distant places is a matter of definition was not known before Einstein based his special theory of relativity on this logical discovery.

The definitions employed for the construction of space and time are of a particular kind: they are co-ordinative definitions. That is, they are given by the co-ordination of a physical object, or process, to some fundamental concept. For instance, the concept "equal length" is defined by reference to a physical object, a solid rod, whose transport lays down equal distances. The concept "simultaneous" is defined by the use of light-rays which move over equal distances. The definitions of the theory of relativity are all of this type; they are co-ordinative definitions.

In the expositions of the theory of relativity the use of different definitions is often illustrated by a reference to different observers. This kind of presentation has led to the erroneous conception that the relativity of space-time measurements is connected with the subjectivity of the observer, that the privacy of the world of sense perception is the origin of the relativity maintained by Einstein. Such Protagorean interpretation of Einstein's relativity is utterly mistaken. The definitional char-

acter of simultaneity, for instance, has nothing to do with the perspective variations resulting for observers located in different frames of reference. That we co-ordinate different definitions of simultaneity to different observers merely serves as a simplification of the presentation of logical relationships. We could as well interchange the co-ordination and let the observer located in the "moving" system employ the time definition of the observer located in the system "at rest," and vice versa; or we could even let both employ the same time definition, for instance that of the system "at rest." Such variations would lead to different transformations; for instance, the last mentioned definition would lead, not to the Lorentz transformation, but to the classical transformation from a system at rest to a moving system. It is convenient to identify one definitional system with one observer; to speak of different observers is merely a mode of speech expressing the plurality of definitional systems. In a logical exposition of the theory of relativity the observer can be completely eliminated.

Definitions are arbitrary; and it is a consequence of the definitional character of fundamental concepts that with the change of the definitions various descriptional systems arise. But these systems are equivalent to each other, and it is possible to go from each system to another one by a suitable transformation. Thus the definitional character of fundamental concepts leads to a plurality of equivalent descriptions. A familiar illustration is given by the various descriptions of motion resulting when the system regarded as being at rest is varied. Another illustration is presented by the various geometries resulting, for the same physical space, through changes in the definition of congruence. All these descriptions represent different languages saying the same thing; equivalent descriptions, therefore, express the same physical content. The theory of equivalent descriptions is also applicable to other fields of physics; but the domain of space and time has become the model case of this theory.

The word "relativity" should be interpreted as meaning "relative to a certain definitional system." That relativity implies plurality follows because the variation of definitions leads

to the plurality of equivalent descriptions. But we see that the plurality implied is not a plurality of different views, or of systems of contradictory content; it is merely a plurality of equivalent languages and thus of forms of expression which do not contradict each other but have the same content. Relativity does not mean an abandonment of truth; it only means that truth can be formulated in various ways.

I should like to make this point quite clear. The two statements "the room is 21 feet long" and "the room is 7 yards long" are quivalent descriptions; they state the same fact. That the simple truth they express can be formulated in these two ways does not eliminate the concept of truth; it merely illustrates the fact that the number characterizing a length is relative to the unit of measurement. All relativities of Einstein's theory are of this type. For instance, the Lorentz transformation connects different descriptions of space-time relations which are equivalent in the same sense as the statements about a length of 21 feet and a length of 7 yards.

Some confusion has arisen from considerations referring to the property of simplicity. One descriptional system can be simpler than another; but that fact does not make it "truer" than the other. The decimal system is simpler than the yard-foot-inch system; but an architect's plan drawn in feet and inches is as true a description of a house as a plan drawn in the decimal system. A simplicity of this kind, for which I have used the name of *descriptive simplicity*, is not a criterion of truth. Only within the frame of inductive considerations can simplicity be a criterion of truth; for instance, the simplest curve between observational data plotted in a diagram is regarded as "truer," i.e., more probable, than other connecting curves. This *inductive simplicity*, however, refers to non-equivalent descriptions and does not play a part in the theory of relativity, in which only equivalent descriptions are compared. The simplicity of descriptions used in Einstein's theory is therefore always a descriptive simplicity. For instance, the fact that non-Euclidean geometry often supplies a simpler description of physical space than does Euclidean geometry does not make the non-Euclidean description "truer."

Another confusion must be ascribed to the theory of conventionalism, which goes back to Poincaré. According to this theory, geometry is a matter of convention, and no empirical meaning can be assigned to a statement about the geometry of physical space. Now it is true that physical space can be described by both a Euclidean and a non-Euclidean geometry; but it is an erroneous interpretation of this relativity of geometry to call a statement about the geometrical structure of physical space meaningless. The choice of a geometry is arbitrary only so long as no definition of congruence is specified. Once this definition is set up, it becomes an empirical question *which* geometry holds for a physical space. For instance, it is an empirical fact that, when we use solid bodies for the definition of congruence, our physical space is practically Euclidean within terrestrial dimensions. If, in a different part of the universe, the same definition of congruence were to lead to a non-Euclidean geometry, that part of universal space would have a geometrical structure different from that of our world. It is true that a Euclidean geometry could also be introduced for that part of the universe; but then the definition of congruence would no longer be given by solid bodies.[1] The combination of a statement about a geometry with a statement of the co-ordinative definition of congruence employed is subject to empirical test and thus expresses a property of the physical world. The conventionalist overlooks the fact that only the incomplete statement of a geometry, in which a reference to the definition of congruence is omitted, is arbitrary; if the statement is made complete by the addition of a reference to the definition of congruence, it becomes empirically verifiable and thus has physical content.

Instead of speaking of conventionalism, therefore, we should speak of the relativity of geometry. Geometry is relative in precisely the same sense as other relative concepts. We might call it a convention to say that Chicago is to the left of New York; but we should not forget that this conventional statement can be made objectively true as soon as the point of refer-

[1] Poincaré believed that the definition of a solid body could not be given without reference to a geometry. That this conception is mistaken, is shown in the present author's *Philosophie der Raum-Zeit-Lehre* (Berlin, 1928) §5.

ence is included in the statement. It is not a convention but a physical fact that Chicago is to the left of New York, seen, for instance, from Washington, D.C. The relativity of simple concepts, such as left and right, is well known. That the fundamental concepts of space and time are of the same type is the essence of the theory of relativity.

The relativity of geometry is a consequence of the fact that different geometries can be represented on one another by a one-to-one correspondence. For certain geometrical systems, however, the representation will not be continuous throughout, and there will result singularities in individual points or lines. For instance, a sphere cannot be projected on a plane without a singularity in at least one point; in the usual projections, the North Pole of the sphere corresponds to the infinity of the plane. This peculiarity involves certain limitations for the relativity of geometry. Assume that in one geometrical description, say, by a spherical space, we have a normal causality for all physical occurrences; then a transformation to certain other geometries, including the Euclidean geometry, leads to violations of the principle of causality, to *causal anomalies.* A light signal going from a point A by way of the North Pole to a point B in a finite time will be so represented within a Euclidean interpretation of this space, that it moves from A in one direction towards infinity and returns from the other side towards B, thus passing through an infinite distance in a finite time. Still more complicated causal anomalies result for other transformations.[2] If the principle of normal causality, i.e., a continuous spreading from cause to effect in a finite time, or *action by contact,* is set up as a necessary prerequisite of the description of nature, certain worlds cannot be interpreted by certain geometries. It may well happen that the geometry thus excluded is the Euclidean one; if Einstein's hypothesis of a closed universe is correct, a

[2] Cf. the author's *Philosophie der Raum-Zeit-Lehre* (Berlin, 1928), §12. It has turned out that within the plurality of descriptions applicable to quantum mechanics the problem of causal anomalies plays an even more important part, since we have there a case where no description exists which avoids causal anomalies. (Cf. also the author's *Philosophic Foundations of Quantum Mechanics,* Berkeley, 1944), §§5-7, §26.

Euclidean description of the universe would be excluded for all adherents of a normal causality.

It is this fact which I regard as the strongest refutation of the Kantian conception of space. The relativity of geometry has been used by Neo-Kantians as a back door through which the apriorism of Euclidean geometry was introduced into Einstein's theory: if it is always possible to select a Euclidean geometry for the description of the universe, then the Kantian insists that it be this description which should be used, because Euclidean geometry, for a Kantian, is the only one that can be visualized. We see that this rule may lead to violations of the principle of causality; and since causality, for a Kantian, is as much an *a priori* principle as Euclidean geometry, his rule may compel the Kantian to jump from the frying pan into the fire. There is no defense of Kantianism, if the statement of the geometry of the physical world is worded in a complete form, including all its physical implications; because in this form the statement is empirically verifiable and depends for its truth on the nature of the physical world.[3]

It should be clear from this analysis that the plurality of equivalent description does not rule out the possibility of true empirical statements. The empirical content of statements about space and time is only stated in a more complicated way.

III

Though we now possess, in Einstein's theory, a complete statement of the relativity of space and time, we should not forget that this is the result of a long historical development. I mentioned above Occam's razor and Leibnitz' identity of indiscernibles in connection with the verifiability theory of meaning. It is a matter of fact that Leibnitz applied his principle successfully to the problem of motion and that he arrived at a relativity of motion on logical grounds. The famous correspondence between Leibnitz and Clarke,—the latter a contemporary defender of Newton's absolutism,—presents us with the same type of discussion which is familiar from the modern discussions

[3] This refutation of Kantianism was presented in the author's *Relativitätstheorie und Erkenntnis Apriori* (Berlin, 1920).

of relativity and reads as though Leibnitz had taken his arguments from expositions of Einstein's theory. Leibnitz even went so far as to recognize the relationship between causal order and time order.[4] This conception of relativity was carried on at a later time by Ernst Mach, who contributed to the discussion the important idea that a relativity of rotational motion requires an extension of relativism to the concept of inertial force. Einstein has always acknowledged Mach as a forerunner of his theory.

Another line of development, which likewise found its completion through Einstein's theory, is presented by the history of geometry. The discovery of non-Euclidean geometries by Gauss, Bolyai, and Lobachewski was associated with the idea that physical geometry might be non-Euclidean; and it is known that Gauss tried to test the Euclidean character of terrestrial geometry by triangular measurements from mountain tops. But the man to whom we owe the philosophical clarification of the problem of geometry is Helmholtz. He saw that physical geometry is dependent on the definition of congruence by means of the solid body and thus arrived at a clear statement of the nature of physical geometry, superior in logical insight to Poincaré's conventionalism developed several decades later. It was Helmholtz, too, who clarified the problem of a visual presentation of non-Euclidean geometry by the discovery that visualization is a fruit of experiences with solid bodies and light-rays. We find in Helmholtz' writings the famous statement that imagining something visually means depicting the series of sense perceptions which one would have if one lived in such a world. That Helmholtz did not succeed in dissuading contemporary philosophers from a Kantian apriorism of space and time is not his fault. His philosophical views were known only among a small group of experts. When, with Einstein's theory, the public interest turned toward these problems, philosophers began to give in and to depart from Kant's apriorism. Let us hope that this development will continue and eventually include even those philosophers who in our day still defend an apriorist philosophy against the attacks of the mathematical physicist.

[4] For an analysis of Leibnitz' views see the author's "Die Bewegungslehre bei Newton, Leibnitz und Huyghens," *Kantstudien* [vol. 29, 1924], 416.

Although there exists a historical evolution of the concepts of space and motion, this line of development finds no analogue in the concept of time. The first to speak of a relativity of the measure of time, i.e., of what is called the uniform flow of time, was Mach. However, Einstein's idea of a relativity of simultaneity has no forerunners. It appears that this discovery could not be made before the perfection of experimental methods of physics. Einstein's relativity of simultaneity is closely associated with the assumption that light is the fastest signal, an idea which could not be conceived before the negative outcome of such experiments as that by Michelson.

It was the combination of the relativity of time and of motion which made Einstein's theory so successful and led to results far beyond the reach of earlier theories. The discovery of the special theory of relativity, which none of Einstein's forerunners had thought of, thus became the key to a general theory of space and time, which included all the ideas of Leibnitz, Gauss, Riemann, Helmholtz, and Mach, and which added to them certain fundamental discoveries which could not have been anticipated at an earlier stage. In particular, I refer to Einstein's conception according to which the geometry of physical space is a function of the distribution of masses, an idea entirely new in the history of geometry.

This short account shows that the evolution of philosophical ideas is guided by the evolution of physical theories. The philosophy of space and time is not the work of the ivory tower philosopher. It was constructed by men who attempted to combine observational data with mathematical analysis. The great synthesis of the various lines of development, which we owe to Einstein, bears witness to the fact that philosophy of science has taken over a function which philosophical systems could not perform.

IV

The question of what is space and time has fascinated the authors of philosophical systems over and again. Plato answered it by inventing a world of "higher" reality, the world of ideas, which includes space and time among its ideal objects and reveals their relations to the mathematician who is able to per-

form the necessary act of vision. For Spinoza space was an attribute of God. Kant, on the other hand, denied the reality of space and time and regarded these two conceptual systems as forms of visualization, i.e., as constructions of the human mind, by means of which the human observer combines his perceptions so as to collect them into an orderly system.

The answer we can give to the question on the basis of Einstein's theory is very different from the answers of these philosophers. The theory of relativity shows that space and time are neither ideal objects nor forms of order necessary for the human mind. They constitute a relational system expressing certain general features of physical objects and thus are descriptive of the physical world. Let us make this fact quite clear.

It is true that, like all concepts, space and time are inventions of the human mind. But not all inventions of the human mind are fit to describe the physical world. By the latter phrase we mean that the concepts refer to certain physical objects and differentiate them from others. For instance, the concept "centaur" is empty, whereas the concept "bear" refers to certain physical objects and distinguishes them from others. The concept "thing," on the other hand, though not empty, is so general that it does not differentiate between objects. Our examples concern one-place predicates, but the same distinction applies to two-place predicates. The relation "telepathy" is empty, whereas the relation "father" is not. When we say that non-empty one-place predicates like "bear" describe real objects, we must also say that non-empty many-place predicates like "father" describe real relations.

It is in this sense that the theory of relativity maintains the reality of space and time. These conceptual systems describe relations holding between physical objects, namely, solid bodies, light-rays, and watches. In addition, these relations formulate physical laws of great generality, determining some fundamental features of the physical world. Space and time have as much reality as, say, the relation "father" or the Newtonian forces of attraction.

The following consideration may serve as a further explanation why geometry is descriptive of physical reality. As long as

only one geometry, the Euclidean geometry, was known, the fact that this geometry could be used for a description of the physical world represented a problem for the philosopher; and Kant's philosophy must be understood as an attempt to explain why a structural system derived from the human mind can account for observational relations. With the discovery of a plurality of geometries the situation changed completely. The human mind was shown to be capable of inventing all kinds of geometrical systems, and the question, which of the systems is suitable for the description of physical reality, was turned into an empirical question, i.e., its answer was ultimately left to empirical data. Concerning the empirical nature of this answer we refer the reader to our considerations in Section II; it is the combined statement of geometry and co-ordinative definitions which is empirical. But, if the statement about the geometry of the physical world is empirical, geometry describes a property of the physical world in the same sense, say, as temperature or weight describe properties of physical objects. When we speak of the reality of physical space we mean this very fact.

As mentioned above, the objects whose general relationship is expressed in the spatio-temporal order are solid bodies, light-rays, and natural watches, i.e., closed periodic systems, like revolving atoms or revolving planets. The important part which light-rays play in the theory of relativity derives from the fact that light is the fastest signal, i.e., represents the fastest form of a causal chain. The concept of causal chain can be shown to be the basic concept in terms of which the structure of space and time is built up. The spatio-temporal order thus must be regarded as the expression of the causal order of the physical world. The close connection between space and time on the one hand and causality on the other hand is perhaps the most prominent feature of Einstein's theory, although this feature has not always been recognized in its significance. Time order, the order of *earlier* and *later*, is reducible to causal order; the cause is always earlier than the effect, a relation which cannot be reversed. That Einstein's theory admits of a reversal of time order for certain events, a result known from the relativity of simultaneity, is merely a consequence of this fundamental fact.

Since the speed of causal transmission is limited, there exist events of such a kind that neither of them can be the cause or the effect of the other. For events of this kind a time order is not defined, and either of them can be called earlier or later than the other.

Ultimately even spatial order is reducible to causal order; a space point *B* is called closer to *A* than a space point *C*, if a direct light-signal, i.e., a fastest causal chain, from *A* to *C* passes by *B*. For a construction of geometry in terms of light-rays and mass-points, i.e., a light-geometry, I refer to another publication.[5]

The connection between time order and causal order leads to the question of the direction of time. I should like to add some remarks about this problem which has often been discussed, but which has not always been stated clearly enough. The relation between cause and effect is an asymmetrical relation; if *P* is the cause of *Q*, then *Q* is not the cause of *P*. This fundamental fact is essential for temporal order, because it makes time a serial relation. By a serial relation we understand a relation that orders its elements in a linear arrangement; such a relation is always asymmetrical and transitive, like the relation "smaller than." The time of Einstein's theory has these properties; that is necessary, because otherwise it could not be used for the construction of a serial order.

But what we call the direction of time must be distinguished from the asymmetrical character of the concepts "earlier" and "later." A relation can be asymmetrical and transitive without distinguishing one direction from the opposite one. For instance, the points of a straight line are ordered by a serial relation which we may express by the words "before" and "after." If *A* is before *B*, then *B* is not before *A*, and if *A* is before *B* and *B* is before *C*, then *A* is before *C*. But which direction of the line we should call "before" and which one "after" is not indicated by the nature of the line; this definition can only be set up by an arbitrary choice, for instance, by pointing into one direction and calling it the direction of "before." In other words, the relations "before" and "after" are structurally indistinguish-

[5] H. Reichenbach, *Philosophie der Raum-Zeit-Lehre* (Berlin, 1928), §27.

able and therefore interchangeable; whether we say that point *A* is before point *B* or after point *B* is a matter of arbitrary definition. It is different with the relation "smaller than" among real numbers. This relation is also a serial relation and thus asymmetrical and transitive; but in addition, it is structurally different from its converse, the relation "larger than," a fact expressible through the difference of positive and negative numbers. The square of a positive number is a positive number, and the square of a negative number is also a positive number. This peculiarity enables us to define the relation "smaller than:" a number which cannot be the square of another number is smaller than a number which is the square of another number. The series of real numbers possesses therefore a direction: the direction "smaller than" is not interchangeable with the direction "larger than;" these relations are therefore not only asymmetrical but also *unidirectional.*

The problem of the time relation is whether it is unidirectional. The relation "earlier than" which we use in everyday life is structurally different from the relation "later than." For instance, we may make up our mind to go to the theatre tomorrow; but it would be nonsensical to make up our mind to go to the theatre yesterday. The physicist formulates this distinction as the *irreversibility of time:* time flows in one direction, and the flow of time cannot be reversed. We see that, in the language of the theory of relations, the question of the irreversibility of time is expressed, not by the question of whether time is an asymmetrical relation, but by the question of whether it is a unidirectional relation.

For the theory of relativity, time is certainly an asymmetrical relation, since otherwise the time relation would not establish a serial order; but it is not unidirectional. In other words, the irreversibility of time does not find an expression in the theory of relativity. We must not conclude that that is the ultimate word which the physicist has to say about time. All we can say is that, as far as the theory of relativity is concerned, we need not make a qualitative distinction between the two directions of time, between the "earlier" and "later." A physical theory may very well abstract from certain properties of the physical world; that

does not mean that these properties do not exist. The irreversibility of time has so far been dealt with only in thermodynamics, where it is conceived as being merely of a statistical nature, not applicable to elementary processes. This answer is none too satisfactory; particularly in view of the fact that it has led to certain paradoxes. Quantum physics so far, however, has no better answer. I would like to say that I regard this problem as at present unsolved and do not agree with those who believe that there is no genuine problem of the direction of time.

It is an amazing fact that the mathematico-physical treatment of the concept of time formulated in Einstein's theory has led to a clarification which philosophical analysis could not achieve. For the philosopher such concepts as time order and simultaneity were primitive notions inaccessible to further analysis. But the claim that a concept is exempt from analysis often merely springs from an inability to understand its meaning. With his reduction of the time concept to that of causality and his generalization of time order toward a relativity of simultaneity, Einstein has not only changed our conceptions of time; he has also clarified the meaning of the classical time concept which preceded his discoveries. In other words, we know better today what absolute time means than anyone of the adherents of the classical time conceptions. Absolute simultaneity would hold in a world in which there exists no upper limit for the speed of signals, i.e., for causal transmission. A world of this type is as well imaginable as Einstein's world. It is an empirical question to which type our world belongs. Experiment has decided in favor of Einstein's conception. As in the case of geometry, the human mind is capable of constructing various forms of a temporal schema; the question which of these schemes fits the physical world, i.e., is true, can only be answered by reference to observational data. What the human mind contributes to the problem of time is not one definite time order, but a plurality of possible time orders, and the selection of one time order as the real one is left to empirical observation. Time is the order of causal chains; that is the outstanding result of Einstein's discoveries. The only philosopher who anticipated this result was Leibnitz; though, of course, in his day it was impossible to con-

ceive of a relativity of simultaneity. And Leibnitz was a mathematician as well as a philosopher. It appears that the solution of the problem of time and space is reserved to philosophers who, like Leibnitz, are mathematicians, or to mathematicians who, like Einstein, are philosophers.

V

From the time of Kant, the history of philosophy shows a growing rift between philosophical systems and the philosophy of science. The system of Kant was constructed with the intention of proving that knowledge is the resultant of two components, a mental and an observational one; the mental component was assumed to be given by the laws of pure reason and conceived as a synthetic element different from the merely analytic operations of logic. The concept of a *synthetic a priori* formulates the Kantian position: there is a *synthetic a priori* part of knowledge, i.e., there are non-empty statements which are absolutely necessary. Among these principles of knowledge Kant includes the laws of Euclidean geometry, of absolute time, of causality and of the conservation of mass. His followers in the 19th century took over this conception, adding many variations.

The development of science, on the other hand, has led away from Kantian metaphysics. The principles which Kant regarded as *synthetic a priori* were recognized as being of a questionable truth; principles contradictory to them were developed and employed for the construction of knowledge. These new principles were not advanced with a claim to absolute truth but in the form of attempts to find a description of nature fitting the observational material. Among the plurality of possible systems, the one corresponding to physical reality could be singled out only by observation and experiment. In other words, the synthetic principles of knowledge which Kant had regarded as *a priori* were recognized as *a posteriori*, as verifiable through experience only and as valid in the restricted sense of empirical hypotheses.

It is this process of a dissolution of the *synthetic a priori* into which we must incorporate the theory of relativity, when we desire to judge it from the viewpoint of the history of philos-

ophy. A line which began with the invention of non-Euclidean geometries 20 years after Kant's death runs uninterruptedly right up and into Einstein's theory of space and time. The laws of geometry, for 2000 years regarded as laws of reason, were recognized as empirical laws, which fit the world of our environment to a high degree of precision; but they must be abandoned for astronomic dimensions. The apparent self-evidence of these laws, which made them seem to be inescapable presuppositions of all knowledge, turned out to be the product of habit; through their suitability to all experiences of everyday life these laws had acquired a degree of reliability which erroneously was taken for absolute certainty. Helmholtz was the first to advocate the idea that human beings, living in a non-Euclidean world, would develop an ability of visualization which would make them regard the laws of non-Euclidean geometry as necessary and self-evident, in the same fashion as the laws of Euclidean geometry appear self-evident to us. Transferring this idea to Einstein's conception of time, we would say that human beings, in whose daily experiences the effects of the speed of light would be noticeably different from those of an infinite velocity, would become accustomed to the relativity of simultaneity and regard the rules of the Lorentz-transformation as necessary and self-evident, just as we regard the classical rules of motion and simultaneity self-evident. For instance, if a telephone connection with the planet Mars were established, and we would have to wait a quarter of an hour for the answer to our questions, the relativity of simultaneity would become as trivial a matter as the time difference between the standard times of different time zones is today. What philosophers had regarded as laws of reason turned out to be a conditioning through the physical laws of our environment; we have ground to assume that in a different environment a corresponding conditioning would lead to another adaptation of the mind.

The process of the dissolution of the *synthetic a priori* is one of the significant features of the philosophy of our time. We should not commit the mistake of considering it a breakdown of human abilities, if conceptions which we regarded as absolutely

true are shown to be of limited validity and have to be abandoned in certain fields of knowledge. On the contrary, the fact that we are able to overcome these conceptions and to replace them by better ones reveals unexpected abilities of the human mind, a versatility vastly superior to the dogmatism of a pure reason which dictates its laws to the scientist.

Kant believed himself to possess a proof for his assertion that his *synthetic a priori* principles were necessary truths: According to him these principles were necessary conditions of knowledge. He overlooked the fact that such a proof can demonstrate the truth of the principles only if it is taken for granted that knowledge within the frame of these principles will always be possible. What has happened, then, in Einstein's theory is a proof that knowledge within the framework of Kantian principles is not possible. For a Kantian, such a result could only signify a breakdown of science. It is a fortunate fact that the scientist was not a Kantian and, instead of abandoning his attempts of constructing knowledge, looked for ways of changing the so-called *a priori* principles. Through his ability of dealing with space-time relations essentially different from the traditional frame of knowledge, Einstein has shown the way to a philosophy superior to the philosophy of the *synthetic a priori.*

It is the philosophy of empiricism, therefore, into which Einstein's relativity belongs. It is true, Einstein's empiricism is not the one of Bacon and Mill, who believed that all laws of nature can be found by simple inductive generalizations. Einstein's empiricism is that of modern theoretical physics, the empiricism of mathematical construction, which is so devised that it connects observational data by deductive operations and enables us to predict new observational data. Mathematical physics will always remain empiricist as long as it leaves the ultimate criterion of truth to sense perception. The enormous amount of deductive method in such a physics can be accounted for in terms of analytic operations alone. In addition to deductive operations there is, of course, an inductive element included in the physics of mathematical hypotheses; but even the principle of induction, by far the most difficult obstacle to a radical empiricism, can be shown today to be justifiable without a belief in a

synthetic a priori. The method of modern science can be completely accounted for in terms of an empiricism which recognizes only sense perception and the analytic principles of logic as sources of knowledge. In spite of the enormous mathematical apparatus, Einstein's theory of space and time is the triumph of such a radical empiricism in a field which had always been regarded as a reservation for the discoveries of pure reason.

The process of the dissolution of the *synthetic a priori* is going on. To the abandonment of absolute space and time quantum physics has added that of causality; furthermore, it has abandoned the classical concept of material substance and has shown that the constituents of matter, the atomic particles, do not possess the unambiguous nature of the solid bodies of the macroscopic world. If we understand by metaphysics the belief in principles that are non-analytic, yet derive their validity from reason alone, modern science is anti-metaphysical. It has refused to recognize the authority of the philosopher who claims to know the truth from intuition, from insight into a world of ideas or into the nature of reason or the principles of being, or from whatever super-empirical source. There is no separate entrance to truth for philosophers. The path of the philosopher is indicated by that of the scientist: all the philosopher can do is to analyze the results of science, to construe their meanings and stake out their validity. Theory of knowledge is analysis of science.

I said above that Einstein is a philosopher by implication. That means that making the philosophic implications of Einstein's theory explicit is the task of the philosopher. Let us not forget that it is implications of an enormous reach which are derivable from the theory of relativity, and let us realize that it must be an eminently philosophical physics that lends itself to such implications. It does not happen very often that physical systems of such philosophical significance are presented to us; Einstein's predecessor was Newton. It is the privilege of our generation that we have among us a physicist whose work occupies the same rank as that of the man who determined the philosophy of space and time for two centuries. If physicists present us with implicational philosophies of such excellence, it is a pleas-

ure to be a philosopher. The lasting fame of the philosophy of modern physics will justly go to the man who made the physics rather than to those who have been at work deriving the implications of his work and who are pointing out its position in the history of philosophy. There are many who have contributed to the philosophy of Einstein's theory, but there is only one Einstein.

HANS REICHENBACH

DEPARTMENT OF PHILOSOPHY
UNIVERSITY OF CALIFORNIA AT LOS ANGELES

II

H. P. Robertson

GEOMETRY AS A BRANCH OF PHYSICS

11

GEOMETRY AS A BRANCH OF PHYSICS

IS SPACE REALLY CURVED? That is a question which, in one form or another, is raised again and again by philosophers, scientists, T. C. Mits and readers of the weekly comic supplements. A question which has been brought into the limelight above all by the genial work of Albert Einstein, and kept there by the unceasing efforts of astronomers to wrest the answer from a curiously reluctant Nature.

But what is the meaning of the question? What, indeed, is the meaning of each word in it? Properly to formulate and adequately to answer the question would require a critical excursus through philosophy and mathematics into physics and astronomy, which is beyond the scope of the present modest attempt. Here we shall be content to examine the rôles of deduction and observation in the problem of physical space, to exhibit certain high points in the history of the problem, and in the end to illustrate the viewpoint adopted by presenting a relatively simple caricature of Einstein's general theory of relativity. It is hoped that this, certainly incomplete and possibly naïve, description will present the essentials of the problem from a neutral mathematico-physical viewpoint in a form suitable for incorporation into any otherwise tenable philosophical position. Here, for example, we shall not touch directly upon the important problem of form versus substance—but if one wishes to interpret the geometrical substratum here considered as a formal backdrop against which the contingent relations of nature are exhibited, one should be able to do so without distorting the scientific content.

First, then, we consider geometry as a deductive science, a branch of mathematics in which a body of theories is built up by

logical processes from a postulated set of axioms (not "self-evident truths"). In logical position geometry differs not in kind from any other mathematical discipline—say the theory of numbers or the calculus of variations. As mathematics, it is not the science of measurement, despite the implications of its name—even though it did, in keeping with the name, originate in the codification of rules for land surveying. The principal criterion of its validity as a mathematical discipline is whether the axioms as written down are self-consistent, and the sole criterion of the truth of a theorem involving its concepts is whether the theorem can be deduced from the axioms. This truth is clearly relative to the axioms; the theorem that the sum of the three interior angles of a triangle is equal to two right angles, true in Euclidean geometry, is false in any of the geometries obtained on replacing the parallel postulate by one of its contraries. In the present sense it suffices for us that geometry is a body of theorems, involving among others the concepts of point, angle and a unique numerical relation called distance between pairs of points, deduced from a set of self-consistent axioms.

What, then, distinguishes Euclidean geometry as a mathematical system from those logically consistent systems, involving the same category of concepts, which result from the denial of one or more of its traditional axioms? This distinction cannot consist in its "truth" in the sense of observed fact in physical science; its truth, or applicability, or still better appropriateness, in this latter sense is dependent upon observation, and not upon deduction alone. The characteristics of Euclidean geometry, as mathematics, are therefore to be sought in its internal properties, and not in its relation to the empirical.

First, Euclidean geometry is a *congruence geometry*, or equivalently the space comprising its elements is *homogeneous and isotropic;* the intrinsic relations between points and other elements of a configuration are unaffected by the position or orientation of the configuration. As an example, in Euclidean geometry all intrinsic properties of a triangle—its angles, area, etc.,—are uniquely determined by the lengths of its three sides; two triangles whose three sides are respectively equal are "con-

gruent;" either can by a "motion" of the space into itself be brought into complete coincidence with the other, whatever its original position and orientation may be. These motions of Euclidean space are the familiar translations and rotations, use of which is made in proving many of the theorems of Euclid. That the existence of these motions (the axiom of "free mobility") is a desideratum, if not indeed a necessity, for a geometry applicable to physical space, has been forcibly argued on *a priori* grounds by von Helmholtz, Whitehead, Russell and others; for only in a homogeneous and isotropic space can the traditional concept of a rigid body be maintained.[1]

But the Euclidean geometry is only one of several congruence geometries; there are in addition the "hyperbolic" geometry of Bolyai and Lobachewsky, and the "spherical" and "elliptic" geometries of Riemann and Klein. Each of these geometries is characterized by a real number K, which for the Euclidean geometry is zero, for the hyperbolic negative, and for the spherical and elliptic geometries positive. In the case of 2-dimensional congruence spaces, which *may* (but need not) be conceived as surfaces embedded in a 3-dimensional Euclidean space, the constant K may be interpreted as the *curvature* of the surface into the third dimension—whence it derives its name. This name and this representation are for our purposes at least psychologically unfortunate, for we propose ultimately to deal exclusively with properties intrinsic to the space under consideration—properties which in the later physical applications can be measured within the space itself—and are not dependent upon some extrinsic construction, such as its relation to an hypothesized higher dimensional embedding space. We must accordingly seek some determination of K—which we nevertheless continue to call curvature—in terms of such inner properties.

[1] Technically this requirement, as expressed by the axiom of free mobility, is that there exist a motion of the 3-dimensional space into itself which takes an arbitrary configuration, consisting of a point, a direction through the point, and a plane of directions containing the given direction, into a standard such configuration. For an excellent presentation of this standpoint see B. A. W. Russell's *The Foundations of Geometry* (Cambridge, 1897), or Russell and A. N. Whitehead's article "Geometry VI: Non-Euclidean Geometry" 11th Ed. *Encyclopædia Brittanica.*

In order to break into such an intrinsic characterization of curvature, we first relapse into a rather naïve consideration of measurements which may be made on the surface of the earth, conceived as a sphere of radius R. This surface is an example of a 2-dimensional congruence space of positive curvature $K = 1/R^2$ on agreeing that the abstract geometrical concept "distance" r between any two of its points (not the extremities of a diameter) shall correspond to the lesser of the two distances *measured on the surface* between them along the unique great circle which joins the two points.[2] Consider now a "small circle" of radius r (measured on the surface!) about a point P of the surface; its perimeter L and area A (again measured on the surface!) are clearly less than the corresponding measures $2\pi r$ and πr^2 of the perimeter and area of a circle of radius r in the Euclidean plane. An elementary calculation shows that for sufficiently small r (i.e., small compared with R) these quantities on the sphere are given approximately by:

$$(1) \quad \begin{aligned} L &= 2\pi r\,(1 - Kr^2/6 + \ldots), \\ A &= \pi r^2\,(1 - Kr^2/12 + \ldots). \end{aligned}$$

Thus, the ratio of the area of a small circle of radius 400 miles on the surface of the earth to that of a circle of radius 40 miles is found to be only 99.92, instead of 100.00 as in the plane.

Another consequence of possible interest for astronomical applications is that in spherical geometry the sum σ of the three angles of a triangle (whose sides are arcs of great circles) is *greater* than 2 right angles; it can in fact be shown that this "spherical excess" is given by

$$(2) \quad \sigma - \pi = K\delta,$$

where δ is the area of the spherical triangle and the angles are measured in radians (in which $180° = \pi$). Further, each full

[2] The motions of the surface of the earth into itself, which enable us to transform a point and a direction through it into any other point and direction, as demanded by the axiom of free mobility, are here those generated by the 3-parameter family of rotations of the earth about its center (not merely the 1-parameter family of diurnal rotations about its "axis."!).

line (great circle) is of finite length $2\pi R$, and any two full lines meet in two points—there are no parallels!

In the above paragraph we have, with forewarning, slipped into a non-intrinsic quasi-physical standpoint in order to present the formulae (1) and (2) in a more or less intuitive way. But the essential point is that these formulae are in fact independent of this mode of presentation; they are relations between the mathematical concepts distance, angle, perimeter and area which follow as logical consequences from the axioms of this particular kind of non-Euclidean geometry. And since they involve the space-constant K, this "curvature" may in principle at least be determined *by measurements made on the surface*, without recourse to its embedment in a higher dimensional space.

Further, these formulae may be shown to be valid for a circle or triangle in the hyperbolic plane, a 2-dimensional congruence space for which $K < 0$. Accordingly here the perimeter and area of a circle are *greater*, and the sum of the three angles of a triangle *less*, than the corresponding quantities in the Euclidean plane. It may also be shown that each full line is of infinite length, that through a given point outside a given line an infinity of full lines may be drawn which do not meet the given line (the two lines bounding the family are said to be "parallel" to the given line), and that two full lines which meet do so in but one point.

The value of the intrinsic approach is especially apparent in considering 3-dimensional congruence spaces, where our physical intuition is of little use in conceiving them as "curved" in some higher-dimensional space. The intrinsic geometry of such a space of curvature K provides formulae for the surface area S and the volume V of a "small sphere" of radius r, whose leading terms are

$$(3) \qquad \begin{aligned} S &= 4\pi r^2\,(1 - Kr^2/3 + \ldots), \\ V &= 4/3\pi r^3\,(1 - Kr^2/5 + \ldots). \end{aligned}$$

It is to be noted that in all these congruence geometries, except the Euclidean, there is at hand a natural unit of length $R =$

$1/|K|^{1/2}$; this length we shall, without prejudice, call the "radius of curvature" of the space.

So much for the congruence geometries. If we give up the axiom of free mobility we may still deal with the geometry of spaces which have only limited or no motions into themselves.[3] Every smooth surface in 3-dimensional Euclidean space has such a 2-dimensional geometry; a surface of revolution has a 1-parameter family of motions into itself (rotations about its axis of symmetry), but not enough to satisfy the axiom of free mobility. Each such surface has at a point $P(x, y)$ of it an intrinsic "total curvature" $K(x, y)$, which will in general vary from point to point; knowledge of the curvature at all points essentially determines all intrinsic properties of the surface.[4] The determination of $K(x, y)$ by measurements on the surface is again made possible by the fact that the perimeter L and area A of a closed curve, every point of which is at a given (sufficiently small) distance r from $P(x, y)$, are given by the formulae (1), where K is no longer necessarily constant from point to point. Any such variety for which $K = 0$ throughout is a ("developable") surface which may, on ignoring its macroscopic properties, be rolled out without tearing or stretching onto the Euclidean plane.

From this we may go on to the contemplation of 3- or higher dimensional ("Riemannian") spaces, whose intrinsic properties vary from point to point. But these properties are no longer describable in terms of a single quantity, for the "curvature" now acquires at each point a directional character which requires in 3-space 6 components (and in 4-space 20) for its specification. We content ourselves here to call attention to a single combination of the 6, which we call the "mean curvature" of the space at the point $P(x, y, z)$, and which we again denote by K— or more fully by $K(x, y, z)$; it is in a sense the mean of the curvatures of various surfaces passing through P, and reduces

[3] We are here confining ourselves to metric (Riemannian) geometries, in which there exists a differential element ds of distance, whose square is a homogeneous quadratic form in the co-ordinate differentials.

[4] That is, the "differential," as opposed to the "macroscopic," properties. Thus the Euclidean plane and a cylinder have the same differential, but not the same macroscopic, structure.

to the previously contemplated space-constant K when the space in question is a congruence space.[5] This concept is useful in physical applications, for the surface area S and the volume V of a sphere of radius r about the point $P(x, y, z)$ as center are again given by formulae (3), where now K is to be interpreted as the mean curvature $K(x, y, z)$ of the space at the point P. In four and higher dimensions similar concepts may be introduced and similar formulae developed, but for them we have no need here.

We have now to turn our attention to the world of physical objects about us, and to indicate how an ordered description of it is to be obtained in accordance with accepted, preferably philosophically neutral, scientific method. These objects, which exist for us in virtue of some pre-scientific concretion of our sense-data, are positioned in an extended manifold which we call physical space. The mind of the individual, retracing at an immensely accelerated pace the path taken by the race, bestirs itself to an analysis of the interplay between object and extension. There develops a notion of the permanence of the object and of the ordering and the change in time—another form of extension, through which object and subject appear to be racing together—of its extensive relationships. The study of the ordering of actual and potential relationships, the physical problem of space and time, leads to the consideration of geometry and kinematics as a branch of physical science. To certain aspects of this problem we now turn our attention.

We consider first that proposed solution of the problem of space which is based upon the postulate that space is an *a priori* form of the understanding. Its geometry must then be a congruence geometry, independent of the physical content of space;

[5] The quantities here referred to are the six independent components of the Riemann-Christoffel tensor in 3 dimensions, and the "mean curvature" here introduced (not to be confused with the mean curvature of a surface, which is an extrinsic property depending on the embedment) is $K = -R'/6$, where R' is the contracted Ricci tensor. I am indebted to Professor Herbert Busemann, of the University of Southern California, for a remark which suggested the usefulness for my later purposes of this approach. A complete exposition of the fundamental concepts involved is to be found in L. P. Eisenhart's *Riemannian Geometry* (Princeton 1926).

and since for Kant, the propounder of this view, there existed but one geometry, space must be Euclidean—and the problem of physical space is solved on the epistemological, pre-physical, level.

But the discovery of other congruence geometries, characterized by a numerical parameter *K*, perforce modifies this view, and restores at least in some measure the objective aspect of physical space; the *a posteriori* ground for this space-constant *K* is then to be sought in the contingent. The means for its intrinsic determination is implicit in the formulae presented above; we have merely (!) to measure the volume *V* of a sphere of radius *r* or the sum σ of the angles of a triangle of measured area δ, and from the results to compute the value of *K*. On this modified Kantian view, which has been expounded at length by Russell,[6] it is inconceivable that *K* might vary from point to point—for according to this view the very possibility of measurement depends on the constancy of space-structure, as guaranteed by the axiom of free mobility. It is of interest to mention in passing, in view of recent cosmological findings, the possibility raised by A. Calinon (in 1889!) that the space-constant *K* might vary with time.[7] But this possibility is rightly ignored by Russell, for the same arguments which would on this *a priori* theory require the constancy of *K* in space would equally require its constancy in time.

In the foregoing sketch we have dodged the real hook in the problem of measurement. As physicists we should state clearly those aspects of the physical world which are to correspond to elements of the mathematical system which we propose to employ in the description ("realisation" of the abstract system). Ideally this program should prescribe fully the operations by

[6] In the works already referred to in footnote 1 above.

[7] "Les espaces géometriques," *Revue Philosophique*, vol. 27, pp. 588-595 (1889). The possibilities at which Calinon arrives are, to quote in free translation:

"1. Our space is and remains rigorously Euclidean;

"2. Our space realizes a geometrical space which differs very little from the Euclidean, but which always remains the same;

"3. Our space realizes successively in time different geometrical spaces; otherwise said, our spatial parameter varies with the time, whether it departs more or less away from the Euclidean parameter or whether it oscillates about a definite parameter very near to the Euclidean value."

which numerical values are to be assigned to the physical counterparts of the abstract elements. How is one to achieve this in the case in hand of determining the numerical value of the space-constant *K*?

Although K. F. Gauss, one of the spiritual fathers of non-Euclidean geometry, at one time proposed a possible test of the flatness of space by measuring the interior angles of a terrestrial triangle, it remained for his Göttingen successor K. Schwarzschild to formulate the procedure and to attempt to evaluate *K* on the basis of astronomical data available at the turn of the century.[8] Schwarzschild's pioneer attempt is so inspiring in its conception and so beautiful in its expression that I cannot refrain from giving here a few short extracts from his work. After presenting the possibility that physical space may, in accordance with the neo-Kantian position outlined above, be non-Euclidean, Schwarzschild states (in free translation):

> One finds oneself here, if one but will, in a geometrical fairyland, but the beauty of this fairy tale is that one does not know but what it may be true. We accordingly bespeak the question here of how far we must push back the frontiers of this fairyland; of how small we must choose the curvature of space, how great its radius of curvature.

In furtherance of this program Schwarzschild proposes:

> A triangle determined by three points will be defined as the paths of light-rays from one point to another, the lengths of its sides a, b, c, by the times it takes light to traverse these paths, and the angles α, β, γ will be measured with the usual astronomical instruments.

Applying Schwarzschild's prescription to observations on a given star, we consider the triangle ABC defined by the position A of the star and by two positions B, C of the earth—say six months apart—at which the angular positions of the star are measured. The base BC $= a$ is known, by measurements within the solar system consistent with the prescription, and the interior angles β, γ which the light-rays from the star make with the base-line are also known by measurement. From these the *parallax* $p = \pi - (\beta + \gamma)$ may be computed; in Euclidean

[8] "Über das zulässige Krümmungsmaass des Raumes," *Vierteljahrsschrift der astronomischen Gesellschaft,* vol. 35, pp. 337-347 (1900). The *annual parallax,* as used in practice, is one-half that defined below.

space this parallax is simply the inferred angle α subtended at the star by the diameter of the earth's orbit. In the other congruence geometries the parallax is seen, with the aid of formula (2) above, to be equal to

$$(2') \qquad p = \pi - (\beta + \gamma) = \alpha - K\delta,$$

where α is the (unknown) angle at the star A, and δ is the (unknown) area of the triangle ABC. Now in spite of our incomplete knowledge of the elements on the far right, certain valid conclusions may be drawn from this result. First, if space is hyperbolic ($K < 0$), for distant stars (for which $\alpha \sim 0$), the parallax p will remain positive; hence if stars are observed whose parallax is zero to within the errors of observation, this estimated error will give an upper limit to the absolute value $-K$ of the curvature. Second, if space is spherical ($K > 0$), for a sufficiently distant star (more distant than one-quarter the circumference of a Euclidean sphere of radius $R = 1/K^{1/2}$, as may immediately be seen by examining a globe) the sum $\beta + \gamma$ will exceed two right angles; hence the parallax p of such a star should be negative, and if no stars are in fact observed with negative parallax, the estimated error of observation will give an upper limit to the curvature K. Also, in this latter case the light sent out by the star must return to it after traversing the full line of length $2\pi R$, (πR in elliptic space), and hence we should, but for absorption and scattering, be able to observe the returning light as an anti-star in a direction opposite to that of the star itself!

On the basis of the evidence then available, Schwarzschild concluded that if space is hyperbolic its radius of curvature $R = 1/(-K)^{1/2}$ cannot be less than 64 light-years (i.e., the distance light travels in 64 years), and that if the space is elliptic its radius of curvature $R = 1/K^{1/2}$ is at least 1600 light-years. Hardly imposing figures for us today, who believe on other astronomical grounds that objects as distant as 500 million light-years have been sighted in the Mt. Wilson telescope, and who are expecting to find objects at twice that distance with the new Mt. Palomar mirror! But the value for us of the work of Schwarzschild lies in its sound operational approach to the

problem of physical geometry—in refreshing contrast to the pontifical pronouncement of H. Poincaré, who after reviewing the subject stated:[9]

> If therefore negative parallaxes were found, or if it were demonstrated that all parallaxes are superior to a certain limit, two courses would be open to us; we might either renounce Euclidean geometry, or else modify laws of optics and suppose that light does not travel rigorously in a straight line.
>
> It is needless to add that all the world would regard the latter solution as the more advantageous.
>
> The Euclidean geometry has, therefore, nothing to fear from fresh experiments. [!]

So far we have tied ourselves into the neo-Kantian doctrine that space must be homogeneous and isotropic, in which case our proposed operational approach is limited in application to the determination of the numerical value of the space-constant *K*. But the possible scope of the operational method is surely broader than this; what if we do apply it to triangles and circles and spheres in various positions and at various times and find that the *K* so determined is in fact dependent on position in space and time? Are we, following Poincaré, to attribute these findings to the influence of an external force postulated for the purpose? Or are we to take our findings at face value, and accept the geometry to which we are led as a natural geometry for physical science?

The answer to this methodological question will depend largely on the *universality* of the geometry thus found—whether the geometry found in one situation or field of physical discourse may consistently be extended to others—and in the end partly on the predilection of the individual or of his colleagues or of his times. Thus Einstein's special theory of relativity, which offers a physical kinematics embracing measurements in space and time, has gone through several stages of acceptance and use, until at present it is a universal and indispensable tool of modern physics. Thus Einstein's general theory of relativity, which offers an extended kinematics which includes in its geometrical structure the universal force of gravitation,

[9] *Science and Hypothesis*, p. 81; transl. by G. B. Halsted (Science Press 1929).

was long considered by some contemporaries to be a *tour de force*, at best amusing but in practice useless. And now, in extending this theory to the outer bounds of the observed universe, the kind of geometry suggested by the present marginal data seems to many so repugnant that they would follow Poincaré in postulating some *ad hoc* force, be it a double standard of time or a secular change in the velocity of light or Planck's constant, rather than accept it.

But enough of this general and historical approach to the problem of physical geometry! While we should like to complete this discussion with a detailed operational analysis of the solution given by the general theory of relativity, such an undertaking would require far more than the modest mathematical background which we have here presupposed. Further, the field of operations of the general theory is so unearthly and its *experimenta crucis* so delicate that an adequate discussion would take us far out from the familiar objects and concepts of the workaday world, and obscure the salient points we wish to make in a welter of unfamiliar and esoteric astronomical and mathematical concepts. What is needed is a homely experiment which could be carried out in the basement with parts from an old sewing machine and an Ingersoll watch, with an old file of *Popular Mechanics* standing by for reference! This I am, alas, afraid we have not achieved, but I do believe that the following example of a simple theory of measurement in a heat-conducting medium is adequate to expose the principles involved with a modicum of mathematical background. The very fact that it will lead to a rather bad and unacceptable physical theory will in itself be instructive, for its very failure will emphasize the requirement of universality of application—a requirement most satisfactorily met by the general theory of relativity.

The background of our illustration is an ordinary laboratory, equipped with Bunsen burners, clamps, rulers, micrometers and the usual miscellaneous impedimenta there met—at the turn of the century, no electronics required! In it the practical Euclidean geometry reigns (hitherto!) unquestioned, for even though measurements are there to be carried out with quite reasonable standards of accuracy, there is no need for sophisti-

cated qualms concerning the effect of gravitational or magnetic or other general extended force-fields on its metrical structure. Now that we feel at home in these familiar, and disarming, surroundings, consider the following experiment:

Let a thin, flat metal plate be heated in any way—just so that the temperature T is not uniform over the plate. During the process clamp or otherwise constrain the plate to keep it from buckling, so that it can reasonably be said to remain flat by ordinary standards. Now proceed to make simple geometrical measurements on the plate with a short metal rule, which has a certain coefficient of expansion c, taking care that the rule is allowed to come into thermal equilibrium with the plate at each setting before making the measurement. The question now is, what is the geometry of the plate *as revealed by the results of these measurements?*

It is evident that, unless the coefficient of expansion c of the rule is zero, the geometry will not turn out to be Euclidean, for the rule will expand more in the hotter regions of the plate than in the cooler, distorting the (Euclidean) measurements which would be obtained by a rule whose length did not change according to the usual laboratory standards. Thus the perimeter L of a circle centered at a point at which a burner is applied will surely turn out to be greater than π times its measured diameter $2r$, for the rule will expand in measuring through the hotter interior of the circle and hence give a smaller reading than if the temperature were uniform. On referring to the first of formulae (1) above it is seen that the plate would seem to have a negative curvature K at the center of the circle—the kind of structure exhibited by an ordinary twisted surface in the neighborhood of a "saddle-point." In general the curvature will vary from point to point in a systematic way; a more detailed mathematical analysis of the situation shows that, on removing heat sources and neglecting radiation losses from the faces of the plate, K is everywhere negative and that the "radius of curvature" $R = 1/(-K)^{1/2}$ at any point P is inversely proportional to the rate s at which heat flows past P. (R is in fact equal to k/cs, where k is the coefficient of heat conduction *of the plate* and c is as before the coefficient of expansion *of the rule.*) The

hyperbolic geometry is accordingly realized when the heat flow is constant throughout the plate, as when the long sides of an elongated rectangle are kept at different fixed temperatures.[10]

And now comes the question, what is the true geometry of the plate? The flat Euclidean geometry we had uncritically agreed upon at the beginning of the experiment, or the un-Euclidean geometry revealed by measurement? It is obvious that the question is improperly worded; the geometry is determinate only when we prescribe the method of measurement, i.e., when we set up a correspondence between the physical aspects (here readings on a definite rule obtained in a prescribed way) and the elements (here distances, in the abstract sense) of the mathematical system. Thus our original common-sense requirement that the plate not buckle, or that it be measured with an invar rule (for which $c \sim 0$), leads to Euclidean geometry, while the use of a rule with a sensible coefficient of expansion leads to a locally hyperbolic type of Riemannian geometry, which is in general not a congruence geometry.

There is no doubt that anyone examining this situation will prefer Poincaré's common-sense solution of the problem of the physical geometry of the plate—i.e., to attribute to it Euclidean geometry, and to consider the measured deviations from this geometry as due to the action of a force (thermal stresses in the rule). Most compulsive to this solution is the fact that this disturbing force lacks the requirement of universality; on employing a brass rule in place of one of steel we would find that the local curvature is trebled—and an ideal rule ($c = 0$) would, as we have noted, lead to the Euclidean geometry.

In what respect, then, does the general theory of relativity differ in principle from this geometrical theory of the hot plate? The answer is: *in its universality;* the force of gravitation which it comprehends in the geometrical structure acts equally on all

[10] This case, in which the geometry is that of the Poincaré half-plane, has been discussed in detail by E. W. Barankin "Heat Flow and Non-Euclidean Geometry," *American Mathematical Monthly,* vol. 49, pp. 4-14 (1942). For those who are numerically-minded it may be noted that for a steel plate ($k = 0.1$ cal/cm deg) 1 cm thick, with a heat flow of 1 cal/cm^2 sec, the natural unit of length R of the geometry, as measured by a steel rule ($c = 10^{-5}$/deg), is 10^4 cm $\sim$ 328 feet!

matter. There is here a close analogy between the gravitational mass M of the field-producing body (Sun) and the inertial mass m of the test-particle (Earth) on the one hand, and the heat conduction k of the field (plate) and the coefficient of expansion c of the test-body (rule) on the other. *The success of the general relativity theory of gravitation as a physical geometry of space-time is attributable to the fact that the gravitational and inertial masses of any body are observed to be rigorously proportional for all matter.* Whereas in our geometrical theory of the thermal field the ratio of heat conductivity to coefficient of expansion varies from substance to substance, resulting in a change of the geometry of the field on changing the test-body.

From our present point of view the great triumph of the theory of relativity lies in its absorbing the universal force of gravitation into the geometrical structure; its success in accounting for minute discrepancies in the Newtonian description of the motions of test-bodies in the solar field, although gratifying, is nevertheless of far less moment to the philosophy of physical science.[11] Einstein's achievements would be substantially as great even though it were not for these minute observational tests.

[11] Even here an amusing and instructive analogy exists between our caricature and the relativity theory. On extending our notions to a 3-dimensional heat-conducting medium (without worrying too much about how our measurements are actually to be carried out!), and on adopting the standard field equation for heat conduction, the "mean curvature" introduced above is found at any point to be $-(cs/k)^2$, which is of second order in the characteristic parameter c/k. (The case in which the temperature is proportional to $a^2 - r^2$, which requires a continuous distribution of heat sources, has been discussed in some detail by Poincaré, *Loc. cit.* pp. 76-78, in his discussion of non-Euclidean geometry.) The field equation may now itself be given a geometrical formulation, at least to first approximation, by replacing it by the requirement that the mean curvature of the space *vanish* at any point at which no heat is being supplied to the medium—in complete analogy with the procedure in the general theory of relativity by which the classical field equations are replaced by the requirement that the Ricci contracted curvature tensor vanish. Here, as there, will now appear certain deviations, whose magnitude here depends upon the ratio c/k, between the standard and the modified theories. One curious consequence of this treatment is that on solving the modified field equation for a spherically-symmetric source (or better, sink) of heat, one finds precisely the same spatial structure as in the Schwarzschild solution for the gravitational field of a spherically-symmetric gravitational mass—the correspondence being such that the geometrical effect of a sink which removes 1 calorie per second from the medium is equivalent to the gravitational effect of a mass of 10^{22} gm, e.g., of a chunk of rock 200 miles in diameter!

Our final illustration of physical geometry consists in a brief reference to the cosmological problem of the geometry of the observed universe as a whole—a problem considered in greater detail elsewhere in this volume. *If* matter in the universe can, taken on a sufficiently large scale (spatial gobs millions of light-years across), be considered as uniformly distributed, and if (as implied by the general theory of relativity) its geometrical structure is conditioned by matter, then to this approximation our 3-dimensional astronomical space must be homogeneous and isotropic, with a spatially-constant K which may however depend upon time. Granting this hypothesis, how do we go about measuring K, using of course only procedures which can be operationally specified, and to which congruence geometry are we thereby led? The way to the answer is suggested by the second of the formulae (3), for if the nebulae are by-and-large uniformly distributed, then the number N within a sphere of radius r must be proportional to the volume V of this sphere. We have then only to examine the dependence of this number N, as observed in a sufficiently powerful telescope, on the distance r to determine the deviation from the Euclidean value. But how is r operationally to be defined?

If all the nebulae were of the same intrinsic brightness, then their apparent brightness as observed from the Earth should be an indication of their distance from us; we must therefore examine the exact relation to be expected between apparent brightness and the abstract distance r. Now it is the practice of astronomers to assume that brightness falls off inversely with the square of the "distance" of the object—as it would do in Euclidean space, if there were no absorption, scattering, and the like. We must therefore examine the relation between this astronomer's "distance" d, as inferred from apparent brightness, and the distance r which appears as an element of the geometry. It is clear that *all* the light which is radiated at a given moment from the nebula will, after it has traveled a distance r, lie on the surface of a sphere whose area S is given by the first of the formulae (3). And since the practical procedure involved in determining d is equivalent to assuming that all this light lies on the surface of a Euclidean sphere of radius d, it follows

immediately that the relationship between the "distance" d used in practice and the distance r dealt with in the geometry is given by the equation

$$4\pi d^2 = S = 4\pi r^2\,(1 - Kr^2/3 + \ldots);$$

whence, to our approximation

$$(4) \qquad \begin{aligned} d &= r(1 - Kr^2/6 + \ldots), \text{ or} \\ r &= d(1 + Kd^2/6 + \ldots). \end{aligned}$$

But the astronomical data give the number N of nebulae counted out to a given inferred "distance" d, and in order to determine the curvature from them we must express N, or equivalently V, to which it is assumed proportional, in terms of d. One easily finds from the second of the formulae (3) and the formula (4) just derived that, again to the approximation here adopted,

$$(5) \qquad V = 4/3\,\pi d^3\,(1 + 3/10\,Kd^2 + \ldots).$$

And now on plotting N against inferred "distance" d and comparing this empirical plot with the formula (5), it should be possible operationally to determine the "curvature" K.[12]

The search for the curvature K indicates that, after making all known corrections, the number N seems to increase faster with d than the third power, which would be expected in Euclidean space, hence K is *positive*. The space implied thereby is therefore bounded, of finite total volume, and of a present "radius of curvature" $R = 1/K^{1/2}$ which is found to be of the order of 500 million light-years. Other observations, on the "red-shift" of light from these distant objects, enable us to

[12] This is, of course, an outrageously over-simplified account of the assumptions and procedures involved. All nebulae are *not* of the same intrinsic brightness, and the modifications required by this and other assumptions tacitly made lead one a merry astronomical chase through the telescope, the Earth's atmosphere, the Milky Way and the Magellanic Clouds to Andromeda and our other near extra-galactic neighbors, and beyond. The story of this search has been delightfully told by E. P. Hubble in his *The Realm of the Nebulae* (Yale 1936) and in his *Observational Approach to Cosmology* (Oxford 1937), the source of the data mentioned below.

conclude with perhaps more assurance that this radius is increasing in time at a rate which, if kept up, would double the present radius in something less than 2000 million years.

With this we have finished our brief account of Geometry as a branch of Physics, a subject to which no one has contributed more than Albert Einstein, who by his theories of relativity has brought into being physical geometries which have supplanted the tradition-steeped *a priori* geometry and kinematics of Euclid and Newton.

H. P. Robertson

Department of Physics
California Institute of Technology